Crimes of the Krays Omnibus

CALLING TIME ON THE KRAYS:
THE BARMAID'S TALE

MURDER WITHOUT CONVICTION:
INSIDE THE WORLD OF THE KRAYS

D1375335

Crimes of the Krays Omnibus

CALLING TIME ON THE KRAYS: THE BARMAID'S TALE

MRS X

Edited and with an afterword by
James Morton

MURDER WITHOUT CONVICTION: INSIDE THE WORLD OF THE KRAYS

JOHN DICKSON

timewarner
paperbacks

A *Time Warner* Paperback

This omnibus edition first published in Great Britain by
Time Warner Paperbacks in 2002
Crimes of the Krays Omnibus Copyright © James Morton,
Patricia Kelly and John Dickson 2002

Previously published separately:
Calling Time on the Krays first published in Great Britain by
Little, Brown in 1996
Published by Warner Books in 1997
Reprinted 2000, 2001
Copyright © Patricia Kelly and James Morton 1996

Murder Without Conviction first published in Great Britain by
Sidgwick & Jackson in 1986
Published by Sphere Books Ltd, 1988
Reprinted 1988 (five times), 1989 (twice), 1990 (twice), 1991
Reprinted by Warner Books 1992
Reprinted 1992, 1993, 1994, 1999
Copyright © John Dickson 1986

A CIP catalogue record for this book
is available from the British Library.

ISBN 0 7515 3294 0

Printed and bound in Great Britain by
Clays Ltd, St Ives plc

Time Warner Paperbacks
An imprint of
Time Warner Books UK
Brettenham House
Lancaster Place
London WC2E 7EN

www.TimeWarnerBooks.co.uk

CALLING TIME ON THE KRAYS:
THE BARMAID'S TALE

For Dad and Les

1

It was the morning of 17 March last year when I heard on the radio that Ronnie died. Then almost immediately a couple of friends from the East End who knew about it all rang me up. I kept watching the news all that day because I couldn't take it in. He'd always seemed invincible to me, even though he'd been ill on and off the last few years. It was the myths surrounding him and Reggie. Over the years it was almost as though he was immortal. I had mixed feelings. I can't say I was glad he was dead, but it brought all the shooting back again and how scared I was of him. A feeling of relief, I suppose. He was the one I was really afraid of – not Reggie. It was a relief knowing he was mortal same as everybody else.

I couldn't quite believe the funeral. I read it cost £10,000 what with the horses and everything. Such a turnout. I knew it was so newsworthy but I think there must have been curiosity value as well. I didn't like it when I read of those children running along trying to touch Reggie Kray's hand through the window of the car. It seemed to glorify crime, as though it was something wonderful. I didn't go, of course, didn't even think of it, but it seemed like the whole of the rest of the East End did.

I don't think the general public realises how horrific it is when someone gets shot. When people get shot in films, there's a bang and they fall down. It's all so neat and tidy; there isn't any mess and smell like there is in real life.

People liked to say they knew the Twins. I had a friend who had a pub, the Alma in Westbourne Grove, and I was there one night when the barmaid was telling people that she was working there that night of the shooting. I just let it go.

People thought the Krays' glory reflected on them. You can often hear people saying how they were in the Beggars the night it happened, but you know damn well they weren't. I was. So were Ronnie Kray and Ian Barrie.

Recently I went to a car boot sale in the East End and there was a stall which was completely memorabilia of the Krays. Books, photos in frames, T-shirts, the lot. It's amazing how popular they are, even after all these years.

To my knowledge, I first set eyes on the Twins when I was about fourteen or fifteen. That's my earliest memory of them; they were pointed out in the street. I used to go shopping in Bethnal Green

Road and they only lived in Vallance Road, which was ten minutes away at the most. They were pointed out as really hard men. I was born 1939, so they were men when I was just a kid.

I remember seeing a poster for one of their boxing contests, but I don't think I ever saw the Twins fight; I'd be just that bit young. I always liked the fights. I heard Bugner fight Henry Cooper on the radio and when Harry Gibbs gave the decision to Bugner, I was so bloody fuming I broke my iron. For boxing there was York Hall, of course, same place as where the Baths were and I used to go there a lot and to Wembley with my husband. There'd be a crowd of us. I was there the night Henry Cooper fought for the European title and the bandleader Billy Cotton died at the ringside.

In the 1960s it was suddenly like everyone knew the Kray Twins. They were just suddenly there. You didn't pay much attention and it didn't affect my life; I had too much else going on for me to notice. It was only as I got older my mother-in-law would say, the Krays are good boys, they make sure us old age pensioners have a party down the church hall at Christmas. But it was a mentality with her and people like her, like voting Labour. They didn't look any further than their Christmas box.

Then suddenly they became a presence. Over the years when I was in my teens and early twenties you'd be having a drink and someone would say something like X had offended Ronnie and he'd given him a hiding. It was bits you got back from everywhere. Fights here and there. People who said they paid protection money. You knew the Twins had clubs. There were rumours that thieves had to pay them. You heard all these bits. It was like a jigsaw; you put things in place and suddenly you realised they weren't people to be crossed but they were people to be frightened of.

It came out at the trial that the Twins also had the controlling interest in the Regency, a Stoke Newington club run by the Barry brothers, one of whom, Tony, went on trial with them. My husband used to like a gamble, and we'd go there on a Saturday night sometimes. Even though technically it was in North London, it was really the smart place for East Enders to go. There was a nice restaurant in the place, a Chinese if I remember rightly.

Later, the Twins were often featured in the *East London Advertiser*, pictured with film stars and old boxers and organising things for charity. We all read about the trouble they had over that club, the Hideaway, in the West End; they were accused of trying to force the owner to sell it to them and they were pictured in all the papers when they were acquitted of demanding money with menaces.

There was a big splash in the papers as well when Reggie married a girl from a local family – Frances Shea. That was really an East End society wedding, that was; not that I was invited. Then there was the sad time for Reggie when Frances Shea committed suicide about two years later. It was talked about that she had been unhappy with her lifestyle for quite a bit.

You saw them all over the East End, of course and, as I say, you heard all these things but it was not until early in 1965 that I really appreciated just who they were.

2

It was my dad introduced me to Prince Monolulu, the racing tipster, once when we went down Petticoat Lane. The Prince, that was what I thought he really was, had a little poem:

> God made the bees,
> the bees make the honey,
> the public back the favourites,
> the bookies take the money.

He also used to have a cry, 'I gotta horse.' That was his trademark at racecourses.[1]

Just after the war, when I was about six, Dad used to take me with him to sell his pigeons down the Lane and I saw this enormous black man with his feathered head-dress shouting, 'I gotta horse.' If I went down the Lane, he'd be doing his come-on and he'd turn and say, 'Come and have a cup of tea.' I was a bit

[1]See Appendix – Prince Monolulu.

starry-eyed. There were hardly any black people in the East End in those days and he fascinated me. He kidded me up he was a real prince, and so did my dad. I thought he was a wonderful colourful figure. I didn't really know a lot about him. Dad used to say, 'He's a really nice man,' and he was always nice to me. I think he made a lot of money with tourists in the Lane. He was always in his robes and feathers and they used to have their photographs taken with him. I don't know where he came from; that's the only place I ever saw him. It's funny my dad knew him, because he didn't gamble at all except for his shilling bet on the Grand National. That would be with a street bookmaker. I asked if he was a real prince, and he said he'd mixed with royalty. I never knew where he was prince of, but because he was such a novelty I believed everything he said. He used to take me to a café, pay for tea and question me about how I was doing at school.

I loved the hustle and bustle of the Lane. I remember being fascinated watching the stallholder at the large china stall. He would juggle with his china, throw it about and bang the plates together to show how solid they were.

We lived in Portman Place just off Globe Road, Bethnal Green. It would be about ten minutes' walk from where the Twins were brought up. My father, Bill, was a stable-keeper for a coal merchant in Elsden Mews off the Old Ford Road. Occasionally he'd take the cart out if someone was sick, but mainly he used to look after the horses. He was a lovely man. I don't think he was a particularly big man, five feet nine or ten, but he was quite strong through working at the stables and humping the coal as well as looking after the horses. I think he worked for the coal people from when he left school. Then you could walk along late at night, and if he was stopping all night, looking after a horse if it was sick, I could go up with tea and sandwiches and stop with him. We lived about a ten-minute walk from there also. This was just after the war. Also, when he was in the stables, he had to go in on a Saturday. I used to love going in those stables with him. I think they had six or eight horses at a time. I used to go in and stroke them. Funnily, when he'd come home at night, before he washed he'd never smell of the horses. It was always coal and dust.

Dad took me to Hyde Park at Easter to see the Shire horses and carthorses in the parade. The breweries used to have the drays back then, but it all went motorised. Everything after the war was horses – totters and a pony and cart on Sundays came round the houses with winkles, rollmops and shrimps. Dad used to buy winkles, and I loved picking them out of their shells with a pin for him to dip in vinegar and eat. We had a front garden about the size of a postage stamp, along with everyone else in the street, and the men would go out and pick up a bucket of manure when the horses and carts passed to try to get some flowers to grow. My dad mainly used to grow irises

– he called them flags. For years he tried to get a little rosebush to grow, but it never came to much.

Dad once got bitten by a dog which was foaming in the stables. It bit into his leg and he went to have it burned out. The doctor we had came out from Globe Road. It cost 2s.6d. a visit. In the end he was an alcoholic, but everyone liked him even if they knew he was pissed half the time.

Mondays was pawn day. It was fairly regular when I was quite young. It was regular for most people. There was no disgrace; a lot of people like my Nan did it from necessity. She'd pawn her husband's suit and shoes on a Monday and get them out on Friday for him to go out in on a Saturday. It was only shillings she'd get. Something like five bob, but money went a long way. You got a lot of food for five bob. You made a stew, and it lasted three days. A neck of lamb was really cheap to buy. You could make a dinner go a long way then. No one wasted things. I used to watch my Nan peel potatoes, and she'd barely skin them. She lived up on the Butler Estate and would come down to us for Sunday evening. She kept the loan club books under a cushion on her sofa and then would take them over to the club office near St John's School, Peel Grove.

If people thought they could make a few coppers, they would. Buy firewood for tuppence, put it on a pushchair and sell it for threepence to people who didn't want to walk down and get their own. Sell bundles of old newspapers; anything which would turn a penny. I'd do that sometimes for pocket money and then go and spend it on pie and mash.

Dad was always very good with his hands. He just fiddled with anything. He'd buy up broken watches for next to nothing and fiddle with them for hours, sitting with an eyeglass mending them. He also used to take my milk-teeth out when they were loose – a piece of string round the tooth and the other end on the door-handle. He mended the shoes for the family. He had a last, and would buy pieces of leather to mend his own boots for work. He'd have a go at anything. He was marvellous with animals: he had pigeons, chickens and rabbits, bred budgies and canaries. The danger with the pigeons was the rats they attracted, and so he would sit out of an evening with an airgun to shoot at them. When I was a bit older, he got a broken-down bicycle and fixed it up for me. Then, when I got married and my husband bought an Austin, Dad would come over and do the repairs to it. He'd never driven a car before. It was all self-taught.

Generally, to get to the Lane, we used to walk all through Cambridge Heath and to Brick Lane. There was a pet and flower market – a separate market, really. We used to take a couple of hampers with pigeons in. If you didn't have a licence, you stood on a bit of waste ground. Mainly the stallholders would tip you off if the police came. I remember once my dad pushed me in a doorway when the Mosley mob marched through. This was after the war, because I can remember it.[2]

He used to say, 'Never sell to an Indian if I leave you on your own, cos they'll make them into pigeon pie.' They were homing birds, but he used to ring some of them so they'd come back after he sold them. Then he'd sell them again. You'd get three or four shillings for a bird. He was very badly paid at the stables and that used to supplement his income. It was his life's ambition to have a smart pony and trap, but he never got one. His dad, who was a totter, had a pony and cart and when he was drunk he would throw money to the kids. But when he was really drunk, he was nasty. My Nan had very long hair, and he once put it through the mangle in a temper. My dad hit him to stop him, and it really did upset him turning his hand to his own father. My Nan was the one. When I grew up, if the weather was bad, I'd go round about half-past nine to see if there was anything she needed and if she was all right. She wasn't grateful. 'You want to bloody get up in the morning,' she'd say. If things weren't done by seven o'clock, she'd think the day had been wasted.

I was looking in the family Bible the other day. Well, it isn't really a Bible, it's a history of it, but we called it the Bible and it has the birthdays of family

[2]Although the large marches, accompanied by a good deal of fighting and unrest, occurred in the 1930s, even after the war there were smaller demonstrations both in the East End and in Stoke Newington in favour of Oswald Mosley, the fascist leader.

written in it. My grandfather William was born on 24 May 1874, and my grandmother Elizabeth six years later on 29 September 1880. My dad, William jnr, was born on 24 June 1902, just over a year after his sister, Elizabeth jnr, who was born 9 April 1901. She was known as Liley. Sarah, another of my aunts on my dad's side, was known as Aunt Sally. She was a good drinker. Eliza Mary was Aunt Lizzie. She died when I was quite young. I remember, because me and one of my cousins was too small, we weren't allowed to the funeral. She had suffered from convulsions all her life and died having a fit. She lived at home with my Nan all the time.

I had another aunt, this time on my mum's step-side, and she was an alcoholic. The strange part was she only recognised me when she was drunk. I was round yet another aunt's one day, and she was sober and didn't recognise me. Years later, at the time of the trial, I was talking with one of the coppers on the case. He was saying about this woman who was in Bethnal Green Hospital, drunk every day, and it was my aunt.

I used to love going down the Lane, but I hated getting in the pigeon-loft. Dad'd got them so tame they'd take a seed out of your mouth. During the war, my mum had a terrible row with the woman next door because she thought she'd told the authorities about the birds. You had to have a special licence to keep pigeons because they could be used to carry messages. They all had to be destroyed. I remember being frightened because I saw Dad cry. I'd never seen him cry before. After the war he got a lot of new pigeons. That's when he started breeding budgies. He'd kill the chickens at Christmas for the family – he used to see Nan and my aunts had a couple of birds. He would wring their necks and I used to have to pluck them. I hated that. In fact I didn't like the chickens anyway. If you had the scullery window open, trying to have a wash, you'd get one of them flying in through the window and perching. I remember my pet rabbit disappearing. It was called Blackie. People in the Co-op gave it to me. Next day my mum dished up rabbit pie. I wouldn't eat it then, and I've never ate rabbit since.

If we had a good day selling the birds, Dad would treat me to pie and mash. That's what I liked. You got pie and mash and liquor (what they cook the eels in), and if you couldn't afford the pie you could have mash and liquor. I could eat it every day. Last year when I was in hospital, I couldn't eat my pie and mash. My kids said I really must have been ill.

Back when I was a kid, outside the pie and mash shops they'd have live eels, and when they were cut up they still wriggled. I couldn't eat them. I never even liked stewed eels. I don't like things with bones in them. Later, when I went out with my husband, he used to stop at the stall – Tubby Isaccs – and get the good ones. You could have a hot pea soup as well, and when I was a kid there was fish crackling – the bits from the fried fish. They'd scoop up the bits and sell them to you for a penny and you had them in salt and vinegar. It was still late in the forties when you could get pie and mash for fourpence. A large loaf was fourpence. It's still a cheap meal. When you bought butter, you had it patted into shape for you. Sugar was measured for you and the top was folded a special way. It's a shame they don't bring that back, because it's ideal for old people. Nowadays you can starve just trying to get into a pat of butter. I used to get sweets at the shop in Bonner Street, a bag of sherbet or two ounces of liquorice comfits and use the red ones as pretend lipstick. Down the Lane you could get hot apple doughnuts, and there was a drinks stall where the blackcurrant drink was the dearest. On Sunday mornings the Jewish greengrocer's would open up and put their bagels and soused herrings outside. All those lovely smells, particularly Cohen's in Jubilee Street, which had wonderful cakes. I had a friend, and she'd go in and say, 'Good morning, Mr Cohen. How're you going?' She thought it was very funny and so did I, but there was no malice in it. Some days I'd meet my dad at lunchtime and we'd go to Ray's Café off the Lane. It was usually syrup pudding and custard or spotted dog and always a big mug of tea. There was another café we went to which had marvellous saveloy and pease pudding.

My father wouldn't go dancing, but once or twice a year my mother would go to the Labour party. Everyone voted Labour, except the people next door who were a bit posh, and they voted Liberal. People never thought about it. It was because their parents did.

In the war Dad did firewatching. We lived in a square (of course it's been pulled down now), and he'd hose the fires from the bombing. I remember when there was an air raid, people picking me up and taking me to the shelters under the railway bridge on the Hackney line. It was just round the corner. I used to like that because you got cocoa there and I didn't get that indoors. One of my uncles, John, was a little tiny man in the ARP or something like it. He was on duty in the church opposite when the Bethnal Green tube disaster happened. He wasn't actually injured in it, but the shock of helping get the bodies out did something to him, shock or something, and he ended with a paralysed left arm.[3] That was one of my mum's brothers. Dad had three sisters, and my mother had two brothers and some step-brothers and -sisters. I never really knew them very well. On Dad's side, there were two who were a lot older than me and one a bit younger.

[3]On 3 March 1943, after German threats of reprisals for bombing Berlin, some 1,500 people had crowded into the Bethnal Green tube station following a siren at 8.17 pm. Ten minutes later, a battery in Victoria Park seemed to create a panic and a woman with a child fell on the steps. Within seconds, there was a press of bodies five or six deep. There were 173 deaths and another 62 injured. The metropolitan magistrate, Laurence Dunne MC, later the Chief Magistrate, was appointed to hold an enquiry. He reported on 23 March and, apart from making certain recommendations, concluded that the matter was caused by the loss of control by the crowd and that nothing in the way of structural design or police control could be a real safeguard against loss of self-control by a crowd.

I remember after the war we had a VE day party in the courtyard of my Nan's flats and we sat at trestle tables. There was one man with one side of his face blackened and the other side was red, white and blue. I thought he was terrifying at the time. Funnily enough I don't remember there being a Coronation party, but I'm sure there must have been. On the other hand I remember crying in the school playground with my best friend Doreen when we heard the King had died in 1952. It's funny how memory is selective. I know Dad got a small television around that time. Black and white, of course. It was a nine-inch Bush. We had a lot of people in for it and for the Stanley Matthews Cup Final that year.

My mother, she was tiny – four foot six – and wore surgical boots. She'd had a fall off a swing when she was about six and damaged her hip. She worked for a short time at a sweet factory, but apart from that I don't remember her working. I think she always thought she was too good for everybody. She never liked soiling her hands with housework or anything and she was never close to my dad's family either.

She was a children's nanny before she married my dad and travelled all around the world – France, Spain, Switzerland, New York. I've got her passport, and it shows that in 1924 she was in Cuba. I often wonder why she just stopped. I'd have thought she'd have gone for someone out there with a few bob. Her parents lived a couple of doors away in Digby Street, and she used to see Dad in between jobs on her visits home and that's how she came to go out with him. My mother was Catholic and Dad was C. of E., so the marriage wasn't recognised by the Church, but he was always keen for me to go to Sunday school – the Methodist one, at that. When I was older I went to the youth club for the table tennis and dances. It was there I met Les, who was such a support to me in years to come. His family was a great big one which lived on the Kingsmead in Hackney when it was a nice estate. I had a friend, Eddie, when I was about ten, and his parents died within a few days of each other. Les's family more or less took Eddie in and I was always welcome there with him. He had a friend, Roy, and the pair would take me and Eddie on the backs of their motorcycles. He was godfather to all my children.

But me and my friends always tried to go to different churches so as to qualify for their Christmas parties. Christmas evening around eleven o'clock was the time to go shopping down the Roman Road market. That was when you could get cheap Christmas trees and food.

My mother had a step-brother, Bill, who married my Aunt Mary. She was Irish, dark-haired, very handsome, looked a bit like a gypsy, and I was very close to her. She lived in Virginia Road near Brick Lane, and we used to go up there. She had a lovely voice and I loved to hear her sing. She used to sing the whole time she was working. She had this home work, and it was a small cardboard box to put things in. Narrow tubes had to be put in, so many across and so many down. I went to help her. She told us that it was for diamonds, but I don't rightly know. She never paid us. You never took money off family for helping. It stank of glue there. Another job she had was peeling onions ready for pickling. I think the glue was worse.

The day after my step-uncle Bill died, she discovered she had cancer of the breast. She was always cagey about her age and then she gave it as sixty-two, but the doctor said she was nearer seventy. Even on her count, when she re-married she was in her late seventies. She called her new husband her toy-boy. He was Irish, too, and seemed much younger. He was still working at the time, so he must have been. She was a real character. She died in 1994.

The house was much like any in the slum areas. I had a bedroom to myself. There was no carpet but it had a coal fire, although that was only lit in the very cold weather. Although with my dad working in the yard, coal was the one thing which was cheap for us, it still wasn't there to waste. There was a small gas cooker downstairs. The toilet was in the back yard and that was a hazardous trip at night with the rats, but it did have a flush. We would wash in the scullery, cold water only, and have a tin bath once a week in the kitchen. Then as I got older, on a Friday night I'd go with a friend to York Hall Baths, which was about ten minutes away. It was a penny for the soap, penny for the towel and tuppence or threepence for the bath and tuppence left over for a drink of Bovril down by the swimming pool. There was an attendant who turned a great big wheel outside the cubicle which poured in either hot or cold water. 'Hot in number six' or 'More cold in number eight', and you used to call out your mate's cubicle number to annoy them. If the water came, there was nothing you could do about it. They'd bang on the door that time was up. I don't remember great queues to get in. As for the washing, we'd do that down the bottom of Globe Road near Stepney Green station. We'd get there about seven in the morning, put all the whites in the boiler and do the rest in the sinks with the dolly board. Later, they had drying cabinets and big ironing presses for the sheets. I still went there when I had the kids.

I went to the school in Morpeth Street as an infant. I think I was four when I first went. I remember it catching fire in the war and it shut down, so from there I went to Bonner Street until I took the eleven plus. I remember there was a family called the Donovans. Everyone was scared of the boys in the family. They were wild in those days. One of them threw a brick at me, cutting my head open, as I walked to school. There was quite a big family, and the boys would nick lead off roofs. I loved that school. It was named after Bishop Bonner, and the headmistress was a Miss Shaw. Mr Evans, a Welshman, used to lead the hymn singing and he was always looking out to see if you was singing his favourite one, 'Holy, Holy, Holy'. He used to belt it out in a deep booming voice. I won a prize there – a book on Robin Hood. How I loved it. I also got beat in a spelling bee by Johnny Carney. We were just the two left and I had to spell porridge. I got to the first 'r', and he went 'rrr' and put me off. So I lost, but I beat him up outside school after that and knocked his head on the pavement, even though I was much smaller. We met at a party, I don't know, thirty years later, and funny, we recognised each other. Johnny Morgan and Johnny Patience made my life a misery there. They were always trying to kiss the little girls and we didn't want to know at that age. Silly what you miss out on.

On the way home from Bonner Street you'd play on the grass and the swings in Meath Gardens. It was quite a small park like Balmy Park by Bethnal Green tube station, where I used to take my kids to the paddling pool. There were a whole lot of kids' games we played – statues, where you had to stop in a silly position or you were out; jacks – we called them busy stones – where you caught stones on the back of your hand; knock down ginger, which was tying two door-handles together, ringing the bell and running away. If we were lucky, we might get invited to play football with the boys.

Later we took up smoking. A joystick was a big cigarette. It was about 18 inches long and it would last for ages. If you were being daring you'd smoke it going along. They weren't strict on the law about selling to schoolchildren then, and I used to go and get my dad cigarettes.

When I went on to my next school, I didn't see much of my old friends. I'd got a pass for the City of London School for Girls and went to the interview, but I couldn't cope with it. It was so posh. The clothes I went in for the interview stood out. I knew I wouldn't fit in in secondhand uniform. I went to Coborn instead. My mum was very upset. She'd have loved it. She thought it was very snobby and therefore good. She could have told all the neighbours. My dad was more content to sit and talk with me. You could discuss things with him; you couldn't with my mum. She just wanted to be able to brag to the neighbours. I must have looked like something out of St Trinian's. I had secondhand uniforms for Coborn as well. I had a hat which was far too big, and I used to kick it to try and get it into shape so it wouldn't look so funny. We had those navy blue knickers you had to wash out every night and get them dry.

I'd be thirteen when I put a bra on the statue of Venus which was in the foyer of the school, and I got into trouble for that. It was just sheer devilment – being dared to do something. I used to bunk off and go down the Roman Road market. You only had to walk through the back. We had Greek dancing on the lawn, and I used to climb the gates and go and get ice lollies. Our twin school was Coopers, and Douggie Brierley, the brother of my friend Victoria, used to make stinkbombs for us in the laboratory there. I used to love that. That was when I used to bunk off; I'd write a note from my dad saying I'd got a stomach upset. Then one day I was called by the head, Miss Philpot, remarking how similar my writing was to my dad's. It was always, 'This is a school for young leddies.'

The Queen Mother came to look over the school when she was still Queen. It was a celebration of 100 or 200 years of the school. Girls dressed in old-fashioned costume – girls carrying slates. Everything to do with that era. We had to be lined up, and the Queen was going to stop and speak to some of us. I could see Miss Philpot practically praying I wouldn't be one of the ones chosen, but I was. There she was, bobbing behind the Queen, reminding me to curtsy. What I noticed most was how much make-up she had on. It was really pancaked. You could smell it, and not just her perfume.

I remember the only reason I stopped bunking off the Greek dancing was I wanted to go to the ballet, and there was to be a school outing for those who went to the class. I think the teacher was sorry for me. We went to see *Coppélia* at a matinée at Sadlers Wells. It was wonderful. I'd only been to the 'Bughole' cinema in the Roman Road, the People's Palace in the Mile End Road and the Hackney Empire. Later on, the Odeon in the Mile End Road was a favourite because one of us would buy a ticket for the circle and then let the others in.

I wasn't really lonely as a child. I had a very close friend from about the age of four. She lived in Sceptre Road and I used to go in her house a lot. She had a cousin, and we could only have been quite young when he died of meningitis. I remember people crying, although I couldn't take it in all that much. We were always being told how important it was to have injections because a girl at Bonner Street died of diphtheria. My friend eventually became my bridesmaid. I still see her, but she moved to South London. She got married very, very young. She was divorced a few years ago and then took a course in psychology.

I liked the Guides. It was to do with the Methodist Church, and the deaconess, Sister Audrey, ran the troop. She was a lovely woman. Once I went to her flat near the Blackwall tunnel to do my bed-making test. It was so lovely. She took me to see *On Moonlight Bay* with Doris Day. What I didn't like was the camping, because of the insects. I was too scared to go to sleep. I remember we were going for some sort of test over Victoria Park, doing tracking. We had to put different signs on trees. I remember watching a young woman riding a bike and she slipped and fell under a trolley-bus. The woman in charge made us take our scarves off and put them under her arm before the ambulance came. We didn't do our tracking that night. A couple of the girls were really upset, and we were taken back to the Methodist Hall.

The cinema was what I really liked. Apart from the 'Bughole', the place we went to was called the Ben Hur cinema. It really was, and it was over Stepney way. The owner had been a strongman in his time, he was really good with us children. I didn't go to Saturday mornings because, from about the age of ten, I used to have to get all the shopping and then, a bit later, I started working on a Saturday. As we got a bit older, me and my mates used to go to a lot of cinemas because we learned how to bunk in, but I used to go to the 'Bughole' with my dad because it was the cheapest. We'd take a pound of broken biscuits from Jacobs the grocers or two ounces of sherbet. Twice a week it had serials. I remember the only time Dad was annoyed with me in the whole of his life was in *The Beast with Five Fingers*, the one with Peter Lorre. I only got to the bit where the hand got on the piano, and that was enough. He had to bring me out, I was so scared, and he was cross. You could get cheap vanilla brick ice creams from the kiosk, but you never went to the toilet because the water came down part of the aisle as it was. It was a bit like going paddling. Dad was mad on Randolph Scott and he was keen on Johnny Weissmuller in the Tarzan films. He liked the Three Stooges, but I never thought they were funny. Most of the time we saw cowboy films. I remember once he took me to the Paragon, which was dearer, and so as a special treat we saw Sid Fields in *Cardboard Cavalier* about Charles II.

I used to love Joseph Locke on the radio. I loved musicals. I had an absolute crush on Gene Nelson; he was the supporting actor. I carried a little picture of him about in a wallet. I thought he was better than Gene Kelly. That was the other thing my dad liked – Shirley Temple films. At Christmas, which was up at my Nan's, you had to do something and my dad played piano-accordion – he wasn't bad. When he died, my mother gave it away to one of my Irish aunts. He could knock out a tune on the piano – 'You are my Sunshine' – and all the Flanagan and Allen, and me and my cousin Irene used to do the Judy Garland number, 'We're a Couple of Swells'. A bit back, my daughter took me to see the Flanagan and Allen show – one of these tribute shows – in London. It made me cry when they sang 'Underneath the Arches'. It reminded me of all those years ago. My daughter Susan said, 'I brought you out to cheer you up, Mum,' but I still went on crying.

I was ten or eleven when I started work in the sweetshop at the weekends and on holidays. It was owned by a young couple with a couple of kids. Then I worked on the biscuits in a greengrocer's in Bethnal Green Road. You had to go down into a cellar, where they had biscuit tins with water in them to catch rats and mice. I got the sack from there for giving old age pensioners extra biscuits. Working at the hairdresser's was good, because you got your hair done. They had the old-fashioned perming machines with wires in the hood. I turned one of my aunts' hair blue. She'd wanted a light blue rinse and it came out navy. She went mad. I'd used too much of the stuff. We used to do highlights with L'Oréal bleach and peroxide and silver foil. You'd get the hair and bleach it and wrap it in foil, leave it on for a while and you'd get blonde highlights.

Once a year I'd be taken to Southend for the day on a train from Liverpool Street. It was always the same. A ride or two at the Kursaal, a Rossi ice cream, cockles, and a swim in the sea no matter how cold it was. When I was a bit older, I went hopping down in Kent to Whitbread's at Paddock Wood a couple of times. It was just a question of getting out of London for a bit. People made it sound really romantic – waving from the lorries and everybody singing away and telling stories round campfires, drinking cocoa – on the newsreels, but where I went it was filthy, really. It was tin huts; just primitive. Taps for washing and the old trenches for toilets, and I think everyone got fleas and nits when they went. I used to go with my aunts and cousins. My dad would come down after a week or couple of weeks and bring me home.

Back at school, the school nurse was horrible. She was known as Nitty Norah. When you got to school of a morning you had a spoonful of cod liver oil and malt. Then Nitty Norah would look through your hair, and if you had nits you went up the clinic. The stuff she put on your hair really stank, so everyone knew where you'd been. Mind you, headlice were really common then. There used to be a phrase, 'I've got visitors', which was the polite way of saying you had lice or fleas. Your head was pummelled with Derbac soap and disinfectant and everyone knew what had happened to you. After that, my dad went through my hair over a newspaper. He'd get stuff from Massingham's the chemist, or The Old Maids, which was another chemist.

When I was about nine or ten I learned to swim in the Thames at Tower Bridge. The river went past Queen Anne's Steps and you could sit on this little stretch of sand called Tower Beach. It was man-made with about 1,500 tons of sand brought up the river and dumped on the shingle by permission of King George V. You used to get down by a ladder which was raised at high tide. Before the war it was very popular with adults and there'd still be parents with kids, but it was mainly youngsters in my day. You had to learn to swim, because if you went under you got a mouthful of the most horrible oily water imaginable, so you learned quickly. We thought it was like being at the seaside. One time there were two fellows with some girls betting one another they could swim across. They dived to swim across the Thames and we heard one of them had disappeared. I was swimming a few days later and I was doing my dog paddle when I felt something touch my leg, and it was this man. I helped bring him in to the beach. Then they turned us all off and closed the area for the day. I never went back there. After that it was the Lido in Viccy Park.

That was the first real close experience I ever had of death, although when I was very small the first time I saw Wassel Newman (a well-known character in the East End – a real fighting man), there was a funeral passing. Dad had stopped and took his hat off. This big man did the same, and he came over to speak to my dad. Later, Dad told me when they were younger, Wassell'd be bet a slice of bread and jam he would put his hand through a window or a piece of wood, and he'd do it. If you didn't have the slice of bread and jam, then you'd be in trouble. It was said he'd walk miles just to have a fight. I used to talk to him when I was out with my dad. I think, looking back, he was a bit backward – 'educationally challenged' they call it now. He was slow in speech, and it seemed like he was collecting his thoughts before he spoke to you. Like a lot of people like that, I suppose, especially being a big man, he'd solve things easier with his fists rather than with words. But the men of that era seemed very polite, very respectful.

At that age I didn't know anything about queers and lesbians. No one ever discussed homosexuals then, but up Bethnal Green Road I'd go into this café and the men there wore make-up and loads of rings, and – this is what really used to fascinate me – the women used to wear men's clothes.

I got five O levels, but I couldn't stop on at school

for A levels because my mum wanted me to go to work. But before I did, I went to Paris. It was really quite daring for me to go alone in those days, and daring of my parents to let me. Mum'd looked after this French girl as a baby and I went out there and stopped in her apartment. Her husband was in films and they also had a house on the outskirts, and that's where they'd had Marlon Brando to stop. I remember her telling me I'd missed him by a week, but I'd have been too scared to speak to him. Her father was apparently something to do with the Moulin Rouge. She took me to her parents' house and the kitchen there was enormous, what you'd expect to see in a country house, with old-fashioned pans. The toilets were larger than our lounge. There were two opposite each other and they were decorated with cherubs. I stayed four or five weeks. I found at first the French were a bit offish, but then they started asking me if I was German because I was very blonde in those days. Once I said I was English, their attitude was completely different.

I was so disappointed with the *Mona Lisa*. I'd expected a really big painting but it was so small. I had enough French to make myself understood, but I never thought of staying on and trying to learn French properly. I wouldn't have had enough confidence. Anyway, although they had lovely sherbet drinks there, it wasn't the East End and they didn't have pie and mash shops. I liked wandering about and looking at the artists painting their view of Notre-Dame and the Sacré Coeur. I ate in student cafés because it was a lot cheaper. I've never been back.

When I got back, I took a job with an insurance company. I started on the switchboard and then learned bookkeeping. I got £4 7s. 6d. a week before deductions. The next job I had was in a finance company in Chancery Lane – it was allied with the Israeli Banking Corporation. That's how I got to know a lot of the car dealers when I used to help out on reception. They used to call in and we would deal with their HP agreements. My friend Sheila and I started going out with them. We used to go to Maxim's, where they had dancing, and we thought it was wonderful because we used to go by car and there were so many rich people up there.

When I started going out with fellows it was either the pictures or dancing; going in the pub it was more like a family outing. Sixpence in St Peter's Hall, half a block from where my husband lived. I can't remember how much Tottenham Royal was. That was good because it had a revolving stage with two bands. We used to go by train until one of the boys got a car. Cambridge Heath, I think it was, to Tottenham and walk up from there. You could go from Hackney Downs station and all round that way. Then there was the Repton. We used to go there to see if we could get any of the boys who did boxing to dance with us. There was the Hut in Brick Lane – that's all it was, really. There was one in Mare Street; I can't think what that was called. I don't know how I had time to do everything. I'd go out dancing, and when I got home I'd want to read. I'd read until three in the morning but I'd still get up.

My mum always wanted me in early, but sometimes if it was a really good night you'd take your chance and say I lost my fare or they took off a couple of buses; it was generally all right if it was my dad waiting up. I left school at sixteen and I was to be in about half-past ten, but might get an extension at the weekend depending on where I said I was going. If it was Tottenham Royal, Dad would make allowances for the journey and give me a bit of leeway. If we were late, we'd climb the railings into Victoria Park and walk across, singing. If we heard a park keeper, we'd hide under the bandstand. There's a lovely boating lake in that park, quite big with an island, and the game was to get off and then try and get back and row off, leaving someone stranded.

There was the odd little punch-up, but nothing really. There again most of the fellows and girls we'd already met up with at other dance places – our own little circle. One of my mates married very young. She was asked to dance by this Jewish fellow and married him very quickly, which didn't go down well with his family. We was invited over once and he said he knew a good game of cards – three-card brag. I skinted him. Stayed till four in the morning. He never asked us again.

I remember I used to like going to the Hackney Empire for Eric Delaney and his Band. He was the leader and the drummer, which was unusual. He had fingers missing on one hand. I remember being fascinated by that. There was a half-caste boy I knew, Larry, and him and I used to go in for jive competitions. Once I went up there and it was closed. A car came and took me to Stepney Jewish club and Frankie Vaughan was there, and we got to jive with him. He was selling kisses for a shilling a time and I felt so sorry for him the ones he had to kiss. It had to be worth more than a shilling.

Then there was the Ted Heath Band with Lita Roza and Dickie Valentine. Years later I went to see *Oblomov* with Spike Milligan, and Dickie Valentine was in the audience. He died not long after. I thought he was lovely at the time. We had an old wind-up gramophone, and when I went to work I started buying a lot of records. I loved Frank Sinatra. The first record of his I ever bought was 'You My Love'. I'd a crush on Johnny Ray as well. Then when I started going out with my husband, his mum had a radiogram. It was lovely being able to play them without it running down.

A bit after I started work I remember being in a club in the West End and being offered a cigarette. A car dealer came over and took it off me, saying, 'You never take a cigarette off anyone you don't know in a club.' This was how I met Phil Jacobs. He was a terrific dancer. There was one where you do the shimmy, and he was magic at it. But he was such a wind-up merchant I think he was thrown out one night. He had a terrific personality. I think he was in the used car trade at the time. I never went out with him, just in the crowd. I was courting my husband John at the time and he was doing National Service. He had been working for a brewery and after finishing his National Service he went back to it. I got married in January 1959. I was nineteen, and John was a year older. Phil Jacobs went on to get the Plough and Harrow at Leytonstone. I think that's when he was involved with the Dixons. That was his downfall. It was said at his trial that he was the leader, but I don't believe it – I don't think he was the leader.[4]

I remember being up West with the dealers one night and we were going to go into this hotel for a drink, and we were held back. This sheik came down the stairs. One of the guys was absolutely falling about laughing. This was when I first saw Charlie de Silva. Then they told me what was going on. We never got a drink in there because everyone was laughing too much. De Silva was very quietly spoken, really rather nondescript, but at the

[4]Once the Richardsons and the Krays had been dealt with, it was feared that other gangs would take over their empire. Commander Bert Wickstead was given instructions by Sir Robert Mark, then Commissioner of Police for the Metropolis, to ensure that this did not happen. One of the results was the imprisonment of the so-called Dixon gang, of whom Jacobs was said to be the brains, for an East End protection racket. On 4 July 1972 Jacobs and George Dixon received twelve years, Alan nine. Other friends and relatives received lesser terms. Lambert Jacobs, Phil's brother, and Brian Dixon were acquitted.

same time rather distinguished-looking. I suppose that was part of his act. Something came up in the conversation: it was when Macmillan was in power and someone said to him, 'How do you get away with it?' You can go anywhere if you act confident enough. What had happened was he'd been in Downing Street. He said you could sell anything if you were confident enough. You could sell Nelson's column – and I believe he had done.[5]

I'd seen the Twins about before at St Peter's Hall; I used to go there dancing to records, twice a week, and when the Twins would come in the music would stop. They'd speak to some people, leave, and then the music would start again. Although there were fights, it was local lads, and some of the girls were as bad. The man, Gerry, who ran it had the local greengrocer's shop and he was very good at keeping order. There was more trouble at the Glasshouse off the Old Ford Road in the middle of an estate of flats. Once there was a bad fight outside the Repton when a fellow, Peter, was stabbed in the back. He got all the way home to Bomwell Street without realising he'd been done. Three fellows got nicked for that. There were lots of Teddy boy fights at the time but we all thought that was a great fashion. I don't remember the other fashions so much, but I always liked the Teddy boys' style.

We were very clothes conscious. In the East End

[5]See Appendix – Charles de Silva.

in those days you had it so hard as kids; most of it was secondhand from down the Lane. At school, because I used to get a uniform from a girl who was five foot ten, my gymslip always came down to my ankles. Once you started work you bought things. I went mad on shoes. Every month I got paid I got another pair of shoes down Roman Road market. It was known for clothes, and you could really get yourself some nice outfits.

Once I was working in the City I would go shopping in the West End. There were smaller nice little dress shops in them days. We never shopped in the big stores. It was usually down Roman Road, or having things made. My mate and I had these bell-coats made. We'd seen in a magazine how they were coming into style, and we thought we'd have a head-start. We must have looked a right pair because when we tried to walk in them we looked like a pair of ducks!

One of my mates and one of my cousins was on the docks and they brought home material, and we took it to a little dressmaker in Jubilee Street. If a fellow had a suit, it was always made by a Jewish tailor. Most of the East End fellows as I grew up were very particular. For example, I had this mate who fancied a boy called Terry at St Peter's Hall, and one night he actually came over and chatted her up and asked her to dance. She had a dance. When she came back I asked if she was going out with him, and she said no, she'd gone off him. His cuffs were frayed and he'd got wrong socks on. It was so unusual for an East End boy.

My first 'boyfriend' was when I was four or five. His name was Laurence Newman and he used to go to Mrs Cattel – I never knew her first name and I was allowed to call her Nan. She had the Parkfield Poultry Farm in Hanworth in Middlesex, where my mother took me for visits. Laurence's father had a toyshop in Hounslow, and it was like an Aladdin's cave. I thought they must be very rich because there was an electric train going round in the window. He and I used to get told off for chasing her ducks and chickens. She used to make a plum and apple pudding and steam it and put it over an open coal range. I can still taste it. She also had a little shop near a pub called the Brown Bear. The other half of the shop she let, and one of her lodgers was a photographer who took a photo of me and had it in the window. There was another pair of lodgers called Mr and Mrs Morris, who bought me a fountain pen when I passed my eleven plus. I remember my mother and I would go for a week or so and once, when my dad came to see us, he brought me a china doll he'd found on a bomb-site. I called her Debris Rose. Mrs Cattel had a couple of dogs and Mr Morris used to walk them with us over by a big reservoir. There were lovely fluffy feather-beds in the rooms with steps you had to climb to get into them, and a china ewer on the dressing table for washing. This was where my mother went when Dad was dying.

I used to go out with George from the youth club when I suppose I was about fourteen. I called him my boyfriend then, but of course we were much more backward in those days. I don't think he even kissed me. Then I was engaged to a fellow called Alf who did all my mum's electrics. When he'd finished, I broke off the engagement. Horrible little cow!

But, really, my husband John was my first serious boyfriend. I met him first at a dance at St Peter's. He only lived half a block away in a flat at the end of Cephas Street. Now he was a smart dresser. I thought to myself when I saw him a couple of times in the hall, 'You'll do nicely.' He was going out with a girl called Margaret at the time but we soon got rid of her. He always used to walk me home, even though I lived a bit of a walk away. He was working in a brewery as a driver, then he went off to do his National Service. He was a year older than me. I was nineteen and still working for the finance company when I got married. That was from home, and we went to Jersey for our honeymoon. He and I had got a flat in a house over in Howard Road in Leytonstone. It was partly because that was where we found somewhere. It had an inside bath – we had to share, but it was wonderful. It was also to get away from my mother. Dad used to come over on his bicycle, and he even did so when he'd broke his foot and it was in a cast. I used to get the bus to go to the finance company.

I kept on working until my first, Susan, was born. I was still in the same job. I used to get in late because I felt sick if I travelled on the tube and so I went by bus, but then again I couldn't stand it being crowded, so I waited till after the end of the rush hour, but my boss never seemed to mind. He knew I'd make it up at the other end of the day. He was a lovely man. If I seemed down, he'd say to me and the other girl, 'Go over to the pub and get yourselves a drink. I'll come over in a few minutes.' He invited me and my husband round to his place in Stamford Hill once, and when we were looking at his fridge he just said, 'Don't you have one? Take that, I'll get another.' Of course we didn't, but he really meant it. I bumped into him a bit ago and we recognised each other after what . . . thirty years?

John and I were happy in Howard Road, but then the landlord died and left a young daughter, Jill. The relatives came and took her, and we had to get out so they could sell the house. We went back to Mum and Dad because we thought that we stood more chance of getting a council house. There was the three rooms upstairs, and we had those. I had two kids when we moved back to my parents'. Mum and Dad had the front room downstairs, and a bedroom which later got burned out with a wiring fault. We had the upstairs.

It wasn't something I wanted. First, there was no real privacy; second, there was no bath, it was back to a tin bath for the kids; and third, there was my mother. Looking back, the move was a great mistake. Of course if we hadn't moved, none of this would have happened. But there again you can say if I'd had a cold that evening or stopped on the way to see someone or if George Cornell hadn't been visiting his friend Jimmy Andrews in hospital and decided to stop off for a drink, nor would it then. You can play games like that until you're blue in the face.

3

___

Mr Jones: My Lord, I propose to follow the procedure your Lordship sees on the depositions. The name of this witness is known to all defending Counsel.

Mr Justice Melford Stevenson: Yes.

Mr Jones (*To the witness*): Madam, I am going to ask you to look at a piece of paper which we call Exhibit One. May that be handed to her, please? (*Handed to witness*) Does that set out your full name?

A: Yes, it does.

Q: Now will you hand it back, please? (*Handed to Counsel*) Do you know a man by the name of Patsy Quill and his wife?

A: Yes, sir.

Of course I knew Patsy Quill. He had been my boss. Along with his brother Jimmy, he ran the Blind Beggar in the Whitechapel Road where it all started. They had interests in pubs all over the East End.

I got to know Patsy Quill from the time when he was a car dealer. In those days Jimmy, his brother, had more of the playboy image. Patsy was more the serious businessman type. Jimmy went into a lot of things. I think he ran a loan company in Stratford and later he went into promoting boxing down the Walthamstow Town Hall and places like that. They had interests in pubs in the East End, and one of the best known was the Beggars.

It was funny how it got its name. There was some poem or story about a Blind Beggar of Bethnal Green who had a beautiful daughter. Men fell in love with her, but finding out her father was a beggar, they deserted her. Then in true fairytale tradition a young nobleman fell in love and wasn't in the least put off when he discovered her father was blind. He was even less put off when he discovered that the father was really rich and a nobleman himself. He had disguised himself as a beggar so that his daughter would not be married for his money. There's another more realistic version. The beggar's name was Montfort, born in 1400, and he had lost his sight in the Loire valley fighting during the Hundred Years' War. He had a daughter, Bessy, born in 1430, who became a prostitute to keep him. When she retired in 1470 she had a house built for him. Bessy Street off Roman Road is named after her.[1]

At the turn of the century the Beggars had been

[1]In 1959 Tower Hamlets council commissioned Elizabeth Frink to sculpt a statue of the Blind Beggar and his dog. It was erected in the market square on Roman Road but was removed after a fortnight to save it from vandalism. In April 1965 it was relocated in the Cranbrook Estate off Roman Road, where it stands today.

the home of a gang of pickpockets and housebreakers known as the Blind Beggar gang because they used to meet there. By the time I went to work there, it had been renovated, but it was still a fairly dark place altogether with a good deal of red plush. Like a lot of pubs in the East End at the time, the bar was four-sided. On the customer side there was a wall between the saloon bar and public bar, but you could get through the saloon round the back of the bar into the snug and on into the public bar. From the server's point of view, you could work all three bars from the middle. You could see across from the public to the saloon bar. At the back of the bar were steps to the cellar and also up to the landlord's quarters.

The stables where Dad worked had closed down in the late 1950s, and my husband John got him a job with a brewery on what was called the heavy gang, shifting gas cylinders. Dad thought it was wonderful because he'd never earned so much money in his life. That first Christmas he got a bonus but he had his pocket dipped on the way home. He was so upset; he'd been going to buy us extra presents.

He hadn't told us, but he'd been feeling unwell for a little while. We'd moved back to my mum and dad's and that's when I found out how bad he was. I got a doctor, and he was operated on for an ulcer in his food-pipe. He was in hospital the autumn when Kennedy was assassinated. That's when the doctor told me he had cancer. He'd always been a heavy smoker. He used to do forty Weights a day, and they were strong then. The doctors didn't think he'd live long and they said they wanted to see my mother, but instead I went over to see them at the Bethnal Green Hospital. I didn't say anything to him, but Mum would have. She just couldn't have helped it. I looked after my dad until he died. After what the doctors had said, I didn't expect him to see Christmas, but he held on. He had a hard death, although he came out of hospital in the November and actually went back to work for a short time in January. I don't know how he managed it. By the March his skin was turning yellow and I was telling him he had jaundice. After that he didn't go back to work. He just stayed at home and went out less and less until he didn't go out no more.

Whilst he was ill my mother used to go away and stay with Mrs Cattel, the old lady in Hanworth who I'd been taken to visit as a child. I don't think my mother was being deliberately unkind; it was more that she just couldn't face up to things. I had the youngest one christened in March. Dad didn't come to the church, but we had a bit of a tea party upstairs afterwards and he came to that. He died on 15 April 1964, the day before my birthday. I've still got his birthday card. He was a lovely man.

Things hadn't been going well with John and me when we went back to my parents'. Looking back, it wasn't all his fault; it never is. I think a lot of it was he couldn't bear either the house or my mother, who didn't like him – or too many other people for that matter. Also he was gambling heavily at the time. Horses, dogs, cards, you name it, and of course in the long run he wasn't winning. I don't think he was even in the short. Then, while I was having my youngest, my husband and I split up. I found out he'd started seeing another girl, so that was that. He moved out. I went to court for money each week and I think I got £6: £2 for each of the children. I didn't want anything for myself, and I don't think he could have paid anyway. After Dad died, Mum got a flat over in Poplar and I stayed on the top floor waiting for the house to be pulled down and me and the kids to be rehoused. We didn't use the downstairs because there'd been a fire where some electric wiring had gone rotten and burned out.

That was when I went to work for the Beggars. I did Friday, Saturday, two evenings a week and the occasional Sunday. In the day I used to make Christmas tags, and then after I finished in the pub I'd sit up addressing envelopes. I got something ludicrous like £1 a thousand and I was working from a Welsh telephone directory. The Christmas tags which I had to thread were 4*s.* 6*d.* a thousand. It took ages. You had to cut the thread to the length. Then I'd walk to Hoxton with them on a pushchair. It was all off the cards, of course.[2] It wasn't a living, but it was money.

[2]Not declared for tax purposes.

Patsy and Jimmy Quill were very well known as being in the middle, not involved, so to speak, so that East Londoners, North Londoners, South Londoners, anybody could drink in the Beggars. Over the years, with all the stories, it's seemed that the only people in the Beggars were villains, but it wasn't so. You had nice people – not that villains couldn't be nice when they wanted. Most of the local hospital staff went to the London Hospital Tavern, but we did get a few in of a week night. Fridays and Saturdays you got a lot of young people in. It was always packed solid. It was a place for impromptu parties. As the barmaid, you had to have a good memory. There'd be people back in the crowd holding up their money and passing it through, saying 'same again'. Bar work isn't good paid work as such, but then you get tips. There was a glass you could put the tips in. You relied on that to make your money up. You'd be offered a drink and say, 'Thanks. I'll have it a bit later,' and then go and put the money in the glass. When it was packed, nearly everyone would say, 'Have a drink.' Patsy was good in the sense that, when you finished work, him and his wife would always have food laid on for you upstairs. Then I'd get my hat and coat and mainly I'd walk home. Cut through the flats at the back and it was only ten minutes or a quarter of an hour. My cousin Chrissie would be there doing the baby-sitting.

Chrissie was short and dark, very attractive. She was very supportive to me, even though she was only about seventeen. Sometimes she stayed with me but most of the time she stayed with her sister near Victoria Park. She's my mother's step-sister's daughter. Her mother's still alive. I speak to her on the phone sometimes.

Chrissie, she used to live with us when I was at home from the time when I was about sixteen and she was about eight. I shared my room with her when her parents split up. She stayed almost until I got married, and then she went to live with her sister. You might think my mother was quite good to have her, but she was paid for it. She couldn't stand her. I was the one who used to cop a hiding to get Chris out of trouble. If Chris did anything, I'd tell her to get out of the way and defend her. She was mad on Doris Day, and we used to go to see her pictures. I remember I bought her her first party dress. When Elvis came out big, I bought all his records for her. She was really more like a younger sister.

My cousin Jean used to do part-time in the bar, but Ivor and David Richards were the regular barmen and their parents had a shop in Cambridge Heath Road. We'd go in there and have a cup of tea with them, and sometimes Ivor or David, one of them, would walk me home. Go left into Cambridge Heath Road, into Cephas Street, into Globe Road, and I was home: Portman Place at Number 51.

But it was safe to walk round the East End in those days, anyway. I remember when I was young there was a little girl disappeared. Her parents had a dairy in Roman Road, and I think it ended up one of the milkmen had done it. It was such a horrific thing when she was found dead. The whole area was horrified. Nobody talked about anything else. Things like that scarcely ever happened when I was a child.

John Keating was another used to help out behind the bar when it was absolutely packed. I don't really know who he was connected with. He seemed to just come and go; be there some days and some days not. He was an ugly giant of a man; very hard-looking, very comical. 'Nut-Nut' he was known as. He was involved in nicking a bus one night. It ended up down Jubilee Street somewhere, and he and his mate, they'd charged all the passengers their fares. He took over a pub in South London eventually and then I heard he'd died. I think he was called 'Nut-Nut' as having a reputation for being a headbutter when he was young. He was good to work with, because if you got upstarts being Jack-the-Lad whilst he was working, he'd lean over and say, 'Did you say something?' If they had any sense they'd stop, because his appearance was enough to put the frighteners on most people. If Nut-Nut Keating or Eddie the assistant manager came in to help out and they were leaving, they'd give you a lift too. It was all a very friendly collection of people; it seemed like a little family.

Amongst the people you'd call actual villains there wasn't any trouble. Any trouble you got in the Beggars was youngsters from outside the area who came there and wanted to make a name for themselves or got silly on drink. A lot of the trouble was young girls. The boys would be flash, and in turn the girls would wind their boyfriends up. 'That man's looking at me. Do something.' If Nut-Nut wasn't there to give them a look, then Patsy or the barman would jump the bar and stop things before they got out of control.

One night I was serving, and there were five from outside and one was being so obnoxious. Eddie, who didn't have a very bubbly personality – nice, but he was a bit cold – got the drinks they ordered. The next thing, one of the party smashed a glass and went to stab Eddie with it. I was there, and I got my hand in the way. It was cut and bleeding. It was Patsy who asked who'd cut me. I pointed. He picked the man up by the scruff of the neck and his pants and ran with him down the length of the bar and ran him out. Looking back, it was really quite funny. First of all he ran him into the door because he'd forgotten the door opened inwards. Then, when he'd thrown him out, he and Jimmy Quill did first aid on my finger. George Cornell was in that night, but fortunately he didn't see what happened. Patsy said to me afterwards that he'd have gone mad. He'd have done the man properly. But trouble was rare.

Lots of faces used the Beggars, and the Ambroses used to go in there as well. I called Eddie Ambrose 'Ginger'. Johnny, one of the brothers, had the

Barley Mow, a small pub around the corner. He was the boxer, and some people said he was the best middleweight in Britain before he went to prison. Tony Voss was their cousin. He was very well known. He did some time in a French prison with Billy Ambrose. Eighteen months, I think it was. When he got back here, I remember Tony insisted on speaking half French and half English for a few months. He got a thing about wine after he came out of the French prison. Tony mainly went about with Ginger Ambrose. Billy never had anything much to say for himself, but if I went round the Barley Mow he'd send round a drink to me.

I knew George, one of the Dixon brothers. He was another giant of a man who got shot at once by Ronnie Kray in the Green Dragon Club in Aldgate. I don't know what he'd done to upset him, but luckily the gun didn't go off and Ronnie gave him the bullet as a souvenir. George used to wear it round his neck on a chain. They came from a big local family. I've seen his brother Alan Dixon. He was a big man as well, very comical, but as I say it was George I knew. He used to use the Beggars quite a lot. I was in a Chinese in Whitechapel one night and I remember seeing him hitting someone – it was an argument, and he didn't half hit this fellow. But in the East End you could have those things and they didn't ruin an evening or anything. They were really part of life. Over and done with in a minute, and everyone got on with things again.[3]

I was tiny in those days, five two or five three, and I only weighed seven stone. The two brothers Ivor and David Richards I worked with, they were both short as well. David used to take things very seriously and looked for insults which weren't there. He got short with George Dixon once, and Dixon picked him up with one hand and just slapped him. I don't know what it was about, but David complained to the guv'nor, who asked me if George had actually hit him. I said he'd more slapped than hit him. The governor said he'd got away quite light. But Ivor could take a joke against himself. He was much more bubbly. Ivor was convinced he could sing, but he had a dreadful voice. Some of the lads actually had a contract drawn up that he was to sing at the Palladium and he really fell for it. If he'd checked the date, he'd have seen it was for Christmas Day. But they were both very genuine good-natured lads. Anyway, Ivor had a laugh on us. He won £100 on Foinavon's Grand National.[4]

Patsy was a good landlord; always knew what was going on. There was no chance of the staff taking advantage of him, like they do in other pubs I've been in where you could take the optics under the landlord's nose and he'd not notice – not that we'd

---

[3]See Appendix – George Dixon.
[4]In 1967 Foinavon, a 100–1 outsider, was so far behind that he avoided a serious pile-up at the 23rd fence and went on to win.

want to. Patsy wasn't like that. Mainly he used to be on the customers' side of the bar. That way he could both mingle and see what was going on. He always used to say to me, 'I'll accept a drink. I'll have a Dubonnet, but top it up with water. Never make it a double.' That way, he could seem to be drinking all evening, but he wasn't really.

I never spoke to Ronnie Kray and I'd never heard his voice until the court, but Reggie I used to talk to in the Beggars. He used to come in on his own a lot. He'd ask me how I was. He was quietly spoken. The difference between them, so far as I was concerned, was that I never saw Ronnie smile but Reggie would, and ask how you were getting on, how the family was and so on. Pass the time of day. On other occasions he'd come in with all the Firm, and Ronnie would be with them, unlike George Cornell, who'd come in late and stay on his own. Reggie'd come in early of an evening, have a drink, and leave.

Reggie kept order, too. I remember Big Pat Connelly, who was one of the Firm, he was ordering drinks this night and I couldn't understand just what he was wanting. I'd said 'Pardon?' and Pat had repeated it. I said 'Pardon?' again and Connelly banged his fist. Reggie just looked over and said, 'Be quiet', and told me what it was was wanted.

I think if it hadn't have been for Ronnie, Reggie wouldn't have gone the way he did. If you'd not known the history behind them when you met Reggie, even though you'd heard the stories and you knew they were all true, there was part of your mind which would say 'No, it can't be so', because he was always so polite and quiet. There was never any trouble in the pub with either of them. The only occasions when Ronnie came in was when they were in a crowd. He preferred to drink in the Grave Maurice just down the road. The only other times I'd seen him was in the Regency, which the Barry brothers ran. We used to go there for a gamble and then a meal. As they grew older, the Twins got less alike-looking. Earlier, they'd been real identical twins but later it was easy enough to tell them apart. People now think of them as big men, but they weren't, they were only middleweights.

One night I was serving, when a voice came from nowhere ordering drinks. I couldn't see anyone, and then when I looked over the bar it was the midget Roy Smith, who ran around with the Twins. He married a showgirl, a big tall blonde. He used to work for the Twins. Now, he was all dressed up like the rest of the Firm and you got this disembodied voice ordering the drinks. He'd been on TV and had tried to con Hughie Green out of some money. I got to know his daughter quite well later on.[5]

Even though he lived over South London, George Cornell was a regular. I only met his wife Olive a couple of times. I met his brother Jimmy Cornell, but I only knew the other brother as Myers and

[5]See Appendix – Royston James Smith.

I only met him outside the coroner's court. One night George was already well bevvied up when he came in and was winding people up. When he was drinking, he thought he was quite funny and others should think he was too. Like Ivor, he also thought he could sing a bit. Patsy knew Johnny Ambrose wouldn't want George bevvied up, and he wanted me to tell him to go round the Barley Mow, saying there was a singing competition. So I told him there was a good prize and just got him out of our place. An hour later, Johnny was on the phone saying Cornell was on stage causing chaos, and it was our fault; but we reckoned we'd got George out of our bar and the Ambroses were old enough and experienced enough to deal with him.

I remember serving a man sitting at the table one night. He sat quietly reading a paper. You wouldn't give him a second glance, he was so nondescript. Later, Patsy Quill told me it was Alfie Hinds, the famous prison escaper. You could see how he'd actually managed the escape. He'd not have been noticed in the outside world.[6]

---

[6]Hinds, who had been convicted of a robbery at Maples, the furniture store in Tottenham Court Road, continually protested his innocence. He escaped from prison on a number of occasions. Later when Herbert Sparkes, the officer who had arrested him, published his memoirs saying that Hinds was guilty, he sued him and won, although the Court of Appeal would not quash his conviction. Later he went to live in the Channel Islands and became a leading light in Mensa. It is probably correct that Hinds was on the robbery but that Sparkes, as was common in those day, gilded the lily so far as the evidence against him was concerned.

There were all sorts of alliances in the East End. This family met up with that family or these brothers didn't like those brothers – but I've never seen the Quill brothers involved in any sort of group. It seemed to be like the pub was neutral ground. Patsy always said they thought that the Beggars was the last place anything would ever happen involving gangs of any sort.

4

This may seem strange, but it is quite true. Three weeks before the shooting, out of the blue my Irish Aunt Mary came down to my home and said she was really worried about me. She just turned up one evening when the kids were in bed, saying she had very strong feelings that something was wrong. I kept saying to her, 'I'm all right', and I was. The kids were well. I'd got three bits of part-time work and I was coping well.

She took off her hat and coat – it's funny how people used to wear hats in those days and don't at all now – and we had a cup of tea together. She was a bit fidgety and I wondered what she wanted. It wasn't that usual for her to come down uninvited, so to speak. Then she said straight out she'd tell my cards for me. Now, this was also unusual in itself. She had those black Irish good looks and a bit of the gypsy in her, and when I was younger, me and my cousins, we were always on at her to tell our fortunes.

Although she was very very good with the cards, she didn't do it all that often because my Uncle Bill didn't approve of it. Usually you had to plead with her to tell your fortune and she wouldn't always do it for you, no matter how you went on, but that afternoon she laid them out for me. It was an ordinary pack of playing cards she used – I always had several packs lying around. I used to play a lot of patience – I still do, for that matter. She spread them around and first she told me I'd move within a very few weeks. Of course she knew I wanted to be out of the slum clearance area and I thought she was just kidding me along, making me feel good, but she said, 'You want a house, but you'll move to a flat.' She also described a building which I thought she was meaning as the block she thought I'd be going to, but later I realised was the coroner's court. She also said I was in the middle of a group of men, half in uniform and half not. She said I'd have to make a decision, and that it would cost me a lot to do so. She really was genuinely concerned. She'd even brought me a rosary and a relic she said had been blessed by the Pope and, in turn, she blessed the kids with the relic before she left and she gave me the rosary. I wasn't religious at all by then, but the strange part was I did have the rosary on me on the night of the shooting.

I know the books that have been written have said George Cornell was a villain, but in the pub he was just so nice to me. He used to laugh at me about the records I used to play in the pub. I've no idea what the quarrel was about. People have always said it was because he called Ronnie a 'big fat poof', but that was just George. If he'd had a few drinks he'd think that was comical, and that others should think it was as well. Then again it has been said that Ronnie got upset because George had come on his manor. That can't have been right. George was a regular drinker in the Beggars.[1]

The night of 9 March 1966 I was a bit late getting to the Beggars. I can't now remember whether the kids had been playing up or Chrissie was a bit late arriving, or if it was me. It didn't matter, because there was hardly anyone in the place. I went upstairs, took my coat off and had a word with Mrs Quill, Patsy's wife, and then went down and relieved Ivor. At the trial Mr Platts-Mills, who was defending Ronnie, made a great thing about it, however. It was like almost everything he said to me. It was over and over again.

Q: When you arrived at the public house, do you remember what you did?
A: Yes, I ran upstairs and took my coat off.
Q: You were late, were you?
A: Yes.
Q: Are you sure about that?
A: Yes, because I was supposed to be there at half-past seven.

[1]See Appendix – George Cornell.

Q: So you did not waste a minute of time because Ivor the barman was due home for his supper?

A: Yes.

Q: Is that true?

A: Well, I think I spoke to the licensee's wife, but only for a minute or so.

Q: Was that just a moment of time, saying Good Evening to Mrs Quill?

A: I can't remember exactly, it is so long ago, but it could only be for a minute or so.

Q: Could it be that you sat down and had a good chat to her for ten minutes?

A: I doubt it.

Q: Could it have been, according to what you say now?

A: No I don't think so. I don't honestly remember, it's a long while ago.

Q: You were late, and Ivor the barman was in a hurry to get home for his supper, so you would not have spent more than the time to say Good Evening to Mrs Quill?

A: I don't really remember.

Q: You mean you may have spent ten minutes passing the time of day?

A: I doubt it very much if I spent ten minutes with her, but I would have spoken to her automatically if I saw her on the premises.

It was fairly early for the pub, around 8.15 and still quiet, and I was on my own. Ivor'd go round to his parents for supper and wasn't due back for another quarter of an hour or so. Patsy was upstairs in his living quarters. There was nothing I couldn't manage on my own. For a start, there weren't too many people

in the bar. Two men were drinking with George
Cornell. Now I know they were Albie Woods and
Johnny Daley, but I didn't know their names then.
There was an Irish fellow was standing in the next
bit of the bar, and there was also an old boy whom
we called Pop, who was a regular drinker. He didn't
give evidence at the trial. He'd gone ga-ga by then.
A fellow was sitting in the centre, a couple at a table
and a young couple who'd come in for a drink.

When the bar wasn't busy, I had a bad habit. I
would keep putting on a record I really liked – over
and over. The same one, time and again. It would
drive everyone mad. George'd just recovered from
Gene Pitney and 'I'm Going to be Strong', and now
he thought he was going to get the Walker Brothers
singing 'The Sun Ain't Gonna Shine Any More'
for weeks.

I was leaning over the bar talking to George, who
was sitting on a stool, about the Walker Brothers'
record, explaining how he was going to have to hear
it a few more times, at any rate, and then Ronnie Kray
and Ian Barrie walked in. They didn't say anything
at all, just walked over to George, who said, 'Look
who's here,' put his hand in his pocket, and said,
'Let's get a drink,' and that's when Ronnie shot
him. Point blank. George didn't say anything. He
never had a chance either to run or plead. He just
went over backwards toppling off his stool. I know
now that there were three shots fired, but when it
happened I was in a sheer panic. It was just so

terrifying to think someone can just walk into a pub and just do that.

At the time I saw those guns, everything seemed to happen in slow motion. It seemed to take ages. It seemed as though it was like a film being done in slow motion. It was the most awful mixture of feelings. Fear, panic and that this can't be happening. If there'd been an argument it would still have been terrible, but just nothing was said. I should imagine when they shot him they just carried on and out. I was sure I was going to be shot.

One minute I'm putting on a record, and the next Ronnie Kray's shot George, and the man with him's got a gun pointed at me. I think it was the man in the centre dived into the ladies' toilets when it all happened, but I didn't care what the others did; I was too concerned about what was going to happen to me. I thought if I try to go up the stairs to the living quarters, I could get shot in the back. By now, things are racing through my mind. Where can I hide? And the cellar was there at the end of the bar away from the street. I ran along the little corridor to the back of the pub and I went down the cellar steps and hit my back as I landed. I'd tried to jump down, and I landed awkwardly and caught the bottom of my spine. I just went straight down the cellar steps. It was such fear. Then I hid, or so I thought. After a few moments I thought, what have I done? I can't get out of here now. There was nowhere to go; nowhere to hide. I was going behind crates and barrels, just wandering round the cellar. I expected the man with Ronnie to come down looking for me. It was going to be like the pictures where the girl gets stalked through the cellar or whatever, but it wasn't as if the cellars stretched under the next-door houses and shops, like they sometimes do. There was nowhere I could go but up.

I waited a bit more, and now there was absolute silence except for the record, which had stuck and was going backwards and forwards on and on in the same groove. That was all I could hear. There was no screaming or anything. It was so quiet. No one seemed to be coming looking for me, so I thought I've got to go back up, and I did.

The bar seemed absolutely empty of customers except for George, who was on the floor, and the old boy who was still at his table. Patsy was on the hall stairway, using the phone, ringing for the ambulance. He said he'd heard the shots in the living quarters, where he was at the time, and the first thing he'd checked on was his kids, and by the time he came round, the pub was deserted and he didn't even know where I was.

That night, before the police arrived, I told Patsy who it was. He wanted to know what I'd seen. 'Who was it?' he wanted to know, and when I told him 'Ronnie', he asked, 'Was Reggie with him?' 'No,' I said. 'I don't know the other guy.' I don't remember he gave me any advice. He certainly didn't tell me I wasn't to say anything to the police. All he really kept on repeating was, 'I can't believe this has happened.' Neither could I.

I went round from behind the bar, and George was still alive but, looking at the blood and the wound in his head, I couldn't believe he could be. Patsy said, 'I've phoned the police and the ambulance.' I said, 'Give me the teatowels.' They'd been through a machine and were spotless. I loosened George's collar and tie and was trying to stop the blood from his head until the police and the ambulance came. I got blamed for this in the trial. It's interesting how many recollections there are of an incident, particularly when it's a shocking thing like that. Ivor says he was in the bar by the time I came back up the stairs, but now I've no recollection of that at all or even of him being in the pub. I'm sure that I was the one who took George's cigarette away from him, but Ivor says he was the one. The one witness who stayed and gave evidence says it was me. He doesn't even mention Ivor at all. It's easy to see how recollections get all muddled up. I can remember I loosened George's tie, because I was going to unbutton his shirt because with the blood all over the place I thought he must have been shot in the chest, and I was going to try and stanch it. I remember it coming over a police walkie-talkie that George was being transferred to a neurological hospital, I think it was Maida Vale, so a bit of me thought, Good, he is still alive, but then because of the state his head had been in, the other bit of me thought, No, he can't be. The other thing I remember, and I still do really, is how awful the whole smell was with the blood and everything. I don't even really remember the ambulance people arriving and taking over. I got criticised at the trial for being cool and collected as if somehow it didn't mean a thing to me. But you can't panic when you're seeing to a person, can you?

They took George to Mile End Hospital first. It was really just down the road, and then he was transferred to Maida Vale. By the time he was there he was unconscious, and he died about half-past ten on the way to the operating theatre.

Once the ambulance men had taken over, I remember Patsy offering me a brandy, but I couldn't think why on earth he was doing that when he knew I drank gin and lime. I know George's wife Olive came into the pub before the police started questioning people. I don't know how she'd heard so quickly. She came in, screaming out 'Where's George?' and 'What's happened?' and 'Who did it?' I didn't really know her, but I knew who she was. The police had only just arrived, and I wasn't going to answer her in front of them. In fact the pub just kept filling up with police all the time. Apparently they'd been down at a party after a divisional football match. They'd had a telephone call and had come streaming back.

Then I was taken to a room upstairs. Tebbell was one of the police in charge, and he was asking me what happened. I said straight off I was round putting records on and I didn't see what happened. It was just about the first thing that came into my head. I knew I couldn't dare say it was Ronnie – I'd have been dead – so I made up a statement which I thought would satisfy them. I remember the police saying, 'If you were by the records, what did you think the gunshots were?' and I said I thought the gunshots were light bulbs exploding. I didn't know what else to say and it was really the first thing that came into my head. I couldn't say there and then what had really happened.

Even in that half-hour before I was questioned and there was all that coming and going, I knew I had another problem. There was this copper who used to come in regularly and drink with East London villains. He always gave the impression he was very well in with them. Other coppers might come in to the Beggars, but you never got other coppers in there drinking with the villains. When you see someone like that, you worry about making a statement because you never know who the information is going to go back to. Of course it was all part of the mystique that the Twins had the coppers sewn up, but you couldn't be too sure they didn't. It wasn't until twenty years later I saw him again, but I remembered him and he remembered me.

Years later, I was invited to a retirement do for another copper – and this bloke walked in. I was standing talking to people and he came over and said, 'Oh, let's get you a drink, my dear.' I told him to bugger off. I said I didn't drink with people like him; he should pick which side of the fence he was on. I think he was quite embarrassed. He didn't even argue. He just stood there for a moment and then he walked away. The people who was with me said, 'Quite right.' Perhaps it doesn't matter now, but it wasn't all right back then.

The police questioning went on until the early hours of the morning and eventually they said I could go, and I was given a lift home by Jimmy. I think Patsy must have phoned him, because he came round to help with things.

Ordinarily we had to tidy up, generally after we finished and before our supper with Mrs Quill, so I would get in half-eleven, quarter to twelve. That night had all the police coming in and out and it was quite a time before I was questioned by Tebbell, but funnily it wasn't any later than usual when I was allowed to go. On the way home, Jimmy Quill said, 'Thank God you kept calm,' and strangely enough after that initial fear in the cellar, I had. It was like something was happening and you weren't really there; you were detached from it all. The evening just sort of seemed to end like a clock had stopped. It was so horrific seeing the state of George Cornell, and also that you knew you didn't mess with anyone like Ronnie.

The strangest part of it all is that somehow that evening I lost the rosary. I don't know whether it was when I went down the cellar or later when I was helping George, but I never had it back. Later, when the police examined the bar, they found a bullet just about the part of the bar where I'd been standing.

5

What I knew I mustn't do was let myself go in front
of Jimmy Quill whilst he was driving me home. Not
that he wouldn't have been kind, but I knew, once I
started, I wouldn't have stopped. I think I kept my
cool quite well whilst Jimmy was there. I simply
wouldn't let myself cry in front of him, but I had
the key out before I got out of the car and I ran
up the stairs into the kitchen and was sick in the
sink. I just threw up all over. I was in a terrible
state, shaking and sobbing. I should have gone to
the outhouse, but I just didn't think.

Chrissie'd always stay until I got home, and I think
before I'd gone out I'd taken it she was stopping the
night. She quite often did. She would be up waiting
for me. When you're younger, a bit before midnight,
that's not a late night.

She took one look at me and said, 'What on earth's
happened?' and I started being sick again and crying.
We didn't have any booze in the house. I couldn't

afford drink indoors, but I could have done with one then. So she made some tea and I sat shivering on the settee which made up into a bed and said, 'Ronnie just come in and shot George Cornell.' She'd no need to ask, 'Who's Ronnie?' Everyone knew. That was what was so funny in the trial, Mr Platts-Mills asking me why I called him Ronnie as if I knew him.

I don't think we slept at all that night. We sat up all night on the edge of the sofa, drinking tea and me going off to be sick, discussing what I could do. I was all for packing up and just running away, but at the same time I was also waiting for someone to tell me what to do. When it came to it, there weren't many options. You can't just run off, not with no money and three young children. Every time we heard a car drive past the end of the road, I just couldn't believe it wasn't going to stop there and someone come in for me. People did disappear in the East End. I don't say it was the Krays were involved, but over the years Mad Teddy Smith, one of their friends, went missing, so did Ginger Marks, so did Billy Stayton, and there was a bank manager in South London who just vanished. There were always stories about mini-cabs being sent round late at night; when the man went to the front door after hearing the bell, the driver would say 'mini-cab'. The man would say, 'I didn't order one,' but he would be bundled in the back seat and off. Maybe it was legend, like those stories of dogs being found choking with burglars' fingers bitten off in their throats, but we believed in it.

Next day, however bad I felt, it was kids to school. Things had to carry on as normal, in the sense that I had to take them, get some shopping and go home. When I got back, I just sat there and cried. I couldn't read, eat, even think straight. Chris worked at the time, and she had to go to her office. She was marvellous. She was back after work, and from then on she spent as much time as she could with me. I was just sitting shivering, trying not to show to the kids how bad I felt. That first evening, we discussed what I was going to do. Was I going to go back just like nothing had happened? I couldn't think about going back to the Beggars that next night. Then I didn't go at the weekend, and I knew I'd never go back and work there. By then, there didn't even really seem to me to be a choice. I said to myself I wasn't going to go back behind the bar. Logic tells you you're not going to be shot just by going in the place, but you still think you might. There hadn't been any arrests. You just don't know what's going to happen. I think that even if Ronnie had been arrested that night, I could never have gone back in there and served again. Not after seeing George like that.

That first evening Mr Axon, the officer who first took charge of the enquiry, sent someone down to take my fingerprints for elimination purposes. He wanted me to go to the police station, but I wouldn't go. It wasn't long before he had me up there, though.

I thought perhaps someone like Patsy Quill or his

brother would come round to see me, advise me what to do or how to cope with it all, but no one did. The nearest was when Jean, my cousin who did the part-time barmaiding, came round, but she never said anything outright like, 'When are you coming back?' I suppose it was really taken for granted that I was too scared to return. I think Jean tried to detach herself from it, as though it has happened, but no one's going to be nicked, so keep your head down and that's it. Word must have got round the East End, because by then it was just about an open secret which everyone shared. I'm pretty sure she knew it was down to Ronnie Kray, but she didn't get it from me. I think she could have been a bit more supportive, because she'd lived with me and my husband when we were over in Leytonstone because her father was a bit nutty and started beating up my aunt and his daughters. Then they all got rehoused eventually. She was younger than me. The last I heard, she was living in Kent on the coast somewhere. I never saw any of them again. I don't know what happened to the rest of them.

So I stayed at home, collected the kids from school, and life went on. I also had a couple of people in the street I knew at the time with small kids themselves. One of them would come in during the day, and we'd take the kids over the park together. But I didn't tell her what had happened. I was still jumping at my own shadow every time a car door banged.

Those days were like living on your nerves waiting

for something to happen. I didn't dare to ring my ex-husband John when I went out, but he'd heard soon enough. Just before the previous Christmas, he'd got in touch and started coming round to see the children, who adored him. There was no question of our getting back together then, but he came round often and he came to see me within a couple of days of the shooting. I told him straight away that I knew what had really happened. I wanted his advice. His view was that I was going to be all right because they would know I was going to be too frightened to do anything, and I should just try and keep out of it. It was now John started popping in, on and off at all times, just to see if things were all right. Not that he could have done that much if they weren't. I mean he didn't know Ronnie personally to go up and say, 'Pat's not talking.' He certainly didn't have enough clout to go up and say, 'You leave her alone,' and he didn't know anyone big enough to do it for me.

I didn't even think of moving out of the East End. I couldn't go to the people at the Housing and say to them, 'I need a move on compassionate grounds.' 'Why?' 'Because I've seen Ronnie Kray kill George Cornell.' I didn't have the money to move privately and rent a flat for myself, and it wasn't like having your own home and being able to put it up for sale. Fortunately, it was a time when a lot of people round the East End were being rehoused by the council because of slum-clearance policies. It was an automatic rehousing by the council.

So, just like Aunt Mary had said, I was in a new flat within three weeks after the killing. Some people in the street had already gone and so I suppose it was always only a matter of time, but, out of the blue, I got a letter from the council saying you're being moved on the following Monday. Les, our friend from the Methodist Youth Club, and John got hold of a van to put my stuff in, not that there was a lot to move.

The block, Withey House, hadn't been up very long, and I was in the caretaker's flat. It was really nice in there. We had a bathroom and an airing cupboard with a drying cabinet, and a balcony at the back of the lounge with three bedrooms. John helped me buy a new three-piece and carpet. My daughter's and the boys' bedroom Les decorated to make them more like kids' rooms. But I still didn't have a telephone.

The baths were just along the road where you could take your laundry. You could get up really early and go and get your washing done before anyone was awake. Like my Nan did. There were big drying cabinets which dried the sheets in minutes. You had big presses where you could put your sheets and towels through.

A lot of this is what I have been told or found out later. At first Jim Axon was in charge of the investigation and Ted Tebbell, the officer who'd interviewed me in the Beggars, was the 2 i/c, but not for long. Axon was applying to be Chief Constable of Jersey – I think eventually he became the Chief

Constable of Guernsey – and anyway there was a move to get the Yard in. I hated Axon. I didn't like his attitude, and I didn't like his getting me up to the police station to confront me with the fact that one of the people in the pub said that I wasn't by the record-player but that I was drinking with George.

The police came late one night and told me I was wanted at Arbour Square station for questioning. I said I couldn't go because of the children. In turn they said they'd leave a policewoman. I said no, and so I got a girl from over the road. She came and stopped in with the kids. I was taken to the police station. There was Tebbell and Axon. They kept saying to me they knew it was Ronnie Kray and they'd had people saying that I was standing talking to George Cornell and not over by the record-player. A young man, Johnny, had said he was there. I opened a door and there was Johnny Dale. He said 'Hello' and I said, 'Sorry, I don't know him,' although, of course, I did. I kept insisting I was round the other bar, and they kept telling me they knew I'd seen it all and could name the people who did it. It just went on like that for ages and finally they told me I could go. I remember Axon on the steps to Arbour Square as I went down, and he was being friendly. He put his arm round my shoulders. I didn't appreciate that at all, as I was sure people would be watching and the word would get about. I seemed to think that Ronnie would have spies staking out Arbour Square police station. I knew Bobby Ramsey lived opposite and he was a friend of the Twins, although he never did me any harm. But what could have happened if he'd seen me in a cuddle with the Bill and reported back? If I was seen talking to them, the police, then Ronnie would know I'd gone against him and my life would be worth nothing. In truth, I was in such a worry I didn't know what to think, except what a shit to do that with a woman. Axon may not have meant any harm, but he should have thought before he did it. It really put my back up.

Mr Axon didn't know how to talk to East Enders. You don't have to be an East Ender to do it, but you have to know how. He gave me the impression that he was the officer who said he'd go by the book and, therefore, I would answer his questions, but I wouldn't.

I didn't realise it at the time, but I now suspect Axon must have had a hand in getting me rehoused, because that was the only ground-floor flat which made it ideal to watch back and front. They didn't have to think of anyone going up the stairs or in the lift. It was completely on its own.

A police van was there, parked outside, almost from the time I moved into the flat. I'm sure Jimmy Axon wanted to know who came to the flat rather than give me the comfort of protection. If they had come up, it would have been over and done before the police could have done anything. Anyone could have come across the green at the back and over the balcony and done me before the police got out of their van. There was a walkway as well, backing on to the Mile End Road.

When I went anywhere out of the flat I knew there was police following me, and I was being treated as a hostile to them. That was all very well, but, again, if anyone had seen this from the Krays' side they could easily have thought I was talking to the police. I thought it was a bit naughty me being the sprat to catch a mackerel. The police should have put more pressure on the men drinking in the pub that night than bullying me. I know I didn't have any convictions and some of them may have had or been allied with some friends or others and so not been such a good witness, but it seemed unfair to me.

One night my friend Doreen came round and said, 'I see you've got the van opposite with effing old Bill.' She was a bit put out because of the thought anyone else seeing them parked there might think I was talking. She said she thought I'd been stuck in the place on my own too long, not going out of an evening, and that I should go out and have a drink. Chris was there, and she said she'd stay and look after the kids. As we went across, Doreen just knocked on the van, said, 'We're going in the pub, the Horn of Plenty in Globe Road, does anyone feel like coming in and buying us one?' But no one answered.

After that, curiously enough, things got a bit easier with the van. The coppers inside were under strict instructions from Axon not to talk to me, but I began to feel a bit sorry for them cooped up in that van.

After all it was Axon's decision, not theirs, to sit outside my flat the whole night. It was pretty cold at night in early April that year, and so I just went to the front door round about eleven o'clock one night and made a sign that I was making tea. Did any of them want any? At first nothing happened and I went back in, but then a few minutes later one of them came over and from then on I would always give them teas or coffee of a night. That was what broke the ice. They never presumed like knocking on the door and saying could they have a cup of tea. Well, one did. He knocked on the door around midnight and asked if I'd like to go to the pictures. He got short shrift. I mean it wasn't their fault. I always asked them to come. They had been told at the time under no circumstances were they to talk to me, but that went by the board with the coffee. One of them later became a very good friend. In fact he was the one who came and took my fingerprints right at the start.

Then, at first in the street, the police had had to walk behind me when I went out, but if you've had coffee with someone and want some more that night you can't watch them struggle with three children and bags, so after a bit they carried the shopping and pushed one of the kids in his chair. We'd had a bit of an incident where one of the officers walked behind me. I thought one of my kids who was in nursery school at the time had dived in the men's toilets and didn't come out. I wasn't going in, and so I called one of the coppers to go and have a look. In the meantime one of the stallholders had said he'd gone off in a car. That threw me into a panic, but it turned out he'd just gone off back to school.

One day I collected Michael, the elder boy, from infant school and I found toy cars which weren't his in his pocket. He'd obviously taken them, and so, after I'd given him a dressing-down and a slap, I got the police to walk me back with him and put him in front of the headmistress. I said what I'd done, and she was all sympathetic to him, saying I shouldn't have touched him but that I should have used psychology with him instead. When I got back, I heard a rattling in his pocket. This time what he'd done was he'd taken the keys from her drawer. The policeman had to walk back with me and Michael again. Really I was quite pleased with the boy! She didn't really have a lot to say the second time. I think her psychology must have failed her.

Tebbell came round quite a lot, but I wouldn't have Axon at all, and I still wouldn't co-operate. I was also furious with 'this person's said this and this person saw you'. He'd never name them. I thought these 'persons' must have seen what happened so why didn't they come forward? When it went to court, it was none of these bloody customers who came to give evidence. If two men were drinking with George, they must have been friendly, and so why didn't they go forward? I saw Tebbell and Axon again, and I was taken up Arbour Square for questioning yet again, and I still lied. Also I'd got to the point of thinking, who do I trust? They, the Twins, seemed to be able to do what they wanted. In the back of my mind was, 'Well, the police have never put a stop to them. Why will they now?' You know the saying, 'You may be paranoid but it still doesn't mean they're not out to get you.'

I have to admit also that the other thing at the back of my mind was what had been instilled in everyone growing up in the East End. You didn't go to the police to solve your problems. Now my dad had a great respect for the police. I remember once I was brought home by a copper for riding a bike without lights. I was punished by Dad not for riding a bike without lights but for the disgrace of having a copper at the front door. I wasn't brought up to hate the police, but it was a cultural thing. You solved your own problems.

If my dad had still been alive, then it might have been different. I could have talked to him and he might, I don't say he would, but he might have said, 'Go and tell them what you really saw.' I couldn't have talked to my mother. It would have been like taking an advertisement out in the *East End Advertiser*. On everyone's doorstep within twenty-four hours. She just couldn't have resisted helping herself to the bit of fame I didn't need.

My ex-husband's attitude was still: 'You know how dangerous they are – don't say anything.' But there again that was the general feeling in the East

End with everything that had gone on over the years. The Krays were so powerful, the police were never going to nick them. They were going to walk away from it anyway. It had been the same when Nipper Read first had tried to get them over the Hideaway Club in the West End. He'd failed, why should anyone succeed now?

Then Jim Axon either moved to the Channel Islands or changed jobs, and Tommy Butler took over the enquiry. He was the first copper out of any of them I had any liking for. He was straightforward and down to earth, and I thought, Here's a man who if he says something means it. He was really at the height of his fame. He was the one who had chased the Train Robbers down all over the world, it seemed. Now he was on the Beggars case. He inspired confidence, but I still wasn't prepared to go along with him. The Twins and the Firm were driving about in their cars and walking the streets then. And the cars they had were better than Tommy Butler's.

First of all he came round, with Axon to introduce him. I said I didn't really want to speak to Axon any more, and Tommy Butler said to wait outside for him; he'd talk to me on his own. I really thought he was a diamond of a man.[1] I was really impressed with him from the start. He said, 'I can understand why you're sticking to this story and you're in a very difficult situation being on your own with kids, but

[1]See Appendix – Tommy Butler.

81

I'm determined we're going to put the whole Kray Firm behind bars.' He said he hoped he wasn't going to have to use me but, if it came to it, he would. If I persisted, he said, I could be charged with perjury. 'I hope it isn't going to come to that, but eventually you're going to have to make a decision.' He came to see me quite a few times. He just turned up; he had to. I hadn't got a phone. I still said I was changing the record-player.

On 4 August 1966 Tommy Butler pulled in Ronnie and Reggie. In the 1960s there were lots of editions of the evening papers, and I saw the Twins had been arrested. In his book, *Our Story*, Ronnie Kray makes a big thing about how I didn't pick out either him or Reggie on that ID parade. He's right. I didn't, because I never went on it. I didn't even know who did go on the first identification parade that summer or even where it was held, although I suppose it must have been Arbour Square police station. The police came round and I was told I was going, but I didn't. Tommy Butler didn't make me. He didn't think it was necessary because he knew I could tell them – Ronnie and Reggie – apart. Butler came to see me a few times, and I had an observation van parked outside my flat. It left me with mixed feelings. In one way you thought the police are there and they would be about if anything did happen, and then there was the other that would the people from the pub think I'd been talking to the police. All you worry about at the time is your kids. The youngest was only two. You just didn't know what was going to happen, whether it was the Krays or the police. That was the horrible part. Later I heard there'd been a big parade with both Ronnie and John Barrie standing to be recognised. Albie Woods, who'd been with Cornell, went to the parade along with Michael Flannery, but they didn't pick anyone out. That was a big point at their trial. It was only me out of all these dozens of men who pointed them out then. How could they fail to recognise them and me get it right?

After the ID parade when everyone failed to pick out Ronnie, from then on the squad was run down. In fact the van outside Withey House never moved. It was there for three or four months, and then, when the police tried to start it to drive off, they couldn't and it was eventually towed away. That would have been useful if there had been someone attacking me and there had had to be a chase. But even after the obbo on me finished, over the months one or two of the officers would pop in to see if I was all right and I kept in touch with them.

Funnily, Tommy Butler helped me no end. I'd been feeling rotten with my stomach, and I'd been taken into Bethnal Green Hospital where the surgeon came round, prodded me, and told me it was just wind. But I knew it wasn't. Tommy said, when he came on one of his visits to try and make me change my mind, how thin I looked and that I ought to go and see someone again. So I did. I got taken in and I had fibroids. This was what all the fuss would be about at the trial.

There was no doubt in my mind that the Twins were looking at, if not for, me, if only to see what I was going to do. They must have known where I lived and, even if they didn't, it wouldn't have been difficult to find out. Albert Donoghue says that they gave Patsy Quill £100 for me, but he never gave me up. Donoghue says Patsy never found me but he, of everyone, knew where I lived. I mean, his kids had been to a birthday party with mine, so there was no way he couldn't know.

In fact it was when I was at Withey House that Patsy actually came round. Now I can't remember why he came, but I went and sat out in the car with him. I said I was really upset, and you must be because George was a friend of yours. He said, 'Yes, but you live by the sword, you die by it.'

What Donoghue also says is that the Twins wanted me picked up by him and that he arranged with me to go to a meet in the Three Swedish Crowns over in Wapping, which was another one of the Quills' pubs, to see if I was going to talk to the police. He goes on to say that it never came to anything: '. . . one, she wouldn't show up, and two, if they did she would never leave.' He's wrong in that. I never saw Donoghue to speak to after the killing. No one put it to me I should go and see Ronnie, and I certainly wouldn't have done. Not voluntarily, anyway.[2]

In fact I only ever saw the Twins twice after the shooting. I don't know if Reggie continued to drink in the Beggars – I only ever went back there one night, but that wasn't to work or socially to have a drink. It was just that I'd got myself so worked up being questioned by the police and being scared what was going to happen that I felt I had to go round.

I left Chrissie with the kids and walked round with a mate, Lorraine, who waited at the door. As I saw it, Patsy Quill had only been in touch with me once. Looking back, it may have been sensible that he didn't get in contact, but at the time I felt that it was being dumped on me and I went to have a go at him. I didn't know the Firm was going to be in the pub that night, but there they were. It was mid-evening when I got there, and the place was crowded. I went in the saloon bar. Bobby Ramsey was there, and he offered to buy me a drink, but I said no.

It was desperation really; I wanted someone to tell me how I was supposed to cope with the situation. I was getting all the pressure from the police and I just didn't know where it was all going to end. It just boiled up in me. Patsy came over because I think he thought I was going to make a right scene, and I started having a row, shouting at him in front of

[2]Albert Donoghue and Martin Short, *The Krays' Lieutenant*, (London, Sidgwick & Jackson, 1995) p. 122, and James Morton, *Gangland*, (London, Little, Brown, 1992) p. 122.

everyone. I can't even remember what I was saying, but I was slagging him off. He was trying to quieten me down. I was in the middle of the saloon with the Firm right down the end where George was shot, just before you get to the snug. They didn't say anything. Ronnie just stared as usual.

Fortunately, one of the Ambroses was in that night. It was Ginger (Eddie) Ambrose, and I think he genuinely liked me and didn't want to see me get further into trouble – which I know I was asking for. He and Tony Voss came over and stood by me. Ginger said, 'I think the girl's put up with enough.' Then he said they'd see I got home all right. I hadn't even considered how I was going to get home. It was one of those occasions when you think facing everybody and giving vent to your feelings is less frightening than waiting for something else to happen. Lorraine was waiting at the door. She was trembling, absolutely terrified something would happen, and so was I when I got out. Tony and Ginger walked us part of the way home, then, when it was clear no one was following, I said we'd be all right, and they left us. When I got home and told Chrissie what I'd done, she said, 'Girl, don't ever do that again.' Even though she was years younger than me, at times like this she'd got much more sense than I had.

The only other time I saw the Twins was a bit after that when I was with John, my ex-husband. He'd gone to pay some car insurance in Clapton and we'd taken the kids for the ride. The office was on the first floor, and whilst I was waiting for him, two cars pulled up on the other side of the road. There was Reggie and Ronnie and other members of the Firm in them. They didn't say anything, just looked over at me, and as John came down they drove away. I was scared about that, but I never saw them again.

Reggie put in his book that he came round to me on Ronnie's behalf and had had a quiet word with me, telling me that it would be in my interest to forget what I'd seen and that he'd given me money, which he thought would keep me happy. That never happened – he never did. He's confusing things, and he's got the wrong witness. Looking back, I wish he had. I'd have emigrated.[3]

One of the questions I've always thought about is why the Myers brothers or some others didn't have a go at the Twins. Of course the answer is that whilst they were hardmen, the Myers weren't killers. The other reason is that it would have been hard to get to both the Twins at the same time. It seemed that once there had been a bit of trouble, they weren't seen together unless there was women around or they were taking Judy Garland out for dinner and a bit of publicity. It would have been very hard to catch them together and the fear was, I think, that if you got one, there was still the other left.

Of course, Olive Cornell did have a go at them. She

[3]Reg Kray, *Born Fighter*, (London, Arrow, 1991), p. 99.

was brave as a lion. She went round once, if not twice, to Vallance Road where Violet Kray lived and broke her windows. Her and Violet were having a slanging match on the front step when the police arrived. Olive got fined something like £1 at the magistrate's court the next day.

I was bringing up kids on my own and basically that's all you're worried about, is them. No one was advising me. I still had to go shopping, walk along the street, see people. I kept hoping it was like a bad dream and it would go away.

I gave up threading tags and writing envelopes and went on the dole. I was just concerned with getting through each day as it came. My cousin Chrissie stuck by me all the time, and John came round all the time. I had a very good friend, Doreen, who'd knocked on the police van and who died last year. She was always there. I wasn't going out socially. I had my own set of friends. Ivor and David used to come round occasionally to see me, and they helped me out a bit financially. Apart from Chris, Patsy, my ex-husband and later Les, I hadn't told anybody what I knew. My husband, he was still strongly against me giving evidence against them. Rumours were now going round that it was both Ronnie and Reggie, which it obviously wasn't, and it shows how things build up wrongly.

It was whilst I was at Withey House that I met the dwarf Roy Smith again. I didn't realise how close he was to the Twins, because people liked to drink with the Firm just to say, 'I drank with Ronnie and Reggie.' My Peter was with me when we met him in the street and came right out with, 'Why are you so small?' I was embarrassed more than him and said straight away, 'Because he didn't eat his dinners.' I suppose, over the years, poor Roy, he'd got used to questions like that, and not only from kids. All he said was, 'That's right. Always eat your dinners or you'll be small like me.'

He and his daughter Karen lived opposite. She was a really pretty child with lovely red hair, but it was very sad because she was a dwarf as well. The whole family looked after that little girl. She was always very well dressed; she was a lovely kid. The people on their side did not encourage their kids to have anything to do with her, but I started having her in to play with my daughter, who was about the same age, and his whole family were very, very nice to me. One day they knocked on the door, and when I opened it there they were with a load of groceries. Said it was because I was doing good for their Karen. After that, the family kept me supplied in fruit and veggies for ages.

I'd seen him before when I lived in Bethnal Green, but it wasn't until I moved into this flat that I saw more of him and his brothers. The other brothers were of normal height. They always seemed close as a family. One day there was a terrible fight with some people in which his family was involved. To get him out of harm's way because he was so little, someone had put him up sitting on top of a wall, but he was determined to join in. He was calling, 'To me, to me,' and he was hitting them from the wall if anyone came within arm's length.

I remember going to the coroner's court. Ivor told me Jimmy Myers had gone into the Beggars in a furious temper and said that people in there should give evidence, but when I spoke to him outside the coroner's court he was very nice. In a way, I'm surprised the Myers never came to see me, but there again they may have thought I'd got enough grief as it was. I lied all the way through those proceedings. Funnily, they weren't held in the East End where George was shot but in Westminster in front of Gavin Thurston. I suppose that's because he died in Maida Vale. I recall going up the steps and being put in a side room, and Patsy Quill was there. I told the coroner what I'd told the police: that the bang I had heard was something like a light bulb. I had been out of sight, and I came out and saw the man going off the stool. I also told the coroner that I didn't notice the colour of Ronnie Kray's clothes. You had the Cornells there, you had the police, Patsy was there. It was obvious there would be people listening in on behalf of the Krays. I remember the coroner didn't seem too impressed with my evidence. I'm sure he didn't believe me, but he didn't say much. But I thought, now it's all going to go away, because no way will they ever go to prison after this. Everyone knew who'd done it,

Left Me aged about nine, Mum took this.

Above I'm about eleven in this, with Dad.

Below This is Mum in her nanny's outfit before she was married.

Left I often dreamed Mr Kelly was my father so I could have free pie and mash. *(Helen McCormack)*

Prince Monolulu at Epsom, 1936. *(Topham)*

Boxing and bathing down at the York Hall Baths. *(Helen McCormack)*

St Peter's Hall. This is where I used to go dancing and where I met my husband. *(Helen McCormack)*

A lone policeman stands guard outside the Blind Beggar in 1969.
(Popperfoto)

The Blind Beggar today.
(Helen McCormack)

Above The Blind Beggar stands guard.
This is the sculpture by Elizabeth Frink which now stands in the Cranbourne Estate, off the Roman Road.
(Helen McCormack)

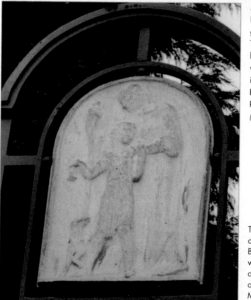

This is the plaque dedicated to the Blind Beggar which hangs on the gates of the Craft School Memorial Gardens.
(Helen McCormack)

Above I think gin was about two and six in those days.

Below The Bar at the Beggars. *(Topham)*

Left John Barrie outside Bow Street Court with Reggie Kray. *(Syndication International Ltd)*

Below This is one of the pictures which started the trouble. Ronnie Kray with Lord Boothby. *(Syndication International Ltd)*

Below From the left: Cornelius Whitehead, Reggie, Harry Jewboy, unnamed, Sam Wederman *(standing)*, Billy Daniels, Jack Dickson, Charlie Clarke, Ronnie, unnamed. *(Syndication International Ltd)*

Above George Cornell. *(Popperfoto)*

Left Reggie with Frances Shea before their marriage. *(Topham)*

Below The motorcade at Bow Street. *(Topham)*

Nipper Read. *(Popperfoto)*

Mr Justice Melford
Stevenson. *(Topham)*

and it just built up their reputation even more. So when I was told by one of the barmen that Jimmy Cornell came in the pub shouting and hollering why wouldn't anyone come forward, I wasn't surprised when no one did.

It was outside the coroner's court when Ivor told me that, and he said no doubt I'd heard it already, but I hadn't. Jimmy Myers was there, and he was nice; he said I was the only one to try and help. He said, 'You've got no problems with us. If we can ever try and help you, we will.'

It was shortly after that I had a great blow. Chrissie went to Australia. She had a brother who was already out there working as a dentist on the west coast, and she decided to go out to him. Things weren't going really well for her. She hadn't got any boyfriends. It wasn't that she wasn't good-looking or bubbly or anything, it was just she didn't seem to be able to settle in to a relationship, and one day she came round and said she'd made up her mind she was off. John, my ex-husband, gave her a £10 note to help her a bit. A tenner was several weeks' rent in those days, but what she did was she bought herself a bloody big hat with the money. I didn't go and see her off. I couldn't bring myself to. I think I'd have disgraced myself.

From the time of the coroner's court on, the police left me alone for a couple of years after that and I began to think that, after all, perhaps, it had gone away. I kept living my life with my head down. I stuck with the same three or four friends I could trust and feel safe with. Then, suddenly, there it was over the evening papers: 'Twins arrested'. That was 8 May 1968. Nipper Read had had this dawn swoop and pulled them in. I thought, so what? They'd got away with things for so long I didn't have any confidence that things would change. I thought, even if they go down on other things it won't be for long, and it's not going to be me who does them. They were only arrested on fraud charges, anyway, and that certainly was nothing to do with me.

So I didn't hear anything until the last week in May, when suddenly Ted Tebbell turned up on my doorstep with a man I hadn't seen before, but whom he introduced as Chief Inspector Henry Mooney. He was an Irishman with all their charm and blarney. I knew exactly what he wanted and it made me go cold thinking of it, so although I gave him tea, I still wasn't having anything of it. My attitude was that it was still my head on the block, not his. And so he got to me another way.

He would turn up of a Sunday with a woman police officer, Pat Allen, who was also on the Kray squad, and take me and my kids to Heathrow airport. Pat would go off with the kids to look at the planes whilst he'd buy me tea and biscuits and we'd sit at a quiet table in one of the cafeterias and talk. For a lot of the time it was general things. Nothing about the case, but there'd always be a bit towards the end. It was all 'Are you scared of bullies, then?' and of course I was, dead scared. Quite apart from that, there was the problem of the perjury. I was worried that I could get sent down myself if suddenly I admitted I'd lied on oath, and I tried to get him to promise me an amnesty sort of thing, but he wouldn't. He kept saying he wasn't going to threaten me nor was he going to make any promises because, if he did and I was asked about them in court, then if I said, 'Yes, I've been told I won't be prosecuted,' my evidence wouldn't be worth anything. Him and Pat Allen would bring me back, and a few days later they'd turn up and take us out again. I think they were putting more and more pressure on me, by the continual visits and saying they were determined to bring the Twins to court on quite a lot of charges.

Really, you read in thriller books that no one innocent ever gets hurt, but to do it as Ronnie did it in the pub that night, innocent people could have got hurt. Someone could have run in a panic into the line of fire. I mean, that old man who used to sit in there – the shock it must have been to him. You don't expect to be out for a quiet drink and have someone killed in front of you. When you get it so blatant and you can walk in and kill someone – where do you go from there? They must have started off as small villains, and then it built up until it came to things like George Cornell and Jack the Hat. Where do they go from there? They're just going to get more and more complacent until they're a complete law unto themselves.

It must have been five or six visits before Henry Mooney began to make real progress and I began to think really seriously. He still wouldn't give me any promises. 'I dare not run the risk of any promise,' he would say. 'It has to be voluntary.' He suggested that I go and see a solicitor and get his advice, and eventually I did just that. I suppose I knew in my own mind that I wasn't actually going to be done for perjury, but I couldn't actually rule it out. I mean the worst was going to be me giving evidence against the Twins, their being acquitted and then me getting sent down for a few months for lying to the coroner. What sort of a mess would I have been in then?

Actually, first, I went to see a friend – well, a friend of my husband who was a villain – to ask for advice. He wasn't a thief, but he'd been a hardman in his time. I didn't tell my husband I was going. The man didn't live far away, and so one evening I walked down to see him and said, 'I just don't know what to do. The police are on the scene and I'm under pressure.' He was really quite firm with me. He said, 'If it was my wife, I'd be taking her to Bethnal Green police station now to make a statement.' He'd got two reasons, he said. The first was, 'They've got to be put a stop to.' His attitude was that things had got out of control. If things could be done like that in a pub, innocent people could get caught up in shootings. What was going to happen next – a shooting in the street? Now, a shooting in the street seems an everyday happening, but it wasn't then. He thought that now the police had shown they were determined to put a stop to the Twins, there was a real chance they would win and so there weren't going to be the opportunity for reprisals. They could therefore be helped. The second reason was, if necessary, the police could take me to court as a hostile witness. I was still worried about the perjury, but he thought that if I co-operated, there was less likelihood of that than if I didn't.

One day in the second week of June, I said 'Yes.' I'd talked to my Chris quite a lot before she'd gone to Australia, and after the first few weeks her attitude had always been that I should do what was right. When you have kids growing up there, if things keep going like that, they'll think that's the way of life – no respect for the police if they aren't doing anything to stop it. Doreen would stand by me whatever I did. She thought that I was doing the right thing, but she was frightened for me if it all went wrong. So far as Les was concerned, he was the sort of person who would always do what was right. He'd have gone to the police that night and taken his chance.

After I spoke to my husband's friend, as a sort of back-up I went to see a solicitor like Henry Mooney had suggested. I just walked in to Breeze Benton's offices off the street and talked with the solicitor about my perjury. He made me realise that whilst there was no way that anyone was going to make promises or put things in writing, if I made a statement and went on to give evidence, no one was going to do anything to me about lying to the coroner. It was one relief off my mind. When it came to it, seeing that solicitor was one of the smartest things Henry Mooney ever suggested to me.

So on 10 June I began to make my statement. Doreen came with me to the police station and waited for me for hours. That first night, before Henry Mooney introduced me to my guards, he gave me a pretty stern warning. 'Don't tell anyone what you're doing. If people ask, don't tell them, just say you know nothing about anything.' Then he shook hands with me and it was out of the station and into the street, but I wasn't a free woman for the next year.

6

Mr Howard (*for Ian Barrie*): When you attended an identification parade in July of last year – you remember that?

A: Oh, yes.

Q: You were not certain, were you, that this was the man who was present when the shooting took place?

A: Oh, yes.

Q: Oh, no, you were not, were you?

A: Yes.

Q: Did you say to the police officers when there was a query about identification – my Lord, I am looking at the Notice of Additional Evidence dated the third of December, Sergeant Davies. When you were asked after the parade if you had recognised anyone upon the parade, did you say, 'I think that is the man. I am not absolutely sure'?

A: Excuse me, can I explain myself?

Mr Justice Melford Stevenson: Yes, you may say anything you like.

What he was referring to was the identification I made that afternoon of Ian Barrie. When it got to things like I had to go on the Barrie ID parade, Harry and Helen (the police officers sent to mind me) had to cope with me. I was like a nervous wreck. I was worked up about going and they had to put up with me and try and keep me calm.

I didn't want to know until the last minute. If you know something a month away, you're just going to brood, keep thinking about it. I was still going through it. Part of me was saying it was all going to go away; something was going to put a stop to it all. But it didn't.

It was just before lunch on 3 July, a Wednesday. We – that's me and Helen and Harry – had taken the kids to school that morning, and now I was out shopping down in Romford where I was buying a suit. Whilst I was in the shop, Helen or Harry must have had a telephone call. Helen said, 'Come on. Just get in the car. You're going somewhere.' I said, 'Where?', and she said, 'You're going to West End Central for an ID parade.' I said, 'I'm not.' They said, 'You've got no choice,' and off we went. This was it. I was in their hands. If I didn't play along, there was the perjury and the certainty that they'd take the protection away from me. It was the first ID I'd ever been on. It was also really the first test I was being put through. I'd never had to go on an ID parade with Ronnie. I'd refused the one with Tommy Butler, and Nipper Read hadn't thought it necessary. He'd seen me a few days earlier, when I'd gone up to Tintagel House where he had an office looking over the river. He'd sat me down, perfectly charming, had a cup of tea brought and then asked straight out if I could identify the second man. I said that, to be honest, I was still terrified, but now I'd made up my mind I was going to see it through. I told him I wasn't so scared of the second man as I was of Ronnie. I told Nipper that all I had to do was look at Ronnie's face, and I was scared.

I think what Nipper wanted was for me to say I'd seen the second man before, and then he wouldn't have had to put me on an ID parade where I might make a mistake. If the man was known to me, then there was no need for it, but I told him I'd seen him just that once. What I didn't know at the time but I learned later was that there'd been a major row between Nipper and Mr Leonard, who was running the case from the legal side.[1] Mr Leonard had said that there had to be a parade, but Nipper thought there was sufficient evidence to go along without one. But, of course, I wasn't privy to all these things. I was just put in the back of the car and driven to the ID, and then to the house. It was as if I had no mind or will of my own now. I was just a puppet dancing to the strings they pulled. Yank this string and I nodded, pull this one and I waved my left arm.

I thought it was going to be like on the films, where you walk along a line with a police officer beside you

---

[1]John Leonard QC, together with Kenneth Jones QC and James Crespi, conducted the case for the prosecution at the Central Criminal Court.

and touch someone, or like that film *Robbery* with Stanley Baker where the witness goes and slaps the person who nearly knocked her down, but it wasn't like that at all.

We drove up to the back of West End Central police station a bit after one o'clock and Helen made me wait whilst she went in to tell the officer in charge of the parade we'd arrived. Then she took me into a room and I met a woman police sergeant. There was nothing about her attitude to put me at my ease. She just seemed officious and full of self-importance. She made me feel like it was me who was the criminal. I hear everything possible is done nowadays to make a witness feel safe and comfortable, but there was nothing like that then.

I was told only to speak to the inspector, and I was sat behind a table. Ralph Haeems, the solicitor's clerk who was representing Barrie, was standing on my left-hand side and they had a line-up of men over against the wall. I can't remember now how many there were. Each one of them had a bit of lint and sticking plaster by their right ears because Barrie had a scar and it was to cover it up. It was quite right, because if there'd only been one with a scar, then it would have been obvious who it was I was meant to be picking out, but, even so, it made them all look different, a bit sinister.

They had to come out one by one and stop in front of the table, turn and look – which was really what happened that night in the pub – and then walk back to their original place. There were some chalk-marks on the floor, like on a film set, to show them where to stop and turn.

Then they all went back and stood in line. Then this uniformed copper – he was a sergeant – said did I want to see anyone again? And as I said 'Number Five' immediately and he'd just started to move forward, I realised I'd counted wrong and said, 'No. Number Six.'

I'd recognised Ian Barrie immediately. I never forget people's eyes, and he'd turned round and stared at me. At the trial it was suggested I'd recognised him from drinking in the pub. But when I saw him to remember him, he didn't have a glass in his hand; he had a gun. There was no way I was going to forget him. But I just wanted to make sure, and that was another mistake that let them get at me. I knew sure enough which one he was, and I should never have said I wanted to see any of them again. Barrie came forward to the chalk-marks at the front of the desk, and I said, 'Yes.' And that's where the second bit of confusion started. You wouldn't think so many things could go wrong in such a short space of time.

The men stayed up against the wall and I was taken into a side room and there was Bert Trevette, who was in charge of witness and jury security, and Nipper Read, and that's when I first actually remember seeing Ralph Haeems, who was from the solicitor's firm for the Twins, although he'd been standing next to me at the parade. He was upset that I'd said Number Five first. I was so nervous, and I'd corrected it straight away. He then said, 'Did she say no?' because I hadn't kept my voice up. The sergeant said that as far as he was concerned I'd said yes. I wasn't asked what I'd said, and it became even more confused because instead of asking me if I'd said yes or no they started round in circles again and I was asked if I recognised anyone. The police have it down that I said, 'I think that is the man. I'm not absolutely sure, I think that is him.' It's almost impossible to explain the panic I was in and how I came to say that because it's not what I meant at all. Once I looked at Barrie's eyes, I didn't doubt it at all. There were only two of them that night, and it was something which was going to stand in my mind for ever. He'd stood in an almost identical position as he had in the Beggars but, of course, he didn't have a gun with him.

It's no use saying, as they did at the trial, that because I was surrounded by policemen there was no need for me to be frightened. I was. I'd been surrounded by policemen from the time I decided to make a statement, and I was still frightened. All I wanted to do was get out of the police station and be back safe with Helen and Harry.

No one amongst the police seemed to blame me for what happened. I think they were quite pleased that I'd made the ID satisfactorily as far as they were concerned, but if they were, they didn't say. It was really as though it was nothing to do with me. Mr Haeems never said anything to me, and I went back to the car with Helen and Harry and off we went back home to collect the children. Nothing to it – for them. Funny enough, Mr Haeems never gave evidence at the trial to say that I'd made a mistake. The judge commented about that.

7

At first I didn't have a lot of confidence in the idea of having policewomen guarding me. Thirty years later, people would say that was sexist, but it was my life and I was worried. Henry Mooney and Bert Trevette who organised the protection of witnesses made a very good choice by having Pat Allen around me from the start. It made it easier that the kids had already met Pat when she'd taken them to see the planes. Then Helen came along and we hit it off together straight away. Not only was she doing her job very efficiently, but we also did have a lot of things in common – reading, crosswords and competitions, that sort of thing. Then there was another policewoman, Rosemary, who I got on very well with. The main policeman was Harry. The kids came to love him. The routine was to have two officers on for twenty-four hours and then another two with replacements when the main four went on rest days and holidays.

Even before the statement, Pat Allen had come and stayed the night. The idea was to see how I got along with a policewoman. By then I knew in my own mind I was going to do it. But the main priority was knowing the kids would be all right. Being so young, they didn't really know what was going on, but I had to be sure that there was people there the kids would be happy with. In fact they settled down straight away. I think you can over-estimate problems with kids. My lot had had Chrissie staying over the years, and they were used to people in the house. So it was easy to say this is Uncle Harry and Aunt Helen, and they'll be staying here for a bit. The kids were very young at the time, don't forget. They called the two favourite ones aunt and uncle right from the start.

There was still a few weeks of school term to go, and the police were with me when I went to school and collected and delivered them. The headmaster had been told what was going on, and so he didn't let them out if we were a bit late in fetching them; but it didn't last long. By the end of the month we were gone, down into Essex.

From the police point of view, the flat at Withey House was completely indefensible. What they didn't like was it being on the ground floor and having a balcony at the back which made things more difficult for them. As I said, you could come straight across the back, in and out, and no one would really be any the wiser. The senior officers hadn't minded when they were just watching, but now there was a new régime and they were guarding me, things were different. The other thing was there was no telephone, and the police didn't have mobile radios back in 1968. If they wanted to report in or keep in contact, it was down to the telephone box at Stepney Green tube station a couple of hundred yards away.

Bert Trevette just came round one day and simply said, 'You're packing.' There wasn't all that much to take – clothes, the kids' toys, the tele. The furniture was left there to make like I was still around and I went on sending the rent, but we were off to Brentwood, to a big house with a garden on its own down a lane, and a conservatory with spiders. The kids loved it, but the spiders must have been the biggest you could ever find. I was doing the ironing one night and I saw this mouse. Now I don't mind mice at all, after all I'd seen plenty of them when I was a child, but, as it got nearer, I realised it was a spider. I was on the table when Harry found me. He had his uses.

It was really the end of term, and so I didn't send the kids to school down there. We all took turns at teaching them lessons for those weeks. For them it was an adventure, a holiday. Here they were out of the East End for more than a day for the first time in their lives and into the country. Tell them you're not going to go to school, and they're happy enough.

Sometimes the officers went to report to Tintagel House [Read's office], and I would go along for the ride. It was really to break the monotony of things.

Bert Trevette would come round to make sure things were running smoothly. Now there was a man who inspired confidence.

There's a funny story about the officer, Ray, the police officer who came to take my fingerprints. Over the months, on and off, I'd kept in touch with him. He was one of the officers who still looked in to see if I was all right after the observation van had been pulled off. In the summer of 1968 he was going out with a policewoman, Maggie, who was one of the relief guards for me at Brentwood.

By then, Ray'd been promoted and had been posted to the Yard to C1, then part of the Murder Squad. Apparently he'd met Maggie in the canteen at Romford when he went back for a promotion do. She was in the CID as well, and one day she told him, 'I've been seconded to a special squad' – guarding me. Of course, she wouldn't tell him what it was. One day I went to see Nipper Read at Tintagel; I was walking down the corridor with Henry Mooney, and there was Ray. I said 'Hello', and we went down in the lift. He walked me over to where my car was parked and there in the front seat was his fiancée. That's how cover gets blown. Now that was all right as it turned out, but it could have been very dodgy. The Krays were meant to have good contacts in Scotland Yard.

We didn't stay long in Brentwood. It was the summer holidays now, but what I wanted was the kids to be settled. They'd had three homes in the past couple of years, gone away from their friends in the East End, and I wanted them to have somewhere more permanent if it was at all possible. They were getting older and were needing proper schooling, and it was better for them to start making friends. So the police liaised with various councils and we went to look at various houses. There was one over in Wembley I went to with Harry. We were due to be shown round at eleven in the morning, and no one had come by quarter past, so I suggested we go round the back and look in the garden. The back door was open, and so we went in. The place was a tip, rubbish all over, clothes left around. It smelled of cooking. I didn't even bother to go upstairs. I said I wasn't going to have that one. Just as well. We'd gone to the wrong place, and it was someone's house.

We moved at the end of the summer and the kids started in regular schooling. No one knew me round there and we carried on more or less as before. They still had their dad coming to see them regular, and they started to make separate friends, although I often wonder what the other parents thought when there was always an uncle and aunt along with me when I took them to parties. There was one woman who, seeing the number of different men coming in, suggested I should have had a red light outside the place. I presume she must have thought all the different women were to help me accommodate them!

In fact, life was pretty claustrophobic with the

police. First, I had to let them know who'd be calling, and there weren't that many. Ivor had come round to see me at Withey House, and got the most terrible shock one evening when he was pulled in, put up against the wall and searched before I could tell them who he was. Even if we'd not moved so quick after that, it might have ended that beautiful friendship. Chris had gone to Australia by then, but I kept in touch with my friend Doreen by phone. Until the police had gone, long after the case was over, she never came round to visit. If I went to see her, the police came too. If I wanted to go and see a Doris Day film, well, they didn't have much of a choice. At worst I got a lift. I remember one night I wanted to go to the boxing at Wembley – cheap seats away from the ring – and they grumbled and grumbled, but they had to come along.

A lot of the time was spent watching television. Callan was a favourite, and there was a fantasy between Helen and me that if we went out in a foursome, who was going to have Callan and who'd have Lonely. The rest of the time we didn't sit there not speaking. We'd sit playing quiz games, doing crosswords. We also used to play a lot of Scrabble. There was one relief officer who couldn't spell words with more than three letters. I used to like playing with him. It was a doddle.

I chose the menus, and the police chipped in. They didn't get a lot of choice, but it can't have been bad because some of them still come over to eat. Helen was an East End girl – in fact she'd been at school with Ray, whose girlfriend was guarding me – and of course, she loved pie and mash, so we had quite a lot of that.

As you might expect, there was some trouble with the police guards. It wouldn't have been human if there hadn't been. There was one who wore dirty jerseys and just pulled them on inside out when they got too filthy. He was a creep. He never cleaned his teeth. I played him at cards one night and he did his money. He didn't half have the hump. I used to cook for everyone, and he'd just put sauce on everything, slop it over really. I remember one Sunday I cooked a lovely roast for us all and there he was with the bottle all over the plate. What was worse was, he fancied himself as a romantic, and I found one of the policewomen sitting on the stairs, head in hands, one night. He had a go with his roving hands at me in the kitchen one evening, as well. I was doing the cooking, and I just said, 'If I were you, I would never do that again whilst I'm boiling the kettle for tea, otherwise you'll sing soprano.' I wasn't having that, and so I asked to be taken to see Nipper Read at Tintagel House. Even though I didn't think I was showing it, he must have known I was upset.

He had me sit down beside him and asked what was the matter. I didn't want to cause trouble, and I muttered something about a clash of personalities. 'What you mean is he tried his bloody luck and came unstuck,' said Nipper, and he had him moved by Bert

Trevette straight off. Mind you, it was nothing like the trouble they had with Lisa, the girl from the nightclub who was a witness in the Frank Mitchell part of the case. Apparently if she got in a temper she would take all her clothes off, and one evening the policewoman guarding her was in such a rage that she took her down to the local police station and locked her up overnight. I may have felt like doing it, but I never did. I think overall I'm too placid by nature.

But, generally, we managed to fit in. I shared the bedroom with Helen or one of the other women officers and and the police officer slept on the settee. If we went out, it was all together or with at least one officer. My ex-husband would want to take the kids to the zoo but we all went, always with a policeman. It was lucky I got on with my ex-husband. For weeks he was the only person I saw outside the police and a few shopkeepers.

What I did do was learn to drive. In an evening the policewoman would baby-sit the children and I would go out with Harry with the L plates on. I'm proud to say I passed my test the first time. Harry had a big smart Jaguar then. The kids used to love going in it. He used to tease them he was driving on two wheels. 'Drive on *three* wheels, Harry,' they'd say. They thought it was marvellous.

It was now that the family shut its door on me. They knew what was happening by now because I couldn't otherwise explain the strangers all over the house. One of the things I had been able to do was to go and have dinner with them or have them over occasionally. I'd had a lovely day with Aunt Mary's eldest daughter and her husband, and the next week they were coming over, when I got a letter to say it would be better if we didn't get in touch until it was all over. I never saw them again until Aunt Mary's funeral, when it was mentioned. I said, 'Never mind, it's all over.' I'd never told them my mother had died. You can't get into arguments at funerals. I haven't seen them since. I've no idea what made them do it, and I was too upset at the time to write and ask. You soon find out who your mates are.

We went to Southend for the day, and again to see the lights, and just before Christmas we went up to see the lights in Oxford Street. I'd always taken them to Selfridges because there was such a good show what with Uncle Holly as well as Father Christmas. It was then the boys tried to convince Helen they were entitled to buy a penknife each, but they failed. Christmas itself was pretty subdued. The children had their presents, of course, and the police had small gifts for them. I cooked the lunch, but all the police really wanted to be with their own families, and they couldn't.

But all the time, the trial was getting nearer and I was getting more and more worried about giving evidence and someone trying to stop me from doing so. I've always been a poor sleeper, and now it was nothing but fits and starts. Regular as clockwork I'd be waking up at three in the morning, sweating and shaking and calling out. By five past, I'd be downstairs in the kitchen having a mug of tea. I wasn't having nightmares about the Twins or the killing, I was just having nightmares. And over a long period it's very wearing indeed.

8

I can remember the coroner's court, down in Westminster. It was just like my Aunt Mary had described, and I can remember the Old Bailey, but, for the life of me, I can't just remember the committal proceedings at Bow Street at all. If somebody had said I'd given evidence there, I'd have called them a liar. Obviously I went, because the briefs for Ronnie and the others wouldn't have let the opportunity pass to have a go at me. But I've positively blanked out the magistrates' court. It's as if I was never there. Whether it was the first time I had to face them that's caused it, I don't know. I've tried to think about it recently. I think I must have just been so scared.

Things went on as normal, or any rate what passed for normal, with me waking up screaming and police officers with loaded guns sleeping on the sofa downstairs and going everywhere with me and the children. Then at the beginning of January 1969 I was told the trial was starting, and then on Thursday

9 January I was just told I was going to the Bailey the next day. I didn't want to know when it would be, and Henry Mooney thought I would have less time to brood on things if I was told almost at the last moment. I know as I was being driven to the court I asked Harry, my regular guard, whether I really had to go, and all he said was, 'Yes.'

What had happened was that the trial had been split into two parts. The first was going to be over the murders of George Cornell and Jack 'The Hat' McVitie. The second was going to be the one over the escape of Frank Mitchell from Dartmoor and his disappearance.

I was driven to the court that Friday. We got there early – you can't keep a judge waiting – and I gave evidence straight after the photographer and the plan-drawer who was a policeman named Luger.

I wasn't there all that long before I gave evidence, just about a couple of hours. I know there was a screen leading into the court. The matron came round the screen to see me. I remember her giving me a drink and asking if I was all right. I remember I was so terrified I didn't think I could walk into the court, but it's amazing how, when you take the first step, there's no turning back.

It was very confusing. You had barristers with wigs and people behind them and other people behind them and people looking down from the public gallery. I was never too clear who anyone was. Ending up in the Old Bailey you're overawed,

116

quite apart from being terrified. All those clever people, you think someone's going to come out with a brilliant question which is going to overthrow the whole case. You see court cases which are all over in a few minutes on television, and even the O.J. Simpson case you only got highlights, but really with me it was more a war of attrition than anything else. Mr Platts-Mills, who was for Ronnie, just kept on going over the same questions time after time and I sort of settled in. The judge, Melford Stevenson, was the perfect gentleman to me, and after a bit I began to find it was much less terrifying and simpler telling the truth than it was lying at the coroner's court and never knowing when I was going to be found out. If you tell the truth, you can't be tripped up. I think now there's an effort being made to help witnesses by showing them the court and telling them what to expect in advance, but I don't think it would have helped to be taken to the court first. I think I'd've been just as scared as I was.

I was amazed by the number of people in the court. There were all those people in the dock. Somehow I'd been thinking it was just going to be Ronnie and Ian Barrie. I hadn't realised there was all those other people charged with various aspects of the killings, like cleaning up after Jack 'The Hat's' death, which was nothing to do with me at all. Then they had the barristers, rows of them, and the solicitors behind. I know they let me sit down, but as I'm not very tall I couldn't speak into the microphone and so they pinned one on me. It kept falling off, and one or other of the barristers would say he couldn't hear properly and so the usher would come and try and pin it on tighter. And they'd make me stand up for a bit to see if that worked better, but I was so small they could hardly see me, and the microphone would fall off when I moved my arms and we'd stop and start all over again.

The jury were to my right and behind me. I don't think it would have made any difference with a screen separating me from the people in the dock. They knew perfectly well who I was. I knew who they were, and it was simply just something that was going to have to be done. I think the public gallery made me more nervous. Also I felt an idiot when the microphone kept tipping upside down, as they had to fix that.

Because there was a door behind me, Helen was sitting at my back as a guard, which was a help. There was a desk in the well of the court with police officers, and I saw Nipper Read down there, and that helped too. I thought Melford Stevenson, the judge, was extremely courteous. He wasn't so much protective as courteous, in the sense that he gave the impression he wasn't going to allow anyone to be hectored or browbeaten when they were extremely nervous and not used to a court set-up. In other words, I don't think he would let anything out from under his strict supervision. That did give me a feeling of more security.

I can remember the man who prosecuted, and I can remember the usher, a short chap with dark hair bringing me a glass of water. Platts-Mills wasn't lovely. I thought he treated me as though anyone from the East End who didn't speak properly like him couldn't have any intelligence at all.

Things started off all right. I was allowed to sit down, and then the prosecution asked me about Patsy Quill and George Cornell and how I was working the night he was shot. I was shown some photographs and identified the bar of the Beggars. Everything seemed to take such a long time. After all, the Beggars wasn't the biggest pub in the world, but you'd think from the trouble we had getting it clear where George was, at one side of the bar, and me at the other, that there was miles of distance between us. Then I had to make the identifications of Ronnie and Ian Barrie in the dock. Of course I was able to do that with no trouble, but I was surprised that both of them seemed slightly smaller than on the night of the shooting. Because of what happened, they had seemed to be the biggest people in the pub. Much bigger than they were in real life.

I know barristers have to be clever to get where they are, but I always thought Mr Platts-Mills seemed to be just trying to put me off the way he kept interrupting. Of course he was only doing his best for Ronnie, but it seemed to me that if he could confuse things instead of clearing them up, he was happier. I know when I was asked if I saw the

one who had shot Cornell, he interrupted and said I
hadn't said which of the men had done the shooting.
Melford Stevenson put him right on that one.

> **Mr Platts-Mills**: So far she has said they both had
> guns, and one of them shot George. She did not
> say a particular one.
>
> **Stevenson**: 'I realised they had guns in their hands. The
> first one shot at George Cornell. I saw him fall.' That
> is my note.

Then they went over the identification parade at West
End Central six months earlier and then, just as I'd
finished explaining about how the ambulance took
George away, Platts-Mills decided that he wanted
the jury to go and see the Beggars for themselves.
That put the cat amongst the pigeons, and the judge
said he didn't think it was necessary. Platts-Mills got
some support from the ones who were involved in
the McVitie shooting. They wanted to go and look
at the house where he was killed. I got sent out of
court and told to come back after lunch; not that I
was going anywhere.

They continued arguing for some time after lunch,
and it wasn't till around two-thirty that I got called
back. I'd been with the matron and Helen all that
time. The matron was so nice, a Scotswoman. People
reckoned she could be cantankerous, but she was
lovely to me. She had a room on a level with the
court and she brought me some tea, saying I was
to have something to eat. I said I wasn't hungry.

I'd felt sick all morning and I didn't feel any better then. But she made me have some toast.

Anyway, the judge decided that there wasn't going to be a look – a view they called it – of the Beggars, at least not until I'd given evidence, and so I was brought back into court and this was the time for Platts-Mills to have a go at me. What I found funny was that Mr Jones, who was the prosecutor who questioned me, hadn't said a word about me lying or why I did it. He made no attempt to get me to explain things.

In a way, it was just repetition. He went through my taking my coat off and having a word with Patsy's wife, but I wasn't sure where he was going. I mean, did it really matter that I'd spent one minute or ten with Mrs Quill? There was no suggestion I'd been drinking, and there was no doubt that someone had shot George Cornell. It was just a question of whether I was right in saying it was Ronnie. I was looking at the transcript of his cross-examination the other day, and I see the first eighteen questions he asked me were about talking to Mrs Quill and taking my coat off. I think in a way that was comforting. If he'd gone straight in about my lying, then he might have made me more flustered. As it was he sort of ran me in gently.

Then he started on about me lying at the coroner's court. Did it matter to me that I'd lied on oath? I told him the reason I had done was I was terrified then what would happen to myself and the children.

Q: Are you telling us that at the coroner's court you
said, 'I didn't see anything at all'?
A: Yes.
Q: Did you say that on oath to the coroner?
A: Yes.
Q: You remember swearing on oath?
A: Yes.
Q: That does not matter to you a scrap?
A: It matters a lot.
Q: What matters?
A: Having to tell lies. I was so terrified what might
happen to me or my children I had to tell
lies then.

It all seemed to take a long time to get nowhere. It was
also easier because the microphone kept falling off,
and there were always discussions about what to do
next with it. What Platts-Mills wanted to know was
how it was I was the one who recognised Ronnie and
the others – he said lots of people – who could have
identified him at the parade which Tommy Butler
organised had failed to pick him out.

Q: In fact, there were lots of people there in that bar who
would have known him and could have identified him
if he had been there?
A: I don't know about other people. I know I recognised him.

Of course I couldn't know the answer to why the
others didn't recognise him, but I expect, like me,
they were scared of what might happen if they had.
   Then Platts-Mills got to what he thought was his

best point. I said that you could walk from the saloon to the public bar direct, which you could, and he got very sarcastic because there was a partition drawn on the plan, saying,

> **Q**: This [the plan] was drawn the day after. Did you have the builders in that night – do you remember the builders coming in?

And, of course, I had to say no. Then he was asking me if I stayed overnight, and I said I hadn't. He was sure he was on a winner. If the partition had been there, then, he reckoned, I could not have seen what had happened. But it was all simple, and when we looked at the photographs, it was all clear and the partition didn't block things behind the bar. So he climbed down.

> **Stevenson**: The lady is correct.
> **Platts-Mills**: My Lord, yes. That is splendid.

But, of course, he didn't really think it was, and off we went on being able to see round the bottles in the middle of the serving area. His great idea was that if I was over by the record-player, then I couldn't see what was going on and only heard the shots. But I kept saying I wasn't, and I could see what happened. I felt really good that I'd been right about the partition. It was only a small triumph, but it made me feel a lot better.

Sometimes he got so complicated in his questions

I couldn't understand what he wanted me to say, and the judge had to help out.

> **Platts-Mills**: Your immediate reaction to the question was that you would run and hide if you heard shots being fired. That is an absolutely frank answer?
>
> **A**: Yes.
>
> **Q**: No attempt to make up a story or alter it to fit the circumstances?
>
> **A**: No.
>
> **Q**: Was the thing which frightened you the hearing of the shots being fired?
>
> **Stevenson**: What is being suggested to you is that you did not see any firing at all, you only heard it, and at the time you could not see who was firing. That is what is being put.
>
> **A**: No, I did see it.

But Mr Platts-Mills still kept banging on:

> **Q**: Let me come back to my question. Why do you think you gave that answer about me and my position in the terms, if you heard shots fired, if that was not precisely what happened? You were scared by hearing shots being fired, were you not?
>
> **A**: Well, I had never heard a gun going off before like that, and it frightened the life out of me.

It was then the judge stopped him.

> **Stevenson**: Mr Platts-Mills, you have made your suggestion, and everybody has understood it. Do you want her to say it again?

He still wouldn't let it go. I'd said Ronnie wasn't wearing glasses, and he told me that Ronnie couldn't see without them.

> Q: First of all, do you know that he is virtually blind, that is to get about, without his glasses?
> A: No.
> Q: He has a percentage of sight called by the experts six over nought without his glasses in each eye; did you know that?
> A: No.
> Q: If that be right, and he really is blind as far as moving about is concerned – well – Let us just see if you made any different statements before the Coroner. You said you were there lying on oath, deliberately telling lies on oath?
> A: Yes.
> Q: To deceive the Coroner?
> A: No, I was terrified I would get shot like George Cornell did if I told the truth.

He seemed to get a bit excited at that. He didn't seem to understand that the others might still have been so frightened they wouldn't say it was Ronnie.

> Q: What about the other people there?
> A: I don't know their reasons.
> A: For what?
> A: If they are lying. If they are saying . . .
> Q: Who says they are lying? Are you suggesting they are lying?
> A: No, sir, I am not suggesting anything. All I am saying is my reasons why I lied under oath.

Then it was back to trying to show I'd said one thing to the coroner, another to the magistrate and a third that day. Looking at it now on paper, it seems so insignificant the details he managed to come up with, but it was harrowing for me that day. When I said, as far as I was concerned I'd told the magistrates the same story that I'd told that morning, he pounced on me again.

> **Q**: That only means you are not aware of what lies you have told, does it not? Let us examine it. Will you try and remember whether you said this to the magistrate? 'I look round the court and I see the man who shot Cornell; it is Ronald Kray. That was not the first time I had seen Ronald Kray. I had seen him twice or at the most three times before that. On those occasions I had seen him in the pub, that is, the Blind Beggar.' That means you had seen him two or three times only and always in the Blind Beggar?
>
> **A**: Yes, but I have seen lots of photographs of him.

That morning I'd also said I'd seen him in the East End, and he wanted to know why I hadn't told the magistrate. I said I must have forgotten it. Then he was off again – why, if I had seen it, Albie Woods and Johnny Dale, who were with Cornell, hadn't said they saw the shooting.

Sometimes I just couldn't follow what he was getting at.

> **Q**: What sort of man is Mr Quill? An honest sort of fellow, a typical publican?

A: I don't know his principles. I find him a pleasant enough man.
Q: A responsible and sensible chap, the kind of chap to run a pub?
A: Well, he runs the pub.

That didn't seem to please him.

Q: Are you suggesting he is not responsible and sensible?
A: I don't know. I suppose he must be to run a pub.

Then suddenly it was all over, or that part of it was. He said I'd never told Jimmy and Patsy Quill that Ronnie was the one, and why, if I was frightened, didn't I get the police to take me home. I told him Jimmy Quill had run me home. He'd been asking me about police protection and then out of the blue he said:

Q: You are inventing this, are you not?
A: You should have my nightmares about it; you would see whether I was inventing it or not.
Q: So you suffer from nightmares?
A: Yes.
Q: I am sorry about your nightmares, madam, and I am sorry I have taken so long.
A: Thank you.

Then it was the turn of Ian Barrie's barrister, Mr Howard. Now Mr Howard was a completely different kettle of fish from Mr Platts-Mills, a real smooth piece of work. He started off very solicitous, asking whether I was feeling well enough to continue. In fact I felt like a limp rag. The judge asked if I wanted to go home, come back on Monday. I know he was being kind, but that was the last thing I wanted. I hoped it was all going to be over that afternoon. What he wanted to know was how the identification parade had gone, and why I had said, 'I think that is the man, I am not absolutely sure.' I asked if I could explain myself and when the judge said I could, I went on: 'I was in such a state that day. Once I recognised him on that ID parade, I can remember all I wanted to do was to get out of the room, and I'm not absolutely sure what I said, but I knew it was him.'

And then it was back to the lies at the coroner's court. If ever there was a good example of having your lies put to you, this was it; but I knew why I'd lied and I knew I wasn't lying now.

What Mr Howard didn't exactly know was what had made me change my mind, and he was a bit shaken when I told him the name of the solicitor I'd seen. I think he thought I was making that up and so he asked who it was, and I gave him the name of the firm straight out. Then he got on to what I thought was the best point, and that was the possibility of a mistake.

Q: Have you ever mistaken someone?
A: I don't really know. I haven't thought about it.

Q: Well, think about it now. Have you ever in the street said to yourself or perhaps to someone else, 'That is old so-and-so' or 'That is my friend so-and-so'?

A: I suppose I have.

Q: And then, upon a closer look, you find you have made a mistake?

A: Yes.

Q: According to your recollection, the face which that man bears is the one which you *have* seen before, and you put it upon the occasion of Cornell's death?

A: Yes.

Q: May it not be that you have seen him in that public house on a different occasion and later you wrongly put him there on that night?

A: No, he had a gun in his hand that night.

It looked for a bit after that as though I was going to have to come back, but fortunately the prosecution had only a few points to clear up and the judge said I could go. I think I must nearly have fainted on the way down from the witness box. At least, that was what it looked like to Mr Platts-Mills, and certainly one of the journalists wrote that I looked 'frail, inarticulate, stumbling with a lot of her words'.[1]

I was given a cup of tea in matron's room and then put in the back of the car. The drive getting back seemed endless, although it can't have taken much over an hour. I just remember John was at the house with the kids when I got home. I was just so tired. I didn't have a good drink. None of it was anything to

[1]Nicholas Tomalin, *Sunday Times*, 12 January 1969.

celebrate, not even that it was over. Looking back, I think I'd been a good witness. I was telling the truth and I'd been honest about why I lied. There was not much Platts-Mills had done to me. Now it was just a question of waiting and trying to get back to normal. I think I stayed in bed a lot of the weekend; I was simply exhausted.

But, when it came to it, it wasn't over. Ivor, who gave evidence on the Monday morning following, a couple of witnesses after me, dropped me in it quite by accident when he was being questioned by Platts-Mills. I think bells must have rung and fireworks exploded when he said it. Being fair to Ivor, Platts-Mills led him into it.

> **Q**: I don't know whether you can help us at all. On Friday she seemed terribly ill, so she could not stand up, really very ill, was wanting to faint, and so on, with some real illness. You don't know anything about that, do you?
> **A**: Well, I believe she was very ill.

That gave Platts-Mills the opening he wanted. Of course I wasn't there when he applied for me to be recalled so he could have another go at me. I think that Platts-Mills was hoping I'd been in a psychiatric hospital. But, before that, he was trying to get Ivor to say I must have been playing the gramophone at the time of the shooting. Well, he had to really, but again Melford Stevenson wasn't having any of it.

Q: Something had happened on this night so that nobody had touched it since it started misbehaving?

A: No.

Q: Probably the lady who was touching it at the time of the shot, do you think?

A: I wouldn't like to say. I wasn't in the pub.

Q: It is difficult to think of any other possible explanation, isn't it?

Stevenson: Now, Mr Platts-Mills, there is a limit beyond which even you cannot introduce wild speculation. How can he possibly answer the question?

Then he came back to my illness.

Q: One more question about the lady. You understand she was ill. Do you know what the illness is?

A: No.

Q: Did you just hear about this?

A: Yes.

Q: Does that mean you have not seen her?

A: Since when?

Q: Any time since she left there?

A: I saw her afterwards, yes.

Q: Frequently?

A: Fairly frequently, yes.

Q: In what circumstances?

A: Could you define that a bit clearer?

Q: In the street? Did you go visiting?

A: I used to visit her.

Q: You used to visit the family?

A: Yes.

Q: Perhaps you would tell us about this. Did you there learn that she was ill?

A: Pardon?

Q: By visiting there, did you learn she was ill?

A: Yes, she eventually went to hospital.

Q: I did not hear that at all.

Stevenson: She eventually went to hospital.

Platts-Mills: What was the illness, do you know?

A: I don't know.

Q: When did she go to hospital?

A: I cannot honestly remember.

Q: Was it a year or so ago, or a month or so ago?

A: I suppose it was about a year ago. I wouldn't like to say.

Q: Just let us consider. You went to work in the public house till about March of 1968, didn't you?

A: Yes.

Q: Did she go to hospital while you were still at the public house, or when you had taken up other employment?

A: Yes, when I was at the public house.

Q: So she went to hospital before March 1968?

A: I think so. I really honestly don't know.

Q: Don't want exactly, but did she get better as a result of going to hospital?

A: I don't know. It is a long time since I have seen her.

Q: You stopped going to visit her?

A: I don't know where she lives.

Q: Did she go on to the same hospital for these two years?

A: No, she moved shortly after the . . .

Q: Yes; so you were visiting at the new house, wherever that was?

A: Yes, that is right.

Q: Do you mean she has moved a second time?

A: I think so. I don't honestly know.

Q: How long is it since you visited?

A: Last July.

Q: Can you tell us why you ceased to visit?
A: Well, I think she moved – that's why I ceased to visit.

Poor Ivor! He used to come and see me regularly and tried to help out financially with bits here and there for the kids. So did Dave, but Ivor more especially. He fancied my cousin Chris. He used to take her flowers and chocolates and once he took her to the pictures, but at that time she wasn't keen on getting into any sort of relationship with anybody. Even after she went to Australia, Ivor still used to come round to see me and the kids until the police moved in. It was only then he stopped. What had happened was that when he knocked one time at Withey House he was pounced on and searched, and it frightened the life out of him. Then again, we moved pretty soon after that.

The questioning of Ivor about why he stopped seeing me was enough for the judge. He was getting really sarcastic with Platts-Mills.

Stevenson: It would be a great help to me if you could indicate how this helps the jury.

And now out he came in his true colours:

Platts-Mills: I am anxious to find out what I can about this lady. On Friday we were all very compassionate, all very moderate, with her, didn't really ask her any challenging questions [No, but you tried] because she

133

was in such a state of illness, and now I am trying to see what this witness can tell us about her.

Stevenson: Yes, but I want to understand what issue the jury have to decide these questions relate to.

Platts-Mills: My Lord, it must be to the credit of the lady. If I can make some progress with finding out something about her real character and nature – but my Lord has heard that I challenge her radically in everything she said . . .

Stevenson: Of course you do. I fully understand that. I utterly fail to follow what all these questions have got to do even with her credit.

Platts-Mills: My Lord, I don't know. I want to see what I can find out – what this illness was, if she was really so prostrate when she came into court . . .

I must say I hadn't realised I was prostrate when I came into court. I was terrified, yes, but that's a different thing entirely. I mean, I wasn't carried in on a stretcher.

Stevenson: So you are wandering over a large field in search of casual admissions, is that right?

Platts-Mills: No, my Lord – because of her state, no one was in a position to test her testimony. She was obviously not in a fit state to answer. Perhaps she should be given the chance of getting better . . .

When I first read this little exchange, I wondered if Platts-Mills was talking about the same case even. I mean, if I had been prostrate, then you'd have

thought he would have mentioned it to the judge
that I didn't seem well and perhaps he could delay
cross-examining me, but it had seemed to me he
went full steam ahead.

The judge was trying to push things along a bit
when Mr Jones put his feet in the water:

Mr Jones: May I mention something? I know nothing of
this illness which my learned friend speaks of. I asked
that the lady might sit down. She was obviously
distressed. My Lord, it may be that Mr Platts-Mills
is making his own diagnosis – and certainly one
which escaped me – I don't know.

Stevenson: I think she did say something about feeling
ill, but I think referring to *feeling* ill, and I have no
doubt she did. [emphasis from transcript.]

Platts-Mills: I thought your Lordship had further
information. I asked whether she wouldn't prefer
to stand up, the better to be heard. I think my Lord
said apparently she is suffering from something that
makes it inconvenient.

Stevenson: When I permitted her to sit down, I was
indulging in no more than common courtesy.

Platts-Mills: I accept that at once. One has that at all
times from my Lord – but what I was suggesting
was that the lady really was faint in the box. My
Lord, of course we all saw when she came down,
she couldn't stand up.

Stevenson: She was obviously very distressed. I felt no
surprise about that – perhaps you didn't.

Platts-Mills: My Lord, there was no cause for a lady
who can face up to things within moments of the
killing – she is not so readily distressed as one might
think, thinking back over it . . .

If he couldn't see the difference between helping someone who was dying and standing there being cross-examined by him and the others, well. Anyway, what happened was that Platts-Mills decided he really wanted another go at me although it took him a few moments to come out with it. It seems like he was putting all the blame on me.

> **Jones**: My Lord, my learned friend Mr Platts-Mills has suggested that in some way he was disabled from cross-examining the barmaid fully on Friday. My Lord, may I make it quite clear that, if he makes the application, I will cause that lady to be brought back to Court, subject to your Lordship's direction in the matter, for him to ask any further questions he wishes.
>
> **Stevenson**: Yes, certainly.
>
> **Platts-Mills**: I shall not make such an application now, but if I had any indication from my learned friend that the lady really was better . . .
>
> **Stevenson**: What?
>
> **Platts-Mills**: Better.
>
> **Stevenson**: No one has suggested she was incapable of giving evidence.
>
> **Platts-Mills**: I saw her virtually faint at the steps of the witness box. We all did. Two ladies tried to lift her up, and she collapsed. She was just quite faint.
>
> **Stevenson**: Mr Platts-Mills, it is quite impossible, I think, to manufacture a grievance about this. If you want the lady back, you shall have her back. Do you?
>
> **Platts-Mills**: My Lord, I do, but I would hope that it would be after someone has made enquiries to see that she is in reasonable health.

Stevenson: No one suggests she is incapable of giving evidence. She is naturally distressed, and I should have thought anyone would understand that. But if you want her back, you will have her.

Platts-Mills: I thought she was very weak and very ill, but I am in your Lordship's hands.

Stevenson: You are not in my hands in this respect.

Platts-Mills: She has been to hospital for something.

Stevenson: If you want her back, say so.

Platts-Mills: My Lord, I do. But, my Lord, I hope that, as I say, enquiries will be made to see that she is well first and not faced . . .

Stevenson: I think you can trust the authorities to deal with that aspect of it. When do you want her back?

Platts-Mills. My Lord, I am entirely in my friend's hands. I prefer they choose their own time. Above all, one that suits the lady.

That's what they said in court, but court life isn't real life. The kids had already gone to school and it was late on the Monday morning when I got it dropped on me I was going back up the Old Bailey. I think it was Bert Trevette came round and said, 'You're needed back at the Bailey again.' I was taken straight up. Nothing about my convenience or if I felt well or anything. I wasn't at all happy. I said, 'I feel sick', hoping Harry, who was driving, might turn round and take me home. Instead, all he said was, 'Be sick out the window, not on my seats', and off we went again.

Obviously I had to go back in the witness box but, when it came to it, I wasn't so nervous the second time. Apart from anything, it seems the judge had had a right go at Platts-Mills. What I gathered was that when Ivor had mentioned I'd been in hospital at one point, they jumped the gun and thought it was a nervous breakdown so they could get me on my mental state. Even before I was called into court, there was another little spat between them. For a start, I don't think Platts-Mills thought they'd bring me back up quite so quick.

Jones: I am instructed, my Lord, that Mrs X is now back in the precincts of the Court.

Platts-Mills: I would ask to be excused cross-examination . . .

Stevenson: I thought you wanted her back?

Platts-Mills: My Lord, I really would like an opportunity of considering this for my client's protection.

Stevenson: Well, Mr Platts-Mills, as I understand it, this morning you were complaining that you had not been able to put what you wanted to put to the lady because of her condition.

Platts-Mills: My Lord, I venture to excuse myself.

Stevenson: Here she is back again, and she is available for you. I am not proposing to bring her back and forth more than is avoidable. Now do make up your mind. Do you want to cross-examine or not?

Platts-Mills: I do, but I prefer not to cross-examine her now. I did indicate to my learned friend that I hoped some enquiries would be made first to see that she really was fit. It was really in part so that I might have an opportunity of considering it. I would like to consider it further before cross-examining her.

Stevenson: Well, how long do you want to consider it, because as a matter of human treatment of this woman, I don't want to bring her here more than I must.

Platts-Mills: I accept that at once, but it must be very easy for her to come. I am very grateful for my learned friend taking these steps. I would certainly like an opportunity—

Stevenson: What do you want to put? Can you tell us that?

Platts-Mills: Yes. I want to test a number of points that she told us about. Indeed, I'd rather not elaborate the actual questions I want to put, but I want to cross-examine her as to the accuracy of her statements.

Stevenson: I do regard this as very unsatisfactory, Mr Platts-Mills. Here you are being offered an opportunity to bring this young woman back, having complained that you were prevented from putting all you wished to put.

Platts-Mills: My Lord, I didn't—

Stevenson: Now you ask for further time to consider. How much time do you want?

Platts-Mills: My Lord, I beg your Lordship not to think I complained. I didn't mean to complain. I indicated when my Lord asked why I was asking the witness about her, that perhaps through my own folly, unintentionally really, because I thought she wasn't fit, I hadn't asked all the questions I wanted. That is still the position, but I ask not to cross-examine her now.

Stevenson: When do you expect to be able to make up your mind as to whether you want her back or not?

Platts-Mills: My Lord, I do want her back, but I should prefer not now.

Stevenson: Could you answer my question? When do

you expect to be able to make up your mind whether
you want her back, and when?

Platts-Mills: Immediately I would like her back, but at
some time after today, this afternoon or tomorrow.
Any time that suits my learned friend.

Nothing about whether it suited me! I was just a ball
being kicked around the court.

Stevenson: Tomorrow morning?
Platts-Mills: Not this afternoon.

But although I didn't know it, help was at hand. Mr
Jones put in his threepence-worth. He wasn't having
any of it if he could help.

Jones: My Lord, first of all, we have no grounds
whatsoever for thinking that this lady is ill. My
Lord, all of us who were present in Court on Friday
witnessed the obvious distress and strain which she
was put to. Indeed we all, myself included, went to
some lengths to ensure that her evidence should be
disposed of on Friday.

Platts-Mills: So did I.

Jones: I have caused her to be brought back today. She
is not in a place convenient to the Court. I caused
her to be brought back so that the woman's anxiety
and distress, which she thought had been terminated
on Friday, should not be protracted. My Lord, I am
somewhat surprised to hear my learned friend say
he is not prepared to cross-examine her now when
one would have expected him certainly to have
been prepared on Friday. My Lord, he has had

nearly three days – certainly two days – to cogitate over his own cross-examination and to think what further questions he should ask. He should have been ready on Friday. My Lord, I would take any step which is with propriety open to me to prevent that witness being subjected to the further stress and strain of having to spend yet another twenty-four hours waiting upon the whim of my learned friend. She is here and, my Lord, I would ask, as a matter of common decency, if my learned friend wants an adjournment for ten minutes to discuss the matter with his learned junior, I have no doubt your Lordship would accede to that. My Lord, she is here, and I would ask that she be put back into the witness box this afternoon so that we may try once again to bring this strain to an end.

I don't know what the jury made of it all. It didn't show Platts-Mills up in a good light, and therefore it might rub off on to Ronnie. Anyway, the judge was satisfied. He sent the jury out and gave Platts-Mills ten minutes to make up his mind if he wanted to cross-examine me. He did, but when he came back into court he still wouldn't back down. I suppose he couldn't, otherwise Melford Stevenson would have walked all over him.

Platts-Mills: I am grateful to your Lordship for allowing the witness to be recalled. As it is, I have to make an apology, but I had no information that she was coming this afternoon and I was not ready for her.

And so the judge rubbed a bit of salt on him.

Stevenson: Well, what you said then was 'any time convenient to the prosecution'. Anyhow, here she is. What do you want to ask her?

At first Platts-Mills was all sugar with me.

Q: Madam, I am sorry to trouble you again. Are you feeling in quite good sorts?
A: I am still feeling shaky.
Q: You have been ill over something, have you not?
A: Yes. I was in hospital for a while.
Q: What was that for?
A: It's a woman's complaint.

In fact, as I say, I'd had an operation for fibroids and that was the end of his hopes that I'd been in a mental hospital. He couldn't seem to understand why I'd referred to Ronnie Kray as Ronnie. Sometimes I think Mr Platts-Mills didn't understand the facts of real life outside his own special world.

Q: You speak almost as though you knew him quite intimately.
A: No.
Q: Is it customary for people where you live to speak of him as simply Ronnie?
A: Yes.

There was nothing to it. It was just like referring to Diana and Charles nowadays. He and Reggie were the equivalent of royalty. But a few questions after that, he asked me something which caused him a lot of grief as the trial went on.

Q: You have changed your address several times, have you?

A: A couple of times, yes, a few times.

Q: Why did you do that?

A: Through fear.

Q: How do you mean 'fear'? Fear of what?

A: Of any of the friends of the Krays coming round to have a go at me.

Q: Let us just consider that and see whether it is true or not. In March 1966 you were living at an address, we will call it address 'A' – Mrs X's address A.

A: Yes.

Q: How long did you go on living there?

A: Well . . .

Q: The best part of a year?

A: Yes. I don't know.

Q: What?

A: Yes.

Q: If there is any truth in your suggestion that you were in danger, you were in danger throughout all that period?

A: Well, until I told the police the truth, I had no valid reason to ask if I could move away from that address.

Q: You had no reason for moving and no worry?

A: I had plenty of reason for leaving, but I couldn't get a move unless I came out and told the truth and said I wanted to move.

Q: You mean the police gave you a new house?

A: No, the council gave me a new house.

Q: The council gave you a new house at the police's suggestion?

A: I believe so.
Q: They helped you get a new house?
A: Yes.

What the prosecution thought those questions meant, and the judge agreed, was that although Platts-Mills in so many words didn't spell it out, he was suggesting I'd been bribed with the new house. It was a ridiculous suggestion, really. I mean, one evening Helen and I ran out of cigarettes. I didn't have any money at all and she didn't have any with her. The officer I didn't like was there at the time, and we weren't going to ask him to lend us the money, and so we went scrabbling down the sides of the chairs and the sofas to see if we could find enough to buy a packet of ten. They didn't even bribe me with cigarettes.

And after that, he was left more or less with going over Friday's ground once more, but now I knew what to expect. He went back over why I'd changed my story and made an identification.

Q: And you simply declined to identify anybody?
A: Well, you didn't have all that lot in before.
Platts-Mills: I didn't hear what you said.
Stevenson: 'You didn't have all that lot in before.' She indicated the contents of the dock.

But he did have another little new go at me. I didn't know what help he thought it would do him, and neither did the judge. It just got Platts-Mills another

knuckle-rapping. Maybe he thought if your marriage
had broken up, you couldn't tell the truth.

Q: What is your husband's employment?
A: Well, I am divorced.
Stevenson: I do not know what it has got to do with
this case, but in the interests of saving time perhaps
you had better tell us.
A: He is a lorry driver.
Platts-Mills: In regular employment, is he?
A: Yes, sir.
Q: And how old are the children?
A: One is eight, one is seven, one is five.
Q: Eight, seven and nine?
A: Five.
Q: You are married, are you?
A: No, sir, divorced.
Q: You are not married?
A: No.

Maybe it was he thought I had all these illegitimate
children and that made me a liar, but then he spoke
to one of the other barristers.

Q: Someone said he thought you said you were
divorced?
A: I am divorced.
Stevenson: You will tell us some time what this has
to do with this case?
Platts-Mills: I want to see how the lady lives.
Stevenson: What in the world has the question whether
or not she is married got to do with any issue the
jury have to decide?

Platts-Mills: I want to see who is paying to keep her alive and whether it is the police paying for a story.

Stevenson: Well, if you want to ask whether anybody is paying her you had better do so.

Platts-Mills: Then I will ask that directly. Since you gave your story to the police in July of last year, who has been paying you?

A: National Assistance.

Q: Is that all you have had to live on?

A: The court allowance my husband has to pay into court.

Q: What does that amount to?

A: Six pounds

Q: Does he pay it?

A: Yes, sir.

Q: You have been as needy as any mother with children can be?

A: Well, I think when you're a mother with children, you learn how to manage properly.

But he didn't take it any further and come right out and ask me if I was on a wage from the police. The answer would have been the same. I wasn't. The ones, like Helen and Harry, who were staying with me, all chipped in for food but they were on allowances and they were eating it. But, as for a wage, there was nothing like that.

Anyway, a bit after that, Platts-Mills decided he wanted to try an experiment. I'd been through how it was I recognised Barrie after two and a half years. I said it was that when you'd seen a man killed you weren't going to forget the face of the man who did it, although technically speaking he was just with Ronnie.

> Q: I suggest, madam, it doesn't make one scrap of difference to your memory. Except to drive everything out of your memory. Do you feel composed and settled now enough to make a little experiment?

But I never got to answer that question, because the judge jumped in.

> Stevenson: Well, I don't know what that question means.
>
> Platts-Mills: Well, I am going to ask if she could look at a member of the jury and then describe him — within ten seconds, not within two and a half years. My Lord, if your Lordship says the whole notion of testing this witness's evidence is not sensible, then I will be guided by that.
>
> Stevenson: I can see no purpose in having had this witness back yet. I haven't heard yet in your questions any suggestion that wasn't plainly put to her and dealt with on Friday.

Platts-Mills must have been distracted or thought his experiment wasn't a good idea, because he just dropped that line and went on to question me again about going to a solicitor and lying at the coroner's court. He just kept going over and over the same things and I kept on telling him that yes, I had been lying and now I was telling the truth, and he kept on going on about how I could be so calm-looking after poor George, and in the end the judge got really fed up and stopped him.

> **Stevenson**: Mr Platts-Mills, that is the third time we have had that question and answer. How many more times . . .

The prosecution just wanted one thing out of me, and Mr Platts-Mills did his best to keep it out. It was just who I'd told privately that evening or afterwards who'd shot Cornell. And I answered that I'd told Mr Quill and his brother upstairs in the pub. Of course, as I've said, I'd told Chrissie and my ex-husband and Doreen, and Les and my husband's friend, but I wasn't going to volunteer that and get them into trouble, and no one seemed to want to take it any further.

In between me giving evidence the first time and the second that Monday afternoon, they'd had in some of the witnesses from the Beggars. There was Ivor, of course, who'd put me in it, but there was also Michael Flannery, who'd been in the bar when the shooting took place but who hadn't been able to identify anyone. There'd also been the statement of the man we called Pop read out. What had happened is that over the years he'd gone ga-ga. He was over eighty when it happened. Apparently all he said was that he'd heard one or two shots, stood up, seen me dive on the floor and then sat down again calm as anything.

What I didn't know until I read the papers of an evening was who was giving evidence after me. What seemed to me at the time a real booster to my evidence was John Dickson. I also didn't know then that Dickson had done a deal with the prosecution that he could plead guilty to having knowingly harboured Frank Mitchell, the one who'd escaped from Dartmoor. It had happened on the first day of the trial. Dickson had been arrested on 5 July, almost immediately after the ID parade with Barrie, and on 17 August he'd asked to see Harry Mooney and another officer, Frank Cater, and over the next few weeks he'd made a series of statements admitting his part. What Dickson said had happened to him was that he'd been in the Royal Marines and was discharged with the highest rating of good conduct, and had just been drinking in a club when he ran into members of the Firm and got roped in as a minder-*cum*-bodyguard. He'd been in the 20th Century Club the day after Mitchell escaped, and he'd been recruited into looking after him and getting him and the girl, Liza, from the nightclub. After Mitchell had been taken away from the flat, he'd helped clear it out. Apparently he'd tried to break away from the Twins but he hadn't been able to do so, and then someone had put a bottle in his left eye and now he couldn't see properly. So, what with everything, the judge had given him nine months' imprisonment, which meant with the time he'd been on remand he'd already almost done his sentence. He went back inside to do the remainder, but whether he was in prison proper, I doubt very much. I expect he was in some sort of police custody.

The night George was shot, Dickson said he'd been in the Lion in Tapp Street, which was known as the Widows or Madges, having a drink, when Ronnie Kray had come in and asked him to drive him to Whitechapel Road. He said Ian Barrie had been with him. Ronnie had gone into the Grave Maurice and then told Dickson to drive him to the Beggars, which was really only a hundred yards down the road. Ronnie and Ian Barrie'd both gone into the Beggars, and when they came out, he had been told to drive back to Tapp Street. On the way, Ronnie had said, 'I hope the bastard is dead.' They'd gone back into the Widows, where Ronnie had had a word with Reggie, and then about eight of them had left and had gone to the Chequers in Walthamstow. There had been the Twins and Ian Barrie, Dickson, some brothers called Teale, Albert Donoghue and Nobby Clark. They'd gone into the private bar, and Ronnie had been sick. Then Ronnie had gone upstairs to listen to the radio to hear if there was anything on it about the shooting. Dickson said he'd left after that, and the first time he knew Cornell was dead was when he read about it in the morning papers the next day.

Of course there were efforts to discredit him. Platts-Mills got on to him about how he'd told two different stories about the car he was driving and whose it was, and then when Dickson admitted he'd tried to write short stories, he started going on about how Dickson was a great writer. He got very sarcastic.

> Q: I was asking you, have you shown these stories to anyone?
> A: Well, what sort of stories are you talking about?
> Q: Well, I don't know. Your fame as a writer is very great, but it hasn't reached me.

He then pointed out how in his evidence Dickson had told the court Ronnie had said, 'I hope the bastard's dead.' What he'd said in a statement to the police was, 'I got the fucking bastard.' Which was it, Platts-Mills wanted to know, and suggested that Dickson had made the whole thing up. He went on through his statement to the police and how it was different from his evidence, but Dickson just sort of held on, saying he'd been there and he knew Ronnie had shot Cornell.

Then Platts-Mills came to the alibi bit. What Dickson had done once was to make a statement to say that he'd been with Ronnie all evening in the Widows. Why had he done that? he was asked. Platts-Mills read out a bit of it: 'I don't know if Cornell's name was mentioned because, if it was, it wouldn't have meant anything to me. I have never heard the name before.'

What Dickson said had happened was that one of the other defendants had suggested it to him in prison when he was on remand and he had gone along with it, because, he said, he was frightened to do otherwise.

And then Platts-Mills did manage to get Dickson riled up about what he had said in his various statements, and how the one giving the alibi to Kray and Barrie was the truth. But Dickson wouldn't have it.

> **Q**: Just like you to look at the statement you made to your own solicitors. You made a statement to them with the object of their relying upon it, didn't you – acting upon it?
>
> **A**: They wanted an alibi. I was quite prepared to give them one, because I don't think I'd be standing here now if I hadn't given them that.
>
> **Q**: I don't understand that.
>
> **A**: They wanted as many statements as possible to make sure that everybody made a statement to say they were in the pub all the time, and they had a few false statements from various people to back them up. I made a statement to back them up.
>
> **Q**: Are you saying it was a false statement?
>
> **A**: It was a false statement.
>
> **Q**: Happened to contain the truth?
>
> **A**: No, sir.

And one of the things they got on to him about was the fact that at one time he'd agreed to give Ronnie an alibi. He said that one of the Firm, Tommy Cowley, had said it was the thing to do and that he'd given a statement to the Krays' solicitor. Why was he now giving evidence? Mr Platts-Mills wanted to know.

> **A**: The first [reason] is that Barrie is in there for nothing. He has nothing to do with the murder of George Cornell. He is in the same boat as me. He went in blind and did not know that Ronnie Kray was going to shoot Cornell. Barrie is a stubborn man, and he must think it big to stand there and be convicted of a murder he did not do.

According to Dickson, Ronnie had said to him, 'I hope the bastard's dead,' and later had been sick in the private bar of the Chequers. What Dickson had done was written out a story in prison praising the Twins and Platts-Mills suggested that was the truth.

> **Dickson**: Never mind what's on the paper. I am telling the truth in the witness box. The truth is that Ronnie Kray murdered George Cornell.
> **Platts-Mills**: I suggest you are a liar.
> **A**: Then your suggestion is very wrong.

Dickson had made a statement to Mr Haeems from the firm of solicitors acting for Ronnie which was completely different from what he was telling the court, and when asked why he'd done it, he said he was so frightened of the Twins he had no option.

Mr Platts-Mills did manage to get Dickson in one lie, or at least a mistake. He'd told the police he had hired the car in which he drove Ronnie and Ian Barrie to the Beggars, but at the trial he said it was one he'd borrowed from a friend. The other thing he had a go at him about was the time it took to drive from the Widows to the Grave Maurice, on to the Blind Beggar, and back to the Widows. Dickson reckoned it was twenty minutes, and wouldn't shift.

Q: Stopping, getting in and out of the car and so on it would have made a full half-hour the whole journey would take?

A: I imagine so, twenty minutes.

Q: You will never change?

A: No.

Q: It is just a preposterous invention.

A: You say so, not me.

Q: If you had ever made the journey you would know you could get round there and back in great comfort in six or seven minutes with ample time for stopping at every corner and blowing your horn. We were told in the magistrates' court by the three brothers they were all in the pub about eight or eight-ten.

A: Most probably yes.

Q: Ten to eight or eight o'clock, round about there.

It all tied in somehow with my being late for work that evening, and so discrediting me and him at the same time. Later the police called Henry Mooney to give evidence about how long it took to drive over the route, and he didn't seem to get much change from him. If anything, the whole picture got even more confused. Mooney'd given evidence that he had done the journey from the Lion to the Beggars, driving under the speed limit, in a minute and a half and, taking a different route on the way back, a minute and forty seconds. But Platts-Mills wanted more.

> **Q**: Suppose an experienced driver says it would take ten minutes or twenty minutes each journey, ten minutes or twenty minutes back again. You would say that was nonsense, wouldn't you?
> **A**: No. You could take ten minutes for each journey or twenty.
> **Q**: You must be having a sleep on the corner on the way?
> **A**: You could do it at whatever speed you liked.
> **Q**: But on any normal sort of driving, the time you gave is the more sensible time?
> **A**: For the shortest routes, yes.
> **Q**: If you took the kind of time, twenty minutes, you would simply be drawing attention to yourself, wouldn't you?
> **A**: It depends on the route, sir.
> **Q**: I mean the direct route. If you take in Wigan pier on the way, it would take longer, wouldn't it?
> **A**: Of course.

Even when he was pushing Dickson about how he came to give evidence for the prosecution, Platts-Mills was still having trouble with the judge.

> **Q**: But he [a prison officer] fixed up things for Mr Read to come and see you?
> **A**: He didn't fix up anything.
> **Q**: Fixed up . . .
> **A**: No.
> **Q**: Fixed up . . .
> **A**: No, I requested . . .
> **Stevenson**: Now, Mr Platts-Mills, you know, you must

let him answer when he wants to. A great deal of time is being wasted because while he is trying to answer, you cut in with something else. Let him complete his answer before you go on to your next question.

Platts-Mills: The trouble is, I'd very much like to school him and discipline him out of this extraordinary phrase 'It's all lies and rubbish'.

Stevenson: Try not to interrupt.

Of course it wasn't all lies and rubbish!

After Dickson had finished, three brothers gave evidence. I'd never seen them to my knowledge, but they were sort of hangers-on to the Krays and had been in the Widows the night of the shooting. They all wanted to be referred to as Mr A, and so forth. The first one, Alfred, told the court about how the Krays had driven over to Walthamstow on the night of the shooting and that later they had gone back to brother David's flat, where the Twins, Ian Barrie, all the Teale brothers and David's family had spent the night, most of them on the floor with pillows and blankets. They left after about a week and then returned and stayed some longer time. I suppose this bolstered my evidence, but it also more or less fitted in with Ronnie's defence that he had left the neighbourhood because he was afraid that he would get the blame for the shooting.

Platts-Mills got after him straight away, saying that he'd been convicted of blackmail along with his brothers, and Alfred agreed, although he said he'd been wrongly convicted.

Q: This was only a sample of your normal way of
living, was it not?
A: No.

He was also cross that Alfred was hiding behind
an initial rather than giving his full name when
everyone in the dock knew full well who he was.
He spent a lot of time trying to get Alfred to agree
to use his proper name, but Alfred said he didn't
want his name revealed because he had a little
boy whom he didn't want to know of his life. The
battle continued into the next day and eventually a
compromise was worked out. Alfred's name should
be given in court but not published. Platts-Mills went
through his convictions, getting him to admit he'd
been convicted of living on immoral earnings and
used this to say he shouldn't be believed. He also
went on to suggest a deal had been made, letting
Alfred's father off a burglary prosecution and his
mother getting a light sentence for receiving because
the brothers were giving evidence.

There was also a lot of other supporting evidence,
such as from Billy Exley, who was serving time
for attempted murder and had been one of the real
heavies of the team. In fact he was sent with Jack 'The
Hat' McVitie to shoot Leslie Payne when the Twins
thought Payne was going to grass them. Apparently
they went to Payne's house, and the door was opened
by his wife, who said he was out. They did nothing
else except that McVitie kept the money he'd been

given and went about bragging that he'd overturned the Twins. That's what got him killed down in Evering Road. Billy Exley had a heart condition, and died in prison not long after the trial.

Anyway, Billy Exley was allowed to sit down to give his evidence and he told the court how he'd been to the flat where Ronnie and Ian Barrie were being hidden to bring some fresh clothing, and how Ronald Kray had said of Cornell, 'Fuck him, I'm glad he's dead.' Platts-Mills asked him about Cornell's general bad reputation, and I don't think he got the answer he wanted.

Q: He made for himself many enemies, did he not?

A: A few, sir.

Q: And they were men who hated him so much they were willing to kill him?

A: Yes, sir. Ronald Kray.

Q: Ronald Kray had never been tortured by him, had he?

A: No, sir. Do you want to know why he killed him, sir?

Stevenson: What did you say then?

A: Do you want to know why I think he killed him?

Platts-Mills: Please, I am not asking for your opinion on this, sir.

A: Well, would you like to know why Ronald Kray told me he killed him?

Q: Please answer my question. I am not willing to make myself a party to further absurd exaggerations and inventions.

A: They are not absurd, sir.

Jones: Well, is that a question?

Stevenson: It is a piece of abuse . . .

Platts-Mills: It is a comment, my Lord.

Stevenson: It is a piece of abuse which most of us here would recognise is grossly improper, but there it is.

Platts-Mills: In my submission, when a witness comes and introduces into a case—

Stevenson: You ought to know it is a grossly improper thing to say.

When the prosecution re-examined Billy Exley, they weren't going to miss asking him what Ronnie Kray had said was the reason why he killed George. And the answer was:

A: He said to me, 'You know why I killed him? He told Micky Morris's brother that I only took him to Newcastle to get him in bed.'

There was another argument about that, and the judge said he didn't think it took things very much further, but Platts-Mills asked him why he'd not mentioned it before when he'd said at the magistrates' court that he'd told the court everything he knew about the Cornell killing.

A: At that time. The more you question me, sir, the more I am remembering. You are jogging my memory.

Stevenson: That is a very frequent consequence of cross-examination.

Platts-Mills: With some witnesses.

Stevenson: And some cross-examiners.

The flat was owned by the brothers, and one of them gave evidence about how he'd had a secret meeting with Tommy Butler all that time ago to tell him what had happened. According to this man, when Ronnie had heard that Cornell had died on the way to hospital, he'd said, 'That's good. Dead men can't speak.' He'd also been told to drive everyone over to Walthamstow, and Reggie had told him his brother had shot Cornell. If he was right, and Reggie had said that, then there was no wonder the story was over the East End within twenty-four hours.

Henry Mooney had already given evidence about the arrest of Ian Barrie. He'd been seen in the Lea Bridge Road on 29 June just the day before Nipper Read had had me up at Tintagel to talk about making the identification of him. According to Henry Mooney's evidence, he'd been cautioned, and he'd gone on to make what the prosecution said almost amounted to admission.

Q: And after you'd cautioned him, did he make any reply or comment?

A: He said, 'Oh, I feel sick.' He said, 'I have been like an animal for a few days now.' He then said, 'I knew you'd come for me.' And later he said, 'And such a lovely day, too.' He said, 'You say I was in the Beggars. Have you got any witnesses?' I told him, 'I know you were in the Widows public house just round the corner that night and you went to the Beggars with Ronnie Kray and came back afterwards and, to take it further, you went to a pub in Walthamstow that night.'

Q: What did he say, if anything?

A: He said, 'You know all about it, then?'

Q: Yes?

A: I said, 'Do you deny being in the Blind Beggar when Cornell was shot?' He said, 'No, but I did not kill Cornell – I did not shoot Cornell. I wish I could tell you what did happen, but I'd get shot. I thought he' – indicating Sergeant Cheval—

Q: That was the officer with you?

A: Yes. '. . . had come to bump me off.'

Q: Yes?

A: 'By the way, can you prove you're police officers? Where are you taking me to?'

Q: And what did you say?

A: I said, 'To Bow Street police station to be charged with the murder of Cornell.'

He'd been seen the next day by both Henry and Nipper Read, and Nipper had said, 'I have reason to believe you still have the gun that was used in your constructive possession – in other words, you know where it is.' Barrie had replied, 'Mr Read, I don't know where the gun is, that's the truth.'

Q: Yes?

A: Mr Read said to him, 'I am told that the gun has not been disposed of and you must realise it is a vital piece of evidence. Are you sure you don't know where it is?' and Barrie said, 'I know nothing about it, Mr Read. Nothing at all.'

What Mr Howard said was that Harry and Nipper had made up the bit about Barrie admitting he'd been in the Beggars.

Q: It is my duty to suggest to you that what you have given in evidence as having been said by this man is wrong.

A: It is not wrong.

Q: He didn't say the things you have attributed to him.

A: You are wrong, sir.

The prosecution then called a police officer who had been with Tommy Butler when Robert, one of the brothers, had been at the rear of Hackney dog track, and then it was Nipper Read's turn. He just gave formal evidence of being with Henry Mooney when Barrie was questioned about the gun, and then he was turned over to Platts-Mills. And almost immediately poor Platts-Mills got it in the neck again from the judge. I don't really understand what he meant by the question.

Q: The whole science is called Krayology at Scotland Yard?

A: I have never heard that term before.

Q: Is it not?

A: No, sir.

Stevenson: I hope we shall never hear it again.

Then he started asking about me and why I'd been protected, and why I wasn't giving my name.

Q: Let me turn to the barmaid. She tells us, and that seems to be confirmed by an associate of hers, that a policeman watched her for two months after the Cornell shooting.

A: That is perfectly true, sir.

Q: Can you tell us why that was?

A: Yes, I can, sir, but I don't think it prudent that I should.

Q: Then she was asked to go to an identification parade in August of 1966, was she not?

A: She was invited to attend an identification parade, yes, sir.

Q: In the hope that she might see something?

A: Yes, sir.

Q: She did not go?

A: She refused to attend, sir.

Q: Then she was demanded to attend, I mean ordered, required, to attend the inquest, was she not?

A: Yes, of course sir.

Q: By the appropriate summons?

A: Yes, sir.

Q: And she came under compulsion?

A: Yes, sir.

Q: And there on oath in public she gave her full name, address and occupation, did she not?

A: Well, sir, I am only speaking from the notes that I have seen of the inquest. Of course, you must appreciate that I wasn't there, and I can't speak personally of my own knowledge of that.

Stevenson: Mr Platts-Mills, we have been through it I don't know how many times before, you know. Do you want it all again?

Platts-Mills: My Lord, I—

Stevenson: Do you want to go through it all again?

Platts-Mills: No, my Lord, but I didn't actually put to her that she gave her name and address quite freely at the inquest. I just want to do that—

Stevenson: I don't see how that helps.

But Platts-Mills seems to have done. Of course, if he

couldn't get rid of my evidence, he had real problems so he had another try.

Q: But, from the notes, you gather she had no hesitation then in giving her name?

A: Quite honestly, sir, although I have read the report, I can't say now at this moment whether I noticed she had given her address or not.

Stevenson: And, if you read the notes, you wouldn't know whether she did it willingly or not.

Q: But she gave her name quite willingly?

A: She did, sir, yes, and I understand—

Q: And there was no 'Mrs X' there?

A: No, sir.

So far as I was concerned, there was no problem in that. I wasn't giving evidence against Ronnie at the inquest.

Q: Does that suggest to you that if she had any fear, she had lost it by a couple of months after the shooting?

A: No, it does not suggest that to me, sir, no.

Q: Does it mean that nobody advised her 'You must keep your name quiet because you may be in danger'?

A: I don't know what she was advised, sir. I have no idea.

Q: Do you think the effect of appointing a policeman to watch her day and night would make her feel she was afraid?

A: No, sir: there was a very substantial reason why this was done.

Q: If you say that, I accept it and don't press you

further on that, but in general it is obvious, isn't it, if you place a policeman watching discreetly at a distance following someone all the time, it scares them out of their wits, wouldn't it?

A: Are you suggesting, sir, that it is an ordinary, average, law-abiding citizen or a criminal or—

Q: Well, I am speaking of a very modest, properly behaved, quiet, sensible decent barmaid.

A: Then I think that the reverse in fact would be the truth. In these circumstances she would be comforted and consoled by the fact that a policeman was in evidence and was present in case . . .

And he left things alone after that until right at the end of his cross-examination. When he'd finished, Mr Howard was about to start and there was a real rumpus. The prosecutor got up.

Jones: My Lord, I do not rise to re-examine, but in my submission my learned friend has charged the police with bribing, in particular 'Mrs X', the barmaid, to give false evidence. My Lord, I can quote from the transcript where that suggestion was made. He said he would see whether it was the police paying for the story. He asked her if the police had given her a new house. That allegation is a most serious one, made by a very senior member of the bar, and, in my submission, must either be withdrawn at this stage or put to this police officer.

Stevenson: Yes, certainly. You cannot abandon it, you know, now you have made it.

Platts-Mills: The lady gave us her answer.

Stevenson: Now listen. You made an accusation of corruption by the police in the clearest terms when you were cross-examining Mrs X. Here is the officer in charge of the case. You ought either to ask him about that allegation or you ought to abandon it.

Platts-Mills: If your Lordship thought I was suggesting corruption by the police, your Lordship misunderstood—

Stevenson: What is the provision for a house, also a series of questions as to what she was living on, all the sources of her income, coupled with an express suggestion that the police were paying her money – I think I am right – what is that but—

Platts-Mills: I didn't.

Stevenson: Do listen. If that is not an accusation of corruption against the police—

Platts-Mills: I asked her whether that had happened. I didn't put it to her that I knew it had happened.

Stevenson: What possible justification is there for this question unless there is some foundation in your instructions?

Platts-Mills: It was quite correct in my instructions that she lived on money from the police. I had no idea when I put that that she was a lady who was bereft of her husband and was living on a pittance. I only put that the police had either given her a house or helped her obtain a house. Of course they couldn't be giving her a police mansion. What she said was, 'No. The local authority got me a new house.' And I asked her did the police, by some intervention, help her with that, and she said she did not know.

Stevenson: Are you now prepared to withdraw that suggestion or are you still pursuing it?

Platts-Mills: My Lord, I want to put it to the officer.

But he never quite did. He rather pussy-footed about whether the police had paid me, and Superintendent

Read said no, he hadn't, but then the prosecution suggested Mr Platts-Mills should ask if Mr Read had acted corruptly.

Stevenson: Of course he should.

Platts-Mills: My Lord, it is nonsense. I never suggested it for one moment, and I deny ever hinting it.

Stevenson: However, that is probably as far as we shall get with it. I don't think that within the scope of this trial we can go into questions of that kind.

Platts-Mills: There has not been anything further than to withdraw the suggestion that the police paid her. I had instructions that that was the case, and I asked whether it was the case.

Stevenson: Mr Platts-Mills, if that is your view of proper behaviour, I have nothing more to say.

Platts-Mills: My Lord, this officer denies it and I withdraw it, but if your Lordship thinks I am guilty of some act of improper behaviour I am very surprised indeed. I am very surprised that your Lordship should suggest it in a case of this kind on nothing—

Stevenson: It was not my suggestion, it was your opponent's.

And, apart from a few questions by Mr Howard to the effect that Ian Barrie had denied his involvement with the murder, that was the end of the Cornell case so far as the prosecution was concerned. Well, they did have another go about getting the jury to go to the Beggars, but the judge still wouldn't have it. That was the eighth day of the trial.

9

It wasn't until the seventeenth day, 30 January, that the defence of Ronnie Kray started. There was yet another application for the jury to be allowed to go to the pub and yet again Mr Justice Melford Stevenson had refused. There was also a submission that there wasn't enough evidence that Reggie Kray was an accessory, but the judge thought that, by organising the trip to Walthamstow and finding a flat for Ronnie and Ian Barrie to stay in, that was sufficient. So, after lunch, Mr Platts-Mills began to tell them what Ronnie's case was before he put him in the witness box. He started off in good form:

> . . . the result [of the Crown's witnesses] was that the evidence rolled forward like a juggernaut. I am not sure that I remember exactly what a juggernaut was. I think it was a great chariot in an ancient, barbaric, pagan religious festival, where bacchanalia of a sort, drunken old men roared in stupor on a chariot and drunken young women danced with them, and as it

dragged forward in ecstasy or hysteria people were thrown under the wheels or threw themselves under the wheels in religious fervour. I don't know whether it is a good comparison or not to say a juggernaut rolled forward, crushing all in its path. In examination, it seems to me that the real sacrificial, hysterical victims were not the prisoners in the dock, my client, but the hysterical witness for the prosecution. [I don't think I'd been hysterical. I thought that he was complaining that I hadn't been hysterical enough.] A juggernaut was a sort of ancient tank, a prehistoric tank meant to crush and very often the wrong people.[1]

He went on to suggest that what was happening was all the witnesses, including me, had lied and asking the jury to

. . . judge Ronald Kray on what they pretend is his reputation. As I say, it is not prosecuting counsel – it is not my Lord – who took any part in so trying to present the case, but those who disgraced the scene in this court by their behaviour, every one of them was trying to usurp the position of my learned friends for the prosecution, who usurped the position of my Lord, and run the trial after their manner in a hooligan fashion. That was their real purpose, was it not, and I hope you will be able in due course to judge them on that basis.

He must have included me, because he went on:

[1]In fact 'juggernaut' is a corruption of Jagannath, in the Hindu religion the Lord of the World, the title of Krishna. The idol of the deity was dragged in an enormous car annually in procession at Puri in Orissa, under the wheels of which the devotees are said to have thrown themselves to be crushed.

Every man, and woman too, who said 'I lied', 'I changed my story', 'I made up a new story' or 'I made an old story' because of fear of Ronald Kray, based on his suggested reputation, were doing precisely that. Asking you to decide this case on the very thing which you will not decide it on: someone's reputation.

Then he went on to tell the jury:

> What I say is this – that we treat the giving of evidence on oath in this court as a precious coin, and these witnesses have debased that coin and dishonoured it, so that Ronald Kray will say, 'I am not going in that box where they stood.' He might well say his words spoken from the dock here unsworn were just as good as that coin that they have so gravely tarnished by their stories. So you may well hear Ronald Kray give his evidence from the dock where he sits. It would be the less courageous course, because he can't be cross-examined by my learned friends for the Crown. It is for him to decide, but you may think it would take considerable courage after the course the Crown witnesses have tried to force upon this court – I mean those of whom I spoke, not the responsible ones – you may think it would take considerable courage, which he may not possess.

There was then a great argument about whether his client would actually go into the box. Stevenson was trying to force Platts-Mills to say what would happen, and he wouldn't. Then he said he was going to deal with my evidence, and suddenly changed his mind. He never came back to it, because Ronnie called out from the dock and said he would give evidence. Platts-Mills didn't give him a chance to change his mind again and called him straight off.

He took him through his early life and how he knew Rocky Marciano and Joe Louis and other boxers, and then he got on to Cornell:

A: I never had no animosity towards George Cornell, never, sir. I was in prison with him, sir, and he was a friend of mine, sir. In fact a week before he got shot, sir, I sent a basket of fruit to his son who was in hospital because he had mastoid, sir.

Q: If you're in prison with a chap, what is your experience, does that tend to make you friends of his?

A: Well, I was a friend of his, sir.

He went on to say there'd never been any quarrels with the Richardsons.

A: You can call them in and ask them if you want to.

He also went on to say that he'd asked Frankie Fraser to get Cornell a job in a club. So far as the night of the murder was concerned, it was that he and the others had been in the Widows all night until they heard there'd been a shooting, and off they'd gone to Walthamstow.

A: I got to the Widows about eight o'clock, sir.

Q: At what time did you leave that place?

A: I left there roughly about nine o'clock, sir, roughly, I'm not sure of the time, sir.

172

He denied that he'd ever told John Dickson to take him to the Beggars, and the first he'd heard of the shooting was after nine o'clock.

A: I was in the Widows when Nobby Clark[2] called in and said that Cornell had been shot, that a copper by the name of Vibart told him, and that is when we left.

Mr Jones, for the prosecution, got after him about his previous convictions and how in 1956 he'd been found with a loaded revolver, a crowbar and a bayonet after someone had been stabbed in the back. That was the case where his father had written to the court. He said that was because as a young man he'd been a bit silly. He wanted to know why Ronnie was called the Colonel.

A: You are known as Taffy Jones by all the prison officers; that makes us both equal, don't it? Taffy Jones, they said you ought to have been a miner instead of a prosecutor, you might have done more good. Taffy Jones – we have both got nicknames, Taffy Jones and the Colonel. Mine sounds better than yours.
Stevenson: Kray, listen; you won't do yourself any good with anybody by being impertinent.
A: Yes, sir.
Jones: It is easy to see how I earned that nickname. Would you care to tell us how you earned yours?

[2]See Appendix – Charlie Clark.

A: I don't know, I have no idea, I had that nick-name—

Q: No idea?

A: How can I when I was called it since I was seventeen.

He also asked him about being followed. Ronnie had said the police had followed him for a couple of years.

Q: Except of course, on the night of the 9th March, when Cornell was murdered—

A: To my knowledge I have been followed all the time, sir. I wouldn't know about that.

Q: . . . or indeed on the 28th October 1967 [that was when McVitie was murdered].

A: So far as I know, the police have been following me all the time.

Q: It doesn't look as though they were following you on those days?

A: Well, that's what you are saying, but I am saying they must have been following me for months and months.

Q: You mean that they have deliberately concealed that they knew where you were on those two nights?

A: They knew where I was on those two nights. Don't worry about that.

Q: And they deliberately concealed it?

A: Well, they would, wouldn't they?

Q: Why do you say they would do?

A: Because the police don't like us; that's why.

Q: Are you suggesting in some way you are the object of some conspiracy here?

A: Police persecution, yes, sir.

Q: Police persecution?

A: And Home Office orders, sir. Home Office orders.

Q: Home Office orders to what effect, Mr Ronald Kray?

A: To try and have us arrested on any pretext.

Q: And to try and have you convicted of two murders?

A: As good as, sir. If they can't find anyone else, we'll do.

Q: That comes from the Home Office?

A: Yes, from the Home Office.

Ronnie's line of defence was that the killing had been done by one of the Richardson's torture victims after the main gang had been arrested on the previous Monday, but when this suggestion was put to Exley, he wasn't having it.

A: No, sir. Ronnie Kray did tell me he killed Cornell. The police knew, everybody knew. It was common knowledge in London.

When he was questioned, he said to his knowledge he'd never seen me, and Mr Jones turned to the question of his going to the Chequers in Walthamstow.

Q: First of all, you were trying to get out of the way of the police?

A: We were not trying to get out of the way of the police. We decided to be out of the public house because we didn't want to be near where he was shot in case the police said it was us.

Q: So you were trying to get away from the police?

A: No, we left the pub to go to another pub.

Q: Quite a long way away?
A: No, it is not very far away at all.

And a bit later:

Q: But to run away is almost a confession of guilt, isn't it?
A: Well that just shows what justice you think if that is what you are thinking now. To go from one pub to another you are telling people makes you guilty of murder.

The first witness he called was Frank Fraser, who was serving fifteen years for his part in the shooting at Mr Smith's Club and the torture trial put together. Frank Fraser had had spells in mental hospitals and a long life of violence. He said he was sure that Jack Duvall, who had been a witness in the torture trial, had shot Cornell.

A: Yes, sir. As a matter of fact at Bow Street Magistrates Court about November or October of 1966 I shouted out from the dock that he was the man who shot George Cornell and everybody knows it. Ronald Kray is an innocent man.
Q: You may have shouted it out out of hatred or malice.
A: No, sir – everybody knows. It's common knowledge.
Q: You know Duvall well, do you?
A: Fairly well, sir.
Q: How does he compare in build and appearance with Ronald Kray?

A: Well, I shouldn't think there's too much difference, sir, no.

Q: Is he a darkish chap?

A: Yes, sir. He wears a toupee, but it is a dark one.

Q: And what—

A: Glasses – glasses on occasions, sir.

Q: What kind of build?

A: Stocky build, sir – quite well built.

Q: Would there be any possibility of a person who
   didn't know them [that's me] may just have seen
   them about, confusing one with the other?

A: A great possibility, sir.

Apparently Duvall had been questioned about the
Cornell killing at Bow Street, and he looked, according to Fraser:

A: Terrified, my Lord. Terrified sir. He went white –
   guilty conscience writ all over him.

When he was re-examined by Mr Platts-Mills, he
went on again.

A: Because a man has a number of convictions, sir, it
   doesn't mean he can't tell the truth. Sir, I know
   Ronald Kray is innocent. I know Jack Duvall shot this
   man Cornell and was boasting about it in Wormwood
   Scrubs Prison in July and August 1966.

Mr Platts-Mills went on to call a number of witnesses
including Sammy Lederman, who had said he had
been with Ronnie drinking in the Widows at the
time of the shooting. Later, Henry Mooney gave

evidence again about a conversation he'd had with Sammy Lederman when he'd been with Mr Haeems. Henry had said, 'I understand you are being called as an alibi witness.' Lederman had replied, 'I was not in the Blind Beggars. I know nothing of the Blind Beggar murder,' and a bit later he'd said he was at home with his father, so that wasn't much of a help. What Mr Platts-Mills really wanted was either Patsy or Jimmy Quill or, better still, both, to give evidence. The idea of this, I suppose, would be to get them to say that I hadn't told them it was Ronnie the night of the shooting.

After all his other witnesses were over he said:

> I would still like to call the witnesses Quill, but I gather all the efforts of my instructing solicitors and the police have failed to produce either of the Quills from their hotel or anywhere else.

There was a good deal of toing and froing, and it was more or less agreed that if they could be found by the end of the other defendants' cases he could put them in then. He never did.

Ian Barrie made a statement from the dock denying that he'd killed George, and Reggie Kray also made a statement denying he'd killed McVitie, and particularly that Connie Whitehead was afraid of him. He read out a long poem he'd sent to Whitehead's little boy. And that, so far as I was concerned, was the end of the evidence.

Mr Platts-Mills abandoned his argument about my

being paid by the police with money, but there was still the question of being bribed with a council flat. Of course this was rubbish. Even after I was in the flat, it was another two years before I would say anything. What he did have to say about me was:

> There was not a single prosecution witness who was not stained by switch and change in his or her story. The witness who stood head and shoulders above all the others for the prosecution was the barmaid. But she still stands only knee-high to the sort of stature of witnesses you need to satisfy yourselves with in this sort of case of murder.

His speech to the jury took twelve hours and five minutes. The summing up came on the thirty-sixth day at the end of February, and the judge said my evidence was crucial.

> As you've been reminded time and time again, the witness on whom you have quite plainly to focus attention with all the concentration at your command in relation to that case is the lady we've called Mrs X or the lady we've more often called 'the barmaid'. It is perhaps easier to call and think of her as the barmaid. Now she raises none of the problems about an accomplice.

He ran through my evidence about that night and then went on:

> Well, it is obvious, is it not, that much is going to depend in this case on what you make of her evidence and whether you are content to rely upon it?

He pointed out that there was no question of my being an accomplice or having previous convictions.

But she has been challenged, and challenged on a whole series of grounds. First of all we have to accept the fact that she gave evidence at the coroner's court which she herself says was not true. She says, 'I was deliberately suppressing my knowledge of the matter. The reason I did it was fear for my own safety and that of my children.'

He told the jury that he wasn't going to go through that bit of the evidence in detail, but I had said that I had suppressed the evidence through fear.

You've got to consider on the totality of all the evidence you've heard whether it may be true or was true that she was indeed terrified at the time.

Now here we come to one of the matters that you have got to think about in relation to every witness. A part of the process on which I think certainly judges when they are acting as judges of fact, as we sometimes are, and I am sure juries, rely is the demeanour of witnesses, the way they behave in the witness box, the way they give their answers, the general personal impression they create. I want you to try and go back to that woman in the witness box when she was giving her evidence and ask yourselves what impression did she leave on your minds? Do you think she was lying, and if she was lying why was she lying? What motive has she got to come here and tell what is, if the suggestions made to her are well founded, a tissue of lies? Bear in mind, of course, the suggestions that have been made to her, in effect she had been bribed. You remember, for some time, a suggestion was made that she was bribed with money provided by the police. That, after some time, was withdrawn, but there still remains the suggestion that her evidence was in effect bought by arranging with the local authority to substitute a council house for the council flat she was occupying with her children at the time of the Cornell shooting. [*He got that wrong. I was in a council house at the time of the shooting, and then I went to the flat.*] Well, don't throw it aside, don't reject it out of hand, give it thought, and ask yourselves, having heard the woman in the witness box and bearing in mind she has come here to give evidence with the knowledge of the unpleasant experience that that involves, do you think she has sold her evidence to the police for the occupation of a council house – because that is the suggestion which still remains in this case as a reason for her lying. Now, gentlemen, do you think that this is an opportunity to use that common sense to which I referred earlier, and your sense of fairness, and do you think it is entirely a matter for you, if you do, what impression of the barmaid is left in your minds. Bear this in mind, too. You see, there is no halfway house in relation to her. So often one hears the suggestion made to a witness that they may be mistaken, they may have fallen into human error. It may be a defect of memory, but you are not concerned here with any defect of memory. What is said here is that this woman is lying, attempting to deceive you, and indeed that she has been put up to it by the police for the purpose of securing an unjust conviction against Ronald Kray and later on against John Alexander Barrie.

Which I really thought when I read it in the papers the next morning was putting it very fairly indeed. I was really quite pleased. The other thing he went on about was my identification of Ian Barrie and why Mr Haeems hadn't given evidence.

> You were told, if you remember, that he was only an articled clerk who had not passed his examinations. Gentlemen, you do not have to pass any examinations as solicitors to qualify yourself for telling the truth if there is something useful he can say, and he has not been called. That is a matter which you may think it is worth giving some attention when you are generally assessing the weight of the barmaid's evidence.

I'd thought that the evidence of Dickson would have supported me, but the prosecution had said they didn't rely on his evidence, and the judge said there were good reasons why they shouldn't.

> He was, was he not, a hopelessly unsatisfactory witness? You're asked not to rely on him, and I suggest you don't allow yourselves to be influenced by anything Dickson said, certainly in this case, and you may think it would be equally unwise to place any reliance on him in regard to the next case, the McVitie case.

It shows how you can get it wrong reading the newspapers.

Obviously, waiting for the finish of the summing-up and the verdict was a strain. The jury went out at about a quarter past twelve and we didn't hear the result until after seven o'clock, when someone telephoned to tell us they'd all been found guilty except Anthony Barry, the one who'd been separate from them from the start. Nowadays seven hours seems quite a short time for a jury to be out, but it didn't then. When we heard they'd been found guilty, there was no celebrating. I was just relieved. Relieved and exhausted.

I went up the next day for the sentencing. I couldn't not go. It wasn't out of spite or anything like that. There was still part of me believed that even now they were going to walk away from it all, and I wanted to see them actually go down the steps from the dock and go to prison. Some of the newspapers say I was high up in the public gallery wearing dark glasses, and that Ronnie looked up and recognised me. That's utter rubbish. I wouldn't have survived in the public gallery with all the defendants' relatives. They'd have had me over the top. I was right at the back, sitting with the police behind the dock.

They brought them up from the cells below the court one by one for sentencing. Melford Stevenson was at his most severe. Platts-Mills was still trying his best. Once Ronnie had been convicted of murder there had to be a life sentence, but what he didn't want was for the judge to impose a minimum recommendation. In fact, what he really wanted was the sentencing to be postponed until after the trial over the death of Frank Mitchell. The judge wasn't having that, and after Nipper had told him about Ronnie's convictions and his life, this was when Melford Stevenson said those famous words.

Ronald Kray, I am not going to waste words on you. The sentence upon you is that you will go to life imprisonment. In my view, society has earned a rest from your activities and I recommend that you be detained for thirty years. Put him down.

The next to be brought into the dock was Ian Barrie, and he had a twenty-year recommendation. I didn't jump up and down for joy. I cried at the Old Bailey, upstairs with matron, and then I cried all the way home. I just couldn't stop. But I'm not really sure what it was for. It was mixture of a lot of feelings. It was part relief that I wasn't going to have to walk in the street and bump into them, it was part that I had been believed; but it was also that, apart from hearing and following the other cases and what had happened there, I couldn't forget kneeling down by George on the floor of that pub. I can still see today the mess he was in. It was tears for everybody and the way I'd had to live since then, trying to give the kids as normal a life as possible in very difficult circumstances. You try to give them as normal an upbringing as possible, but with the police being there, losing contact and being so scared, to me it was just a complete and utter mess-up and waste all round.

The funny thing is I'd like some day to go back to the Old Bailey and sit in the public gallery to see them come in with their robes and with the nosegays. Look at things objectively. I wouldn't want to see a murder trial, though.

10

I can't say I remember anything much about the appeal. I didn't go and hear it. It seemed so remote by this time. It wasn't just the George Cornell murder people were sentenced for, so I wouldn't have been all that concerned. All the appeals were dismissed, both against conviction and sentence. A bit after the trial, I went in the Barley Mow when I was visiting the East End, and the next thing a drink came over and Johnny Ambrose came round and put his arm round me and asked if I was all right. I said I was, but I wasn't at all. I was waking up at night screaming.

The police stayed with me for quite a while. They eased it off very gradually. It was partly for the sake of the children, because they'd got used to having uncles and aunts around, and partly because I was still in such a bad way. The officers who'd been with me stayed, and then they gradually tailed off. Every day and night became alternate days and then twice a week and so on. I had their home numbers, but there was no such thing as a hot line.

I wasn't really ever officially thanked in the sense anyone sent me a letter. I was taken to see Commander du Rose at Tintagel and had my hand shaken by him and by Nipper, and Henry Mooney, the old flanneller, would say, 'I realise it took a lot of courage,' which I didn't think was right because I was so bloody scared the whole time.

But as for myself, I began to get more and more depressed. I was on prescriptions, and they weren't doing any good. I was sitting at home doing as little as I could. I would get the children ready for school and then I'd sit still all day doing nothing. I'd always smoked, but now it was getting up to nearly fifty a day. The kids were cared for, of course, but it was a basic minimum. I wouldn't go out or see people. If John came round to see the kids I'd put on a show, but if he didn't there wasn't any need as far as I was concerned. I'd just sit around in my dressing-gown. I think I was missing my father as well. Now I'd learned to drive, John had got me an old mini-van banger and I sat thinking how Dad would have loved me to be driving him round the countryside. It would have been so lovely.

But the worst thing was that I wasn't sleeping. If you've never had trouble sleeping, you don't know what it's like maybe dozing off for an hour at a time and then waking up with a start, never getting any proper sleep. You end up feeling like a zombie, as though the whole world is in a haze. You can't think straight, and one night in early November I thought even less straight.

I was so desperate to sleep I didn't mind how I did it, and I took a whole load of paracetamols. Even then, I didn't get to sleep properly. The phone was just by my bed and when Ray, the police officer, rang up I must have answered it instinctively. With what I sounded like on the phone, he and Maggie came round, and whilst she stayed with the kids he bundled me up and drove me to hospital where they pumped me out. I don't think I was trying to kill myself. It was just that I was so tired. I remember John came round with a bag of apples. I didn't want to talk to anyone, and he was so bloody cheerful I threw them at him. I just wanted to be let alone.

I was in hospital two days, and when they discharged me I was told I had to go and have counselling. I went once, but I never went again, and no one followed up to see why I hadn't. The trouble was that I couldn't tell the man what was wrong and who I was. Already somebody, I suppose it was from the hospital, had let the newspapers know I'd been in, and I didn't want anyone else knowing. I felt ashamed of myself at being so foolish about not thinking of the repercussions.

So it was back to the mixture as before. I still wasn't sleeping properly but I was more careful what I did. I sat in my dressing-gown. I wouldn't even put on make-up. I'd just sit and look at the wall. I was having a bit of a breakdown, really. It went on until nearly Christmas, when another copper and then another of the coppers who'd been guarding me came round by chance and found me sitting there. The kids were out with their father. The place was a mess and the truth is I think I smelled a bit. They made me go and have a bath, and whilst I was upstairs the man's wife tidied up. Afterwards they took me down the road to have a bit of a meal and we had a chat. They stayed for a few days, helping me, and from then on they kept looking in, and so did Ray and Maggie. With it, I began to put myself together. I thought, I've got to make a go of things. It wasn't being fair on the kids, although they were very good about it, helping out; but it took several more months before I was really ready to go out and start living properly. I suppose it wasn't until the spring that I began functioning properly again. I have never really slept well since the trial, but at least I cut down my smoking back to about fifteen a day.

I got a job in a shop as a cashier and did that for quite a few years, and then went back to office work again. We never had that much money, but we managed. One year I took the kids on a caravan holiday and another to Butlin's. That sort of thing. It was years before I told them what had happened; as far as they were concerned, they knew nothing about it at all. We were now well away from the area and no one knew anything about us. I told Susan first, one Sunday afternoon, after lunch. I'd been thinking about it for some time, and I suppose I was having one of my bouts of worry that now she was getting older she'd say something which might trace us. Then I told Michael and Peter, and they took it all very matter-of-factly as if it didn't concern them at all, which I'm glad.

My mother died in the early 1980s. She was still living in Poplar. The people next door rang up to say they hadn't seen her, and when I went over there, she was dead. That was on the Sunday. Someone had been in there and rifled her cupboards and put an electric fire on. The doctor wouldn't come out until the next morning. I stayed over there with her, and during the night I thought there was something under the bed. As I bent down, her hand slipped over and touched me on the head. It was absolutely horrendous.

Eleven years ago my house got burned down. The firemen think it was electric wiring which had rotted through. It started in the corner of the lounge when I was on my own. Fortunately the kids were away, and there was only me and the dog there. I'd gone to bed early and I woke up in the middle of the night to a bedroom full of smoke. I went out on the landing, thinking, if I get a flannel I could soak it, put it round my face and go and get the dog, but when I came out, it was now flames on the landing. I was sinking to the floor and I had to get back in the bedroom and throw myself from the window out of the front. Thank God none of the kids were there. I hit the porch roof first, and came down off of it. It didn't do my stomach a lot of good. I lost everything in that fire. It was very embarrassing with your nightdress burning off you. Someone had already called the ambulance and the fire brigade, and I was shaking all over by the time they arrived. Someone had wrapped me in a rug. I asked the ambulance man for a fag, and he said, 'Haven't you had enough smoke for one night?'

We literally had nothing left. I was brought home the next morning and went round to my son's place. Everyone turned up and brought things. The girl my son was going out with brought loads of stuff, and my mates from the East End turned up with suitcases. The council put me and my daughter and one of my sons in a flat for nine or ten months, and mates came there with beds and a television. The man next door found loads of photos in the garden and he tried to salvage them. When I got in the flat, I found I'd got almost everything – knives, forks but no teaspoons. It was just on Christmas, and a butcher sent round a chicken and some beef. Helen sent round a hairdryer. For months people would say, 'You don't want that, you've got one.' And I'd say, 'It went in the fire.'

I always say to my lot I must be lucky because I survive things. When the house got burned down, my daughter said, 'Bloody hell, Mum, you've had everything. Pub, car accident, fire. Be careful you don't drown.' I went round the house to see what I could salvage, and I was halfway up the stairs when the water tank came through the ceiling and just missed me.

I'm sure I did my back in the pub that evening, but there was no such thing as Criminal Injury Compensation then. Like I said, I'd hit my back on the cellar steps when I tried to jump down, and I'd landed awkwardly and caught the bottom of my back. I used to get backache over the years, and eventually I put the discs out completely. My back gradually got weaker and when one day I lifted something, my legs just went and I fell over. The treatment went on for about three years, on and off trying different things. This was in the early seventies. I was put on traction, put in a plaster cast. I'd tried acupuncture. Then I was in a wheelchair and on a walking frame, but nothing seemed to do any good. Otherwise I was going to have to have my spine operated on. I saw a programme with Katie Boyle about her troubles, so I wrote to her and she gave me the name of her faith healer, a Mr Fricker who had rooms in Wyndham Place. John said it was worth trying anything and he got me an appointment, and he took me to him to see if he could get me walking again.

I got on well with him from the minute I was there. I just threw in my lot with Mr Fricker. There wasn't any laying on of hands or anything like that. He never actually touched me. He just said he had enough faith for both of us. I walked better after the first session, and it got to be OK. He'd be in his late fifties, quite a short man, stocky, always had music in the background. He was a very jovial person and would put you at your ease. He was just lovely. He's since died. Katie Boyle sent me a Christmas card that first year, saying she hoped things had worked out, and I wrote back saying thank you it had.

It was about nine months getting over the car crash. One Sunday, I was driving along minding my own business when the driver of a car coming the opposite way got slammed straight into me. I ended up with the dashboard in my legs. They had to take the roof off to get at me and it took an hour and a half to get me out. There were two lovely paramedicals there. I was under a ground-sheet with one of them, and I said, 'It's the first time I've been under a blanket with a young man for years, and I can't do anything about it.' They had to get the engine out to lift it off me before they could get me out. A helicopter was landed in the grounds of the local school in case I had to be flown to the London Hospital. Mind you, there was no way I would have gone. There was no way you'd have got me up in a helicopter. I told them they'd have to give me a knock-out injection before I went in one of those.

What was funny, was it was just before Sunday lunchtime. The road was blocked off either end. They'd told the whole family, who were out by the car. I was conscious all the time and and my son-in-law said, 'I don't suppose there's any chance of the roast dinner then today?' I won't say what I told him.

I came home on crutches, but I couldn't hardly walk for months and I was confined to my bedroom for six weeks. The furthest I could get was down the landing to the loo. I had a table with jigsaws which people brought me. I just can't lay in bed and do nothing. I'll have to have a knee replacement in a few years.

In 1994 I went into hospital again. I knew there was something really wrong with me, and I kept on going round to the surgery. The young doctor there said I'd got irritable bowel syndrome and I was just going to have to live with it. When I went back, he just commented that he'd been getting a lot of paperwork to do with me. One day I was down the surgery and fortunately my old doctor was there. I told him I felt so ill. He put his hand on my stomach and sent me straight off to hospital. I'd got a growth. It was so big they didn't do a biopsy but just took it out straight off. Fortunately it wasn't malignant. I remember lying there. I felt so ill I couldn't eat the pie and mash my daughter Susan brought me. 'You must be really ill, Mum,' she said, and I was. I went up back to the hospital two or three months after the operation for a check-up. The surgeon said, 'Give it a couple of months and we'll let you start driving.' I didn't tell him I had the car in the car park.

Of course, it hasn't been all bad. I made some good friends with the police. Helen and I have remained close all these years, and one of the best ever friendships came with Ray, one of the police who'd been in the van right at the start, and who was the one who called the night I'd taken the overdose. When he retired in the 1970s and became the manager of the Alma pub over in West London, he would ask me to come and help his wife out with the staff. You never really lose your knack as a barmaid – if you've got one to start with, that is. So I went off and helped out from time to time in the Alma and he'd say stop on for a couple of weeks, and I would do. I hadn't lost me touch. He was there for two and a half years. It was a very different sort of pub from the Beggars. You used to get Marius Goring and Irene Handl in there, along with Sam Kydd, Danny la Rue and Bill Simpson, who played Dr Finlay.

There was a different class of criminal as well, just the odd shoplifter and housebreaker. There was one shoplifter we called Paddy, although I don't think he was Irish. We also used to have some Australians who were on their way round the world in their campers. One of them, Kerry, wanted some special sort of sockets and was talking about getting some. Paddy was in the crowd and said, 'No worry', he'd get them. He brought them back to Kerry and said, 'How about them?' 'No, they're the wrong type,' says Kerry, very particular. 'No problem,' says Paddy, and off he goes. What he did was he went back to Whiteley's, put them back on display and got the right make. Kerry only knew what had happened when he offered to pay, and Paddy refused.

It was in that pub that I heard the barmaid saying

she'd been the one working that night in the Beggars. When I told my friend Ron, he said, 'Did you ask her anything about the shooting and what she did?' I couldn't help laughing. We rolled up over it. It's amazing the number of people who say, 'I was having a drink in there that night.' You'd think the place had been full. The number of people who were in there, I'd have been run off my feet. It's like the Easter Rising in the Dublin post office. Thirty walked in and thirty thousand walked out. If they'd known what I had to put up with, they wouldn't be so keen. You'd be surprised the number of people who were great friends of the Twins. I don't know if they think it reflects glory.

So far I've always said about my mum and dad, but really I was an adopted child. I'd been born in the Mile End Hospital just round the corner from where my adoptive parents were living. I'd have expected to have been born in the East End Maternity Home, which was nearer to Brunswick Buildings, Goulston Street off Petticoat Lane, where my real mother was living with a George and Margaret Ford.

My real mother was Irish by the name of Nancy Kelly, and I found out I was baptised Patricia Kelly at St Mary's and St Michael's, Commercial Road. It was odd how I discovered that church. It wasn't the nearest RC to Goulston Street, but I was passing with Helen and I said I really thought I had something to do with that church. She was sort of humouring me, and said, 'All right, go in, then.' So in I went and saw the priest in charge, Father Francis, and we went through the records together. He couldn't have been nicer, but he couldn't find anything under Kelly. A few weeks later I went back and asked if he would look again under Flannagan, and there it was.

On my birth certificate my father's name appears, but a few weeks later it was deleted. My father's name there is Patsy Flannagan. Originally my mother put her name down as Nancy Flannagan. She used the name Donovan as well, and then reverted to Kelly. On the birth certificate my father's down as Joseph, but I think Patrick is more likely – that's where the Patricia probably comes from. It's all a bit of a mystery. A Margaret Ford went with her when she signed the adoption papers, and I was adopted at about the age of six months.

I knew from very early that I had been adopted. My dad never ever spoke of it to me, but if she thought I was misbehaving my mother would remind me where I'd come from, telling me she picked me out of the gutter, so to speak, and that if I wasn't careful I'd be right back there. When I started school she told the headmistress, and when I started work in the West End, she travelled to the firm I'd started with and told them also. I used to believe it was a disgrace, and she made me think there was a stigma to it. Even at my wedding, she went round telling the guests I'd been adopted.

My mother treated me more as a possession than a daughter, as if she was doing me a favour. When

I was young, I wanted to find my father in case he was rich. When I saw the name Kelly on my birth certificate, I hoped it might be the Kelly who had a lot of pie and mash shops in the East End because I loved pie and mash – I still do, for that matter – and I thought maybe I could inherit them. If my dad had a good day selling his pigeons, he'd treat me to pie and mash. With the family, I didn't miss the aunts because I'd always been reminded by them that I was adopted. My Nan (Dad's mum) never said anything like that.

I think it was my mum's influence. Liley – there was no real harm in her but she was easily influenced. If my mum said I should be grateful, then Liley would think that I should be. I was talking to Christine's mum about a year back [Aunt Flo]. She said they didn't know anything at all about me until I was about two years old. Flo didn't have much to do with my mum. It was a question of meeting up at weddings and funerals.

I decided to find my real mother when I was quite young – when I was in my late teens, early twenties. But I just got nowhere with it at all. I suppose I didn't try hard. It would have upset my dad, and I wouldn't have done that for the world. But in the last eight to ten years I've really started again on it in my spare time because there's slightly more access to information. It was a closed shop when I was younger. Especially with the war years, so many records were mislaid or lost and people moved about. It has made it that much harder. I need a date and place of birth in Ireland. I can't find a marriage certificate in England. I don't even know whether they came from Ireland or from the North. I shall take myself over there and kiss the Blarney Stone and try and get someone to help me.

I've spent a lot of time trying to find what happened to my mother. I went to Brunswick Buildings and tracked down the last couple of really elderly Jewish people who were there. They couldn't remember the Fords, and of course the war had intervened. I've spent hours in Bancroft Road library and St Catherine's House in Kingsway, as well as the Public Record Office in Clerkenwell.

Then I went to the Greater London Council record library at Northampton Row. They won't release the records to anyone but the patient – that's my mother, Nancy Kelly. My argument is that, as the infant, I'm the patient as well, but they don't see it that way. I went to Toynbee Hall, and I was told their librarian had disappeared and they couldn't get into the record library.

Then I was told I had to have a social worker to counsel me, and information would be sent through her. I didn't think in my early forties I needed counselling but I can't go into the GLC records. My social worker, Joan, can go in for me but she can't take photocopies or bring them out. She really hasn't got the time to do extensive searches for me. One of the Mile End Hospital records – which I haven't seen – suggests an estimated age could be around thirty. On the other hand, Aunt Mary always used to tell me that my real mother had me when she was extremely young, so I don't know who's right. Stepney Council said the records from the LCC were in Harford Street, and then a bit later that they were in their new headquarters at Mulberry Street in Poplar, so off I went there. The people in Mulberry Street had no idea. I phoned Ken Livingstone's offices at Tower Hamlets, but they didn't know where records were kept.

I've tried the Catholic Children's Society and Norcap, which I joined, but that seemed to be more of a counselling group and, as I say, at my age I don't need that. The Salvation Army couldn't help, and I'm told the Mormon Church has a massive computer that is better than the CIA. They'll help me if I can get my mother's date of birth!

David James Gilbert is the godfather on the baptismal records. There was a Gilbert Boxmakers in Elsden Mews. They're now in Hackney, but they've no record of there being a DJG. I'd never heard the name before. Nancy had me baptised. I found it difficult to understand why she'd go to the trouble of having me baptised if she wasn't going to keep me. My mother always said she got me from an orphanage, but it looks as though they all knew each other somewhere along the line. It would be nice to have a photograph of some sort. I'd like to see if I look anything like my mother.

Strangely, that's something I can feel sorry for the Krays. Whatever else, they were devoted to their mother. It must have been awful for her and them being separated.

Just before she died, Mary, my aunt, was talking about going back to Ireland when she came out of hospital. She'd been born in India, where her father had been a serviceman. She was always thankful for her education. Towards the end of her life I asked her about my mother, but she started bumming me off. She told me my mother had worked as a manageress at the Gresham Hotel in Dublin, but when my daughter went over to make enquiries, there was no record of their having had any Nancy Donovan, Kelly or Flannagan around that time, so I gave up asking her.

Then one day recently I was talking with Henry Mooney, and he said, 'Well, Ford's an Irish name. Do you think this Margaret Ford could be Nancy Flannagan's sister?' It suddenly began to make a bit of sense. If she was, then it would account for why they were all together at registering the birth and so on. Maybe that line will prove some good.

11

I've often thought about my life. What would it have been like if I hadn't been there that night? It would have been a struggle. I'm glad I got away from the East End for the sake of the kids. It's easy enough if you live there and don't have much money there to be drawn into trouble. I think it turned out for the best, moving away, but I'd have preferred to do that in different circumstances. There again, perhaps I never would have done if I hadn't been forced to. You'd have had to have a jolt to make you move because, for East Enders, there was nothing in life but the East End. So far as we were concerned, everything else was out in the sticks. My friend Doreen wouldn't even move to Ilford because it was just that. I know I worked out of the East End, but I went back every night. It was accepted you'd marry there, raise your children there, die there. Families tended to live on one another's doorsteps.

My kids have all done well. They've always had

full-time jobs, which isn't bad these days. They're all very good to me. Although Susan's gone to New Zealand with her husband, it's a rare day that I don't speak to one or other of the boys, and she keeps in touch regularly. For my birthday the other year my elder son, Michael, gave me a jewellery box and when I opened it there were two tickets for Disneyland. I took Helen with me – now she's retired, we often go on holidays together – and a police officer friend of hers recommended me to meet John Polk, the Sheriff of Sandown County. He arranged for me and Helen to look round a top security prison. I would have chanced a helicopter ride with him! I like America; people put themselves out for you. I went swimming just after the hurricanes. People there thought I was mad. They thought it was too cold to go in the hotel pool – the temperature was only 74°! I want to go back to the Everglades and the Keys.

I always remained good friends with my husband. At first he didn't pay the maintenance, but by the Christmas after my father died he had started to and from then on, as I've said, we got on really well. He was so close to the kids and they really idolised him. I still loved him. He ended up with a girl by whom he'd had some kids. For years I never knew that; he never mentioned it to me, then it came out of the blue. Over all the years coming to see me and the kids, he'd never let slip, and then someone just told me. Next time he came over, I challenged him on it. I wasn't cross, it was more to see what he said, and he admitted it straight away. Then he brought the kids over themselves and they got on well with ours. They're grown up now, but I still see them regularly. It's one good family. We were all absolutely devastated when he died. He'd taken up taxi-cab driving, and done the knowledge and got his cab when he was diagnosed as having lymphoma. He told us he'd been going to the doctor complaining that his neck was swollen. He was told that it was because it had got stiff because he was getting cold through an open window. He had such a big lump they couldn't operate, but he had chemotherapy and radiation. For a while it seemed to be doing him some good and then in 1983, when he was forty-five, he died in Bart's. Whilst he was having his chemotherapy the last time, my daughter spent days with him. I used to go along, and when I left I'd want to put my fist through the wall in frustration. You can be all calm on the outside for people to see, but it doesn't mean you'll be calm on the inside. There was no question of our getting back together. There was too much water under the bridge but we became really good friends. I never remarried. I thought about it once or twice, but no, I'm happy as I am.

All the people I was closest to have all died: Doreen; Johnny; Les, the godfather to my children. He was killed by a drunk driver careering round on the wrong side of the road doing seventy. The two cars in front of Les managed to get out of the way, and the man hit Les head on. I remember Les had always been keen on Rudyard Kipling; he could stand quoting him for hours. He always liked 'If'. Doreen, she died about a year and a half ago of cancer. I'd been close to her and her second husband, Bill. He was so dreadfully cut up.

Tommy Butler died on 30 April 1970. He was fifty-seven. He had been ill for some time with lung cancer and had a chest operation in September the previous year. He'd retired on 31 December 1968 and become the chief security officer for the Midland Bank. Over a thousand attended his memorial service held at St Margaret's, Westminster.

Chrissie stayed in Australia. When it came to it, she only lived with her brother for a few weeks and then she struck out on her own. She got a good job as a secretary in Perth, and things took off from there. Eventually she met a fellow called Geoff, started living with him, and she's still there and still with him. We keep in touch. She still lives in Perth and still does secretarial work. She comes over every second year or so. She never seems to alter much. All she keeps on about is me going out there. I don't know about living for good, but I'd like to go and spend some time with her. When she comes over, there's all sorts of people to see. Her mother's still alive and she's got a brother and two sisters here, so we only really have time for a meal or two. We keep talking about going to Paris together for a few days next time she's over, but I don't suppose we will.

I finally settled down near where three of the coppers who were guarding me lived. I've always like the Medway towns. One of the things which did come out of the whole thing was that I got a family that I never had. I mean when I was younger. My kids and theirs all grew up together, and they still see each other. My youngest said the other day that as far as he was concerned they were his cousins. Even though they're no relation at all, he refers to them like that to other people. I still see Nipper and Pat Read every now and again. Nipper's a big name on the Boxing Board of Control. It was him suggested I wrote this book, and every few months I have dinner with Henry Mooney. He qualified as a solicitor when he left the force. He's nearly seventy now but he's still in practice – specialises in fraud work.

I don't go back to the East End much. It was a Jewish community when I was young, now it's a coloured one. Where there were Jewish people, now there are Bangladeshis. You talk to people, and they tell you that the community spirit isn't like it was. Even now, I don't really like to be there in case I'm recognised. It may seem stupid, but there it is.

I still imagine ridiculous things like thinking it was set up so I'd be on my own in the pub. Normally there'd have been a couple of staff there, but that night there was just me. But I don't think Patsy knew it was going off. Someone must have rung to say, 'It's all right, the pub's nearly empty.' But there again, if Ronnie was determined to shoot Cornell, he'd most probably have done it if there were fifty people there.

I'd have been adamant it was Ronnie, but say I'd made a statement that night, would anyone else have come forward? The person who told Ronnie that Cornell was in the Beggars has a lot to answer for. Whoever made that phone call just walked away. I can see that if I'd made my statement at the time, it would have been an unknown person and Ronnie. Would my evidence on its own have been enough to bring a conviction? I don't think so. I'm not at all sure I'd have lived to give evidence. And, anyway, what about all the men who saw this? If they'd said or done something, then McVitie might have been alive. My memories have been so taken up with the shooting, and how it affected me and the family, that I didn't think about the others. They couldn't lay a guilt trip on me. There must have been a number of people associated that night who must have mentioned it to the police. They were quick enough to do that, but they never actually spoke out.

There's so much of it I can remember and some things I can't at all. However much I try, I can't remember the committal proceedings. I'd say I never went to them, but of course I did. But what I can remember is that evening and George being shot. It's just like an old film run and re-run in slow motion. Him and me talking. Ronnie and Ian Barrie coming in. George putting his hand in his pocket and saying, 'Let's have a drink.' Him toppling over backwards off the stool. Me jumping down the steps.

What's happened to the people in the case? I read that Johnny Dale, who was with George that night, was himself shot. According to the prosecution, he'd been ripping people off over drug deals, and he got shot at point-blank range outside his home in 1991, but he was fortunate – he survived. Two men called Renwick Dennison and Stewart Warne got life imprisonment for it. I've never heard what happened to Ian Barrie when he came out. Reggie's still waiting the thirty years before he gets parole. I expect he will. I rather hope so. Maybe now Ronnie's gone, Reggie deserves a spoonful of mercy. He was never anything but pleasant to me.

A lot of the others have gone on to write books. Ronnie and Reggie wrote a lot, the Lambrianou brothers did, so did John Dickson, and Albert Donoghue's just done one. It's all become part of the Krayology which was a word the judge hated when it was used at the trial. I suppose it could be said I'd jumped on the bandwagon by writing this book but, at least in my case, it's some compensation for the years of misery and hiding away. I didn't ask to be there the night of the shooting. It seems ridiculous, but I still don't want anyone to know my past, who I am and so on. Part of my life stopped with George's, but although I'm bitter, I'm not like the person who left a note on George and Olive's grave: 'One down, two to go. God is slow but sure'.

In a way, I'm ashamed of not speaking out straight off as I think my dad would have wanted me to have done. He was never afraid to stand his ground, but I was scared what would happen to my family if anything happened to me.

Looking back, it was all such a waste for everyone. All right; someone they hate they kill, they spend their lives locked up. I had my life ruined. In my dad's day things were different. I can remember one of his sisters was married to a man who was very erratic and violent to her. She often used to come round and talk. Dad didn't interfere a lot. Then Jack, my uncle, made a mistake of pushing my Nan about. My aunt let it out the next time she come round. Dad didn't have much to say, and the next minute someone said, 'Here's Uncle Jack now.' We had a small path from the gate. Dad said, 'I'll get the door.' The next thing, my uncle was sailing down the path into the road. They did it with their fists then, not with iron bars and guns.

It's all so pointless: just a load of unhappiness. George Cornell – well, his wife had only just had a baby. I became an outcast and I'm still looking over my shoulder. The Twins went to prison and so many with them. It all seems so, I don't know . . .

I read the other day the Blind Beggar was up for sale.

Afterword

Over the years, many criminal trials have been described as 'The Trial of the Century'. The Kray trial was one of the few which did, indeed, justify that billing. There was as much newspaper and public interest as there had been in any of the great criminal trials – Crippen, Seddon, Christie included – of the past. There was a thriving black market in tickets for the public gallery.

Shortly before their arrest, the Criminal Justice Act 1967 had come into effect, bringing with it serious changes in the conduct of criminal trials. For a start, a defendant had now to notify the police that he was proposing to call an alibi. The details had to be supplied to the prosecution within seven days of the committal proceedings, under which a magistrate heard preliminary evidence and decided if there was sufficient to send the case for trial at what was now the Crown Court, but had formerly been Assizes for felony cases and Quarter Sessions for misdemeanours. Once an alibi was given, the police had the right to interview the alibi witnesses. If the defendant's solicitor knew what he was doing, he would always ensure that he was present during this interview.

The committal proceedings no longer needed all the evidence to be taken down by the magistrates' clerk. The prosecution would now serve on the defence such evidence as they needed to establish a *prima facie* case and, if the defence agreed, they could have this rubber-stamped by the court and the case committed for trial without the need for anything more than a two-minute hearing. Obviously, in a case such as this where there was evidence to be given by accomplices and informers, the defence would never agree to that course of action.

Other significant changes included the so-called majority verdict. Until that time a criminal trial required a unanimous verdict of twelve or (in the event of the illness of a juror) eleven. Now, after a retirement of at least two hours in the simplest of cases, a judge could give directions that he would accept a verdict of a majority which must not be less than 10–2. The more complicated the case, the longer the judge should wait before the direction that he would accept a majority should be given. When it came to it in the Kray trial, majority verdicts were not required.

Some research had shown that by 1965 there were hung juries in 4 per cent of criminal trials in England

and Wales, and the then Home Secretary, Roy Jenkins, asserted that many of these disagreements had come about because one or two had been persuaded by bribery or intimidation to hold out against the evidence. There was no research to back up that latter assertion, but Jenkins also had been informed by the Commissioner of Police that there had been six major cases of jury interference in the Metropolitan Police District over the past three years. One of these was undoubtedly the effort by Charlie Richardson to improve the position of his brother in the Mr Smith's affray trial in 1965.

In the twenty-five years since the Kray trial, both investigation and trial procedures have changed almost beyond recognition. The Police and Criminal Evidence Act 1984 provided much more protection for prisoners in police stations. Although in the Kray trial Read ensured that there was almost immediate access to legal advice and there was very little questioning of prisoners before they saw a solicitor or clerk, now there are built-in safeguards for a suspect in the Codes of Practice which accompany the 1984 Act. Before that, suspects could be hidden from their legal representatives for days at a time by being switched from police station to police station in the area, and even from county to county if it was thought to be a serious enough case.

We know now that Mrs X's identification of Ian Barrie was an accurate one, but today the procedure differs considerably from that which existed in 1968.

There are more safeguards against a mistake and there is less pressure on both the witness and the suspect. The court's attitude on the value of identification evidence has also changed.

The excitement that July afternoon which must have hung like a pall of smoke over the parade cannot easily be understood by those who have not experienced it. It is, indeed, almost impossible to convey the tension of an identification parade in the 1960s in a serious case or to recount the number of things which could go wrong with one, from the viewpoint both of the defence and of the police. Often it was Amateursville. I remember taking a suspect into Wood Green police station, where we were told to go and sit opposite a very pleasant elderly couple. After some twenty minutes of silence, the man leaned forward and said, 'We're here for the identification parade. What are you here for?' I suppose his failure to make an identification of my client or me – for it would not have been the first time a solicitor was identified – showed that my client was entitled to walk out of the station without a charge.

Apart from that small hiccough, for a start there was always the problem of getting a sufficient number of men or, more rarely, women, who in any way resembled the suspect. Suspects were not always represented. In the middle 1960s I attended one parade where all the suspects had nylon stockings pulled over their heads. This was the view the woman had of bank robbers running out of the bank. She made an identification and the man received six years. It was, for an armed robbery, a lenient sentence, particularly as the defendant had a number of previous convictions and I have always felt that the discount was given because the judge was not all that happy with the evidence.

There is a story, which may be apocryphal, that on an identification parade in Scotland on a charge of rape, the suspect was the only black man on the parade. Certainly Joe Beltrami, the legendary Glasgow solicitor, recalls that on one occasion he refused to allow an identification parade to go ahead because his client was the only red-haired man on the line-up. He had some difficulty with the officer in charge of the parade making him understand why he objected to the line-up.

One of the difficulties that a solicitor faced in those days was the undeniable and, often, understandable hostility of the police officer. In the main, the parade was organised by the officers who were themselves involved in the case and had a positive interest in an identification being made. Now, the organisation and conduct of a parade is handed over to a uniformed officer of a rank no lower than inspector. The suspect, particularly on a murder case, would be anxious that the parade be held as soon as possible, and the solicitor attending on behalf of his client would be in a two-way stretch, with the police urging him to accept the line-up or threatening to have a confrontation – a face-to-face with the prisoner often flanked by police officers – and the client anxious to get out, pressing him to accept a less than satisfactory line-up. When, as sometimes happened in those days, the identification parade took place in a prison, the witness was subjected to a long and sometimes obscene harangue from the other men on the parade in an effort to intimidate or disturb him or, more probably, her.

The identification parade which Mrs X attended to try to pick out Ian Barrie must have been one of the most electrically charged. She had, after all, seen him only once in harrowing circumstances, and the light in the Blind Beggar on a March evening would be very different from that at West End Central on a July afternoon. It would be fair to say that, at the time, there was no real case against either Ronnie Kray or Ian Barrie, without her evidence. A number of witnesses did come forward, but most of them had a number of previous convictions and many were, in one way or another, tainted as accomplices or accessories either in the murders themselves or self-servers in other aspects of the case. We know now, from his memoirs, that Superintendent Read did not wish her to go on the parade in case she did make a mistake, one which could have brought the carefully erected pack of cards tumbling down on his head. Now, at least, she would have been protected from the sight of the men on the parade and allowed to make her identification through one-way glass.

By 1972, a mere three years later, the Criminal Law Revision Committee produced a report highlighting the dangers of honest and convincing wrong identifications which were accepted. Five years after that, the attitude of the court towards identification parades and their value had changed. The value of identification evidence had been under considerable scrutiny and in that year the Court of Appeal gave what was called the *Turnbull* judgment, which ruled that the judge should warn the jury of the special need for caution before convicting because of the danger that a mistaken witness can be a convincing one.

One of the greatest problems that the defence has at a criminal trial is whether to call the accused and witnesses on his behalf. It is often said that the high-water mark of the defence case is the close of that of the prosecution. From then on, it is very often downhill all the way. Before 1968, the question of whom to call to give evidence was even more of a problem. There were very specific technical advantages in both so doing and not doing so. If a defendant gave evidence and called a witness as to fact, his counsel would then be able to make an opening speech on his behalf. If he did not give evidence at all, his counsel had the right to make the final speech to the jury after the prosecution had had their say.[1]

It was also possible for a defendant not to give evidence but to make an unsworn statement from the dock. This could be used by him to cast about wildly and lambast all and sundry. The great advantage of this was that the defendant could not be cross-examined. Nor did it matter too much that the judge could, and did, warn the jury that untested evidence such as the statement from the dock was not as valuable as evidence given on oath. They had heard what often seemed, and sometimes was, a genuine protestation of innocence. The damage to the prosecution case had been done. The statement from the dock was often very carefully prepared and rehearsed by the defence barrister and solicitors. In many cases, it had to be. The inarticulate defendant could scarcely be expected to put up any sort of show himself. Later it became a matter of professional misconduct to prepare a defendant's statement in these circumstances. The privilege was removed after a former police officer gave a virtuoso performance from the dock, castigating his

[1]To further complicate things, if a defendant was unrepresented and did not give evidence, then the prosecution had no right to make a closing speech at all. This was usually fairly academic because the defendant was unlikely to know this himself and no one told him. It was, however, used to great effect when a former barrister and Member of Parliament, John Ryman, was charged with fraud and quite properly took advantage of this provision. He was later convicted of a not dissimilar offence.

colleagues and the prosecution in general to such effect that what had appeared to the authorities to be a cast-iron case ended in both an acquittal and much bitter recrimination.

After the passing of the Criminal Justice Act 1993, the defendant is effectively required to give evidence. If he does not, then he is likely to face severe comments from both prosecution and the judge over his failure to do so. Today, not only would Reggie Kray and the others not be allowed to make a statement from the dock, but they would also have to give evidence and be subject to the withering cross-examination of prosecuting counsel.

Now, in September 1995, committal proceedings are under considerable threat. They had been in decline for some years as the Divisional Court tightened the rules against general cross-examination of a fishing nature. When the Krays were committed for trial, the old-fashioned committal had just been superseded by the Criminal Justice Act 1968, which allowed for written statements to be handed into the court. Until then, every witness, whether it was the barmaid, Superintendent Read, or the plan-drawer, had to appear and give his or her evidence which was written down in long-hand. Nevertheless, for a variety of reasons, things progressed at a much smarter pace than today. On 14 December 1959, when Ronald Marwood stabbed a policeman, Raymond Summers, at a fight outside a dance hall in North London, thirteen others were arrested and charged with affray. Marwood disappeared, hidden by either the Twins, the Nash brothers or both. By the end of the year all the others had been committed in the old-fashioned way to the Old Bailey. Marwood surrendered on 27 January 1960. The trial was held in March, and on 8 May Marwood was hanged.

Following a series of decisions, the barest minimum of evidence was required before the justices were obliged to commit the case for trial. Nor could they exclude evidence which might have been improperly obtained. This was to be a matter for the trial judge. As a result, the committal proceedings in which magistrates ruled that there was a *prima facie* case to answer has to an extent faded into disuse.

In the Kray case, things proceeded speedily. The arrests were made in May, and the committal proceedings began at the end of June. It was during those weeks that one of the barristers making an application for bail was told by the magistrate that he had been refused the previous week, and that fresh grounds were required before he could apply again. 'There are seven,' said the young and fearless man, for Mr Geraint Rees, the magistrate, could be extremely difficult when it suited him. 'Monday, Tuesday, Wednesday . . .' The trial began in the January of the following year. Today it is doubtful if the trial would begin within two years of arrest.

There were other differences. For example, at the Kray trial, the defendants were allowed to make up to seven challenges each to members of the jury panel without giving any reason. This privilege was reduced to three, and the Criminal Justice Act 1988 removed it altogether after it had been suggested that counsel in the Cyprus Spy trial had banded together to remove from the jury anyone who was thought to be favourable to the prosecution.

On a practical rather than strictly legal level, the conduct of a case requires decisions by the solicitor which can determine the course of the case and the outcome. In the instance of a man charged with murder, the professional rule is that he must be represented by a Queen's Counsel, known in the trade as a 'silk' because of the fabric of his gown, one of the longer-serving and most experienced barristers. The choice of silk and the junior barrister is one of the most difficult for the solicitor.

Although the newspapers described the New Zealand-born Balliol-educated John Platts-Mills QC who appeared for Ronnie Kray as the best-known barrister on display, he was, perhaps, better known for his defence work in political cases rather than the rough and tumble work of the criminal courts. Apart from him, the defence assembled much of the cream of the criminal bar of the day. All were men with years of experience in the day-to-day rough and tumble of serious Old Bailey crime. Of course Mr Platts-Mills had appeared in numerous criminal trials, but the mild-mannered intellectual that he was, he would not necessarily have been the first choice of every defending solicitor in a case which required an all-out attack on the prosecution witnesses. Just as there are horses for courses, there are barristers for cases. A barrister who is a great mitigator or brilliant lawyer is not necessarily a good cross-examiner. This was a case in which the witnesses might not be broken – contrary to what is seen on the cinema and television, they rarely are – but had to be badly damaged. Now this is not necessarily too difficult. The witness box is not the place in which the truth always appears, even if the witness happens to be telling it. Witnesses can be made to look bad even if they are telling the whole truth, but there is an art in making them look liars.

As it was, defending Ronald Kray, first named in the indictment, the burden of the first, and incisive and decisive, cross-examination would fall on him. There is an argument that witnesses should not be left in the witness box longer than necessary as, like a bull in the ring, they become more confident the longer they survive. Incisiveness goes a long way. It would also be Mr Platts-Mills who would have to take the step in the objections made to the conduct of the trial and he who would have to make to the judge the general representations for the defence over the dozens of things which happen in a long trial.

Almost immediately, there had been trouble at the trial. The judge had decided the defendants were going to wear placards to help in identifying them. Not surprisingly, the defendants were not keen on this being done.

Platts-Mills: I invite your Lordship to withdraw that,
at least so far as Ronald Kray is concerned. I would
much prefer to represent him not labelled. I know
this is a well-recognised practice in other courts of
jurisdiction. In fact in the United States I understand
that the President himself had a label . . .

Stevenson: It has been done in my court, in this
court.[2]

Platts-Mills: I invite your Lordship not to do it. In my
submission, the jury are no more acquainted with
counsel than they are with the accused.

Stevenson: They will be.

The next day, arguments broke out at the start of the
proceedings, when all the defendants except Tony
Barry came into the court.

Clerk of the Court: Dock Officer, have we got numbers
for the accused?

Dock Officer: Yes.

Stevenson: Let them be put on.

Ronald Kray: This is not a cattle market.

The prisoners then took off their numbers.

Stevenson: Let them all stand down from the dock and
put those numbers on.

Platts-Mills: My Lord, may I make a further submission
on this matter? My Lord, in many different parts it

[2]And so it had in 1962, in the case of the Mussies, a North London
youth gang.

was the practice to label prisoners in various ways, but it has now been stopped, and in the last of those jurisdictions in Hong Kong the learned Judge finally ruled that such an indignity should not be imposed on the prisoners.

Stevenson: It is not a question of imposing an indignity upon anybody. It is extremely difficult in a crowded dock such as this for witnesses – some of whom may have to give evidence of identification – to give that evidence with certainty and clarity if they have to refer to someone sitting in the second, or, possibly the third row. It is solely for that reason, and that is why it is going to be done.

Platts-Mills: If it is a matter of identification, as your Lordship suggests, then the very last thing one would wish to do would be to put a mark on any individual. Indeed, any possible difference should be eliminated if people are going to identify somebody in court for the first time. It is not like a normal parade, my Lord. I hope the Court will be at pains to avoid any kind of mark, and I urge your Lordship to say it is not necessary in this case.

Stevenson: Mr Platts-Mills, I have heard all you have to say, and it makes no difference. On my discretion, take them down and put them on.

Mr Hudson: My client has his number on, my Lord. May he remain?

Stevenson: Yes, of course he can. Take them down.

Even in and at this stage of the trial Barry was being dissociated from the main group. The quarrel did not last long, and indeed it ended in a minor triumph for the defendants. It was just about the only ruling which would go in their favour throughout the trial.

> **Stevenson**: The numbers are at the front of the dock, and plans are being prepared which will facilitate reference to any of the accused, so exactly the same purpose has been achieved.
>
> **Platts-Mills**: I have been asked to say by one of the accused – I understand on behalf of all of them – to say how very much they appreciate the dispensation the Court has allowed.
>
> **Stevenson**: That is a great relief to me.

That is one of those remarks which appear on the transcript of the trial in a very different way from that in which it is spoken.

Indeed, the appointment of Mr Justice Melford Stevenson as the trial judge must have come as a blow to the defence. In those days there were few, if any, who could be described as pro-defence and Stevenson certainly was not amongst that number. He was a judge who would be called by the Bar a 'robust' judge and by the defendants 'a right dog'. A man well known for his ability to deal with recalcitrant defendants and counsel alike, I once saw him at Birmingham Crown Court when he appeared after the luncheon adjournment. When he entered and posed like a Nietzschean figure on the bench, you could almost hear the rattling of counsel's foreheads on the wooden seats in front of them as they tried to prostrate themselves before him. He lived in a house called Truncheons. It was named that when he purchased it, but it is significant that he never changed its name. He was also regarded as what has, in obituaries, perhaps become euphemistically known as a good after-dinner companion at the Garrick Club, that home, off Covent Garden, of the well-connected lawyer and actor. What he would not tolerate was waffle and, re-reading the case, it is quite apparent that Mr Platts-Mills' thought processes appeared not always to be as clear, focused and succinct as Stevenson required. Three examples will suffice. First, here is Ronald Kray's counsel talking about severing the indictment, something which was crucial to the case.

We see that the indictment is labelled 'Autumn Session', but whether that is a survival from old times I don't know, because, as I understood it, now there is a session almost continuously in your Lordship's court, but whether it is divided into months or not I am not sure, or it may be it is simply a seasonal arrangement, but, nevertheless, this indictment is labelled for the autumn session. Anyway, there was an indictment settled and issued and served relating to that committal in which my client and two others were indicted in this court on the Cornell murder. My Lord, as to the McVitie case, counts three and four, the committal to this court was on the 22 October of last year; it was not even to the current session but to the next following session. If we assume that seasonal matters play any part at all, the current session must have been the autumn session and therefore one must assume the committal was to the winter session. It was a committal at the end of October, the next succeeding session, not for the current session.

Likewise, there was a separate indictment settled, issued and served relating to that alleged murder. My friend says that applies not to three individuals. I don't know, but my friend has a copy of that indictment. I am informed, and I think you may take it as correct, that the terms of the indictment relating to counts one and two were precisely as in the form of the existing counts one and two except, of course, that the title is different. There are only three people in it and the charge is different, but the same three people are charged. Otherwise it is identical.

Stevenson: At the moment I am considering an indictment which is the result of a voluntary bill, am I not?

Platts-Mills: Yes, my Lord.

Stevenson: Well, what does the history matter?

Here he is speaking about the public house, the Grave Maurice a couple of hundred yards along the Whitechapel Road, which had nothing at all to do with the case except that it was a watering-hole which Ronnie Kray favoured and which it was said Ronnie had visited before his fatal appearance in the Blind Beggar. Perhaps it is not fair to say it had nothing to do with the proceedings. If the waters and times could be sufficiently muddied, then it could be shown that John Dickson, a crucial prosecution witness, had wildly overestimated the time Ronnie was out of his ground in the Widows the night of the shooting.

Q: The Grave Maurice was one of his well-known drinking places?

A: Yes.
Q: The Grave Maurice . . . The Graf . . . meaning
prince . . . Prince Maurice . . . the brother of Prince
Rupert . . .
A: The Grave Maurice as I know it.

The third illustrates how by the end of the first week
of evidence Stevenson's irritability with Platts-Mills
was beginning to show. Platts-Mills had been cross-
examining a police officer at some length about
Cornell's long criminal record.

> **Stevenson**: Perhaps you will tell us what it has to do
> with this case?
> **Platts-Mills**: I suggest it indicates in general a life of
> violence.

It could be argued that this showed Cornell could
have had many enemies and so would be vulnerable
to others than the Krays.

> **Stevenson**: That had been established about four wit-
> nesses ago, wasn't it?
> **Platts-Mills**: I didn't realise it was so sustained and so
> well charted.
> **Stevenson**: The last few minutes were a complete
> waste of time.
> **Platts-Mills**: I am sorry, I didn't really know the details
> of this. It is a sustained life of violence, isn't it, six
> for violence?
> **A**: I don't wish to use the term sustained.
> **Q**: Well, intermittent, shall we say? He only appears
> violent when caught.
> **Stevenson**: It is a record which includes a number of

convictions for violence and is still nothing to do with this case.

In those days there was a tendency in a long case for a judge to pick on one of the counsel, often a junior one, to serve as the butt of his jokes and ill-humour. However gracious Platts-Mills had been about the judge's conduct, many felt that on this occasion he filled that role. Of course it is one which can rebound on the judge. The jury may begin to think that the constant picking and sniping is unfair and will tend to begin to sympathise with the defendant whose counsel is having such a hard time.

By the sixth day of the trial, he was being forced backwards by the judge time and again, and he knew it. Here he is trying to cross-examine Mr D, one of the three brothers who were in the Krays' company on the night of the shooting of Cornell.

Q: You were suggesting to this jury that you never went back there [to his flat] for some such reason as the ghastly experience that you had with the Krays, or something of that sort.

Jones: With respect, witnesses don't suggest things. They answer questions put to them.

Stevenson: It is one of the examples of putting words into the witness's mouth which he has not used. I hope it won't happen again.

Platts-Mills: My Lord, I am responsible for it. I am sorry.

Stevenson: You were. I hope you will stop it.

Platts-Mills: I venture to justify my question on this basis—

Stevenson: You cannot justify putting words into a witness's mouth that he has not used.

Platts-Mills: Your Lordship will not permit me to explain. I am always in the wrong in the eyes of your Lordship, but my friend could never conceivably have asked him did he come back to that place unless it was something relevant to this case. It must have carried some connotation that he had left the place in connection with what had happened previously.

Stevenson: The witness used no such words or phrase.

Platts-Mills: My Lord, I am entitled to explore—

Stevenson: You are entitled to explore anything, but you must not put into the mouth of a witness words he has not used. That is all.

Platts-Mills: My Lord, I accept that. I didn't suggest he had said that, I suggested to him that he had indicated it. The reason is because no other ground could make it relevant to this case—

Stevenson: We all know what was said. Let us go on.

Platts-Mills: If I have erred in any way, I am extremely sorry and I will try not to do so again.

Stevenson had appeared for Ruth Ellis[3] and, given

[3]Ruth Ellis, the last woman to be hanged in Britain, was convicted of the murder on 2 April 1955 of her faithless lover David Blakely. She had been the subject of persistent physical abuse and shortly before she shot him to death outside the Magdala public house in Hampstead she had suffered a miscarriage. Her execution was a direct influence on the campaign to abolish capital punishment. [Robert Hancock, *Ruth Ellis*]. Despite directions from the trial judge that there is no defence in law, juries have, on a number of occasions, refused to convict the defendant. A recent example is the case of the defendants accused of assisting George Blake to escape. The thinking behind this seems to have been that the prosecution was oppressive. The authorities had known for some years that the men had been behind the escape, but had done nothing until they wrote a book.

the judge's ruling on the question of murder, had declined to make a closing speech to the jury on his client's behalf. It is a decision which may seem hard to understand now but then, in 1955, it was well within the requirements of conduct at the Bar following the judge's ruling that there was no evidence to support a verdict of manslaughter on the grounds of provocation. He had also held a junior brief for the prosecution in the Bodkin Adams case.[4]

In major criminal trials over matters of law and sentence, it is common for judges to take the advice of their fellow judges and sometimes the Lord Chief Justice. There was no need for Stevenson to seek help. He was well able to take firm decisions without flinching and without advice. Later, towards the end of his judicial career, when asked if he was hurt by criticisms – his sentencing had been reversed three times in one day by the Court of Appeal (Criminal Division) – he remarked, 'A lot of my colleagues are constipated Methodists.'

---

[4]Dr Bodkin Adams was one of the great criminal *causes célèbres*. In 1957 the doctor was accused of poisoning a number of elderly women patients so that he might benefit from their wills, the contents of which had been revealed by them. He did not give evidence, and the prosecution was forced to admit that the amount of pain-relieving drugs given to the women was in line with medical practice at the time. The trial judge, Mr Justice Devlin, wrote an analytical account of the trial, *Easing the Passing*, which some thought unduly harsh on Sir Reginald Manningham-Buller, the Attorney-General who led the prosecution. It is not without significance that *Private Eye* used to refer to the lawyer as Sir Reginald Bullying-Manner.

In the Kray trial, one such decision was going to be crucial. It was called the severance of the indictment. Put simply, what the prosecution wanted was to have the Cornell and McVitie murders tried together. The link between the cases was, so the prosecution said, that Reggie Kray had helped his brother to hide out after the Cornell murder. This would allow all sorts of evidence to come before the jury. There would be unquestionably a good amount of prejudicial material involved and, better still, there was one defendant, Anthony Barry, who was out on a limb and was running the defence of duress. That is that he was terrified of the Krays and, as a result, his actions should be excused because of the immediate fear in which he was placed. It was anticipated that he would be giving evidence which would run totally counter to the united front being presented by the other defendants. There had been some talk of letting Barry out before the trial began, but Read argued against it. A cut-throat defence is what every prosecutor hopes for.

There was also the problem of the accumulation of evidence against them. It is, after all, possible to explain away the evidence of some witnesses by faulty recollection, poor light for identification, and malice. If there are too many, then the sheer weight of numbers against them tends to do for the defence.

It is easy to see why the severance was to be sought by the defence. The number of witnesses in each case would be substantially reduced. In the Cornell case the only untainted and non-expert witness, in the sense that she was not a disaffected part of the underworld who was going to cause them damage, was the barmaid. She had undoubtedly lied.

Mr Justice Melford Stevenson and Platts-Mills had earlier clashed badly in the Angry Brigade trial during which, in his defence, Platts-Mills had tried to show that a fingerprint could be improperly transposed by a police officer. It had brought the wrath of Stevenson down on his head. There was another reason for the antagonism. Although, of course, politics never enter the British courts, Stevenson's politics could probably be fairly described as well right of centre and Platts-Mills, a former Bevin Boy and collier, after being a pilot officer in 1940, was certainly sympathetic to the communist movement. Platts-Mills was also undoubtedly Stevenson's intellectual superior, and neither this nor his politics would have appealed to the judge, who was later described by Lord Devlin: 'Without knowing what bodies, political or other, Melford belonged to, it would be safe to say he was on the right wing of all of them.' It would not make for a happy two months.

Although he was later at pains to deny that he had been treated with anything save the greatest courtesy, many who watched the trial thought that Platts-Mills received unnecessarily rough handling from the judge. It began within the first few minutes of the trial when it commenced on 7 January 1969.

Platts-Mills: Before the indictment is put to the prisoners, I have an application to make to the court on the trial of this indictment which your Lordship will probably think should be made before the prisoners should be asked to plead.

Stevenson: What is the nature of your application? First of all, for whom do you appear?

Of course Stevenson well knew for whom Platts-Mills appeared. It may have been that he should first have uttered the magic words he did a few moments later, 'I appear with my learned friend Mr Ivan Lawrence, for Ronald Kray . . .' but it was the shape of things to come.

Why then was he chosen to lead the way in what was undoubtedly going to be a difficult time? The simple answer is that Ronnie Kray particularly wanted him. Platts-Mills had appeared successfully on his behalf in the Hideaway Club case and, as such, had acquired talismanic status. Criminals are a particularly superstitious bunch and the defenders can be either adhered to or changed on a whim.

I remember acquiring a client who, in the days when things moved faster and it was possible to be arrested, acquitted and re-arrested and acquitted four times in a year, deserted his former solicitors. Why? 'Their luck couldn't last' was the disarming reply. My luck ran for several years before it too evaporated in a raid on a bonded warehouse staked out by the police. The rule of thumb for defence solicitors is quite clear. Provided the barrister does not actually suffer from a speech impediment, and over the years there have been a number who have faced their profession with such a handicap, a client's request for a particular counsel should be honoured. If the solicitor presses his own choice, then, if there is an acquittal, all may be well – although Mr A would have won my case in half the time – but if there is a conviction, the client will always hold the lingering feeling that Mr A would have worked the oracle.

Stevenson was to go on to preside over the trial which followed the notorious Cambridge student riot in 1970. At that trial, at which he handed down what were then considered to be swingeing sentences, he said they would have been longer 'had I not been satisfied that you have been exposed to the evil influence of some senior members of your university, one or two of whom I have seen as witnesses for the defence'. This in turn produced an angry and anguished letter to *The Times*, signed by the six dons who had appeared to give evidence, emphatically rejecting the judge's criticism.

In 1975 Stevenson sentenced a defendant to six months' imprisonment for planning to release laughing gas in the court. The boy's effort at providing temporary entertainment had been interrupted by the police. 'You are a humourless automaton,' said the defendant. 'Why don't you self-destruct?' The Court of Appeal, in one of its more enigmatic judgments, decided that because the plan had been thwarted by the police, there was no contempt of court and released Mr Balogh.[5]

On the other hand, some defendants held him in complete admiration. To have appeared before him was something of a cachet in the criminal circles of the day. I remember defending two youths who, in their late teens, had received terms of some eight or nine years for a series of raids on sub-post offices. Their counsel and I went to the cells afterwards to discuss the possibility of an appeal. 'Who was that ol' geezer?' asked one. 'Which old geezer?' we replied. 'The one which potted us.' 'Mr Justice Melford Stevenson.' 'Aw,' said the spokesman, 'fergit the appeal. We can tell oor mates we wiz put away by Melford.'

Of the others, Kenneth Jones and John Leonard became High Court judges. James Crespi, a man of enormous bulk and charm, was never appointed. Earlier he had contracted a short-lived marriage to a nightclub hostess which, in the social mores pertaining, disqualified him. He, however, sat for a number of years as a recorder at the Old Bailey. Ivan Lawrence, who represented Ronnie Kray with Platts-Mills, became a Member of Parliament and a Queen's Counsel. William Howard QC, who appeared for John Barrie, spent some time in Hong Kong. Paul Wrightson, QC for Reggie Kray, died young. Petre Crowder QC, who represented

[5]*Balogh* v. *St Albans Crown Court* [1975] QB 73.

Christopher Lambrianou, sat at Middlesex Crown Court and was a Member of Parliament. Montague Sherbourne, who appeared with him, was one of the leading defence counsel throughout the 1980s, as was Barry Hudson who appeared for Anthony Barry. Rudolph Lyons QC, who was for Bender, became a Crown Court judge. Desmond Vowden for Charlie Kray was in constant demand at the Old Bailey and was appointed a circuit judge; Roger Frisby QC retired in 1995. Ivor Richards, junior counsel for Foreman, became a European Commissioner. Edward Gardner was the Conservative MP for Billericay, the constituency whose result was one of the first to be announced at an election. Ralph Haeems, who was an articled clerk to the firm Sampson & Co. at the time of the trial and who undertook the great burden of the preparation of the defendants' cases, eventually qualified and went on to found one of the best-known and successful criminal practices in the country. The list of his clients reads like a Debrett of crime.

One of the problems Haeems faced at the time was the defection by so many defendants from the cause. Things are difficult enough when the defence is united. Handling a number of defendants in a high profile case is never easy. To take a seemingly unimportant aspect, it is essential to have worked out in advance of going to prison which defendant should be seen first. If one who believes he ranks higher in the prison pecking order is not seen before the other, hostilities can break out.

With a split defence, the situation quickly becomes grave. Read, in putting together a case against the Twins, had managed to get many of their followers – Leslie Payne, their former *consigliere*, and Billy Exley are two prime examples – to commit themselves to the prosecution even before arrests were made. Worse, from the time of the arrests there was a steady noticeable defection as Read was able to convince a number of the defendants – Dickson, Donoghue and Charlie Mitchell were three – where their best interest lay. Dickson, who had given an alibi for Ronnie Kray in the Cornell murder, was a particularly crucial and, from the defence point of view, cruel defection. The position can rapidly become untenable. Morale can so easily falter the longer the defendants remain in custody. Provided his witnesses came up to proof and, by and large, they did, Read was sure there would be convictions. On the other hand, nothing is ever certain. It is apparent that, despite the torrent of previous adverse publicity, the jury in the Mitchell case were not prepared to convict the Twins of murder on the evidence of the uncharismatic Albert Donoghue.

Through any trial there are dozens of decisions which must be taken. Which witnesses will be good ones? Some will have to be called even though it is thought they may not be good ones. There are some who can be discarded; some whom it is absolutely essential to call. The decision on which a witness is to be called is further complicated in that barristers are not allowed to see witnesses – except expert witnesses – before they are called. The decision is made on the quality of the proof of evidence taken by the solicitor or, often, his clerk. One decision which also had to be taken was whether to call Ralph Haeems, the articled clerk who had attended the identification parade on which Ian Barrie stood. Melford Stevenson made withering comments about the failure to call him, but things were not as simple as that. Unlike in the United States, where there are circumstances when a witness can be cross-examined only on the evidence he has given, in England, once a witness goes into the witness box, he can be exposed to a wide-ranging series of questions. Had Mr Haeems given evidence about the identification parade, he could have been asked quite legitimately by the prosecution about the interview with Henry Mooney and Sammy Lederman, in which the latter appeared to recant the alibi he had given Ronnie Kray.

Additionally, there were all sorts of questions about privileged communications – those said in confidence – which attach to the client and not the solicitor. One or more of the defendants or those who had once been his clients could have exercised that privilege and effectively prevented him from giving evidence or, at the very least, have made it appear he was hiding a number of things if he did so. Certainly, in those days, it was frowned on by the Bar and the judiciary for a solicitor or his clerk to be called by the defence. The reputation of a young solicitor could easily be ruined if he was found in the witness box on behalf of his clients too often. It was by no means as clear cut an issue as Melford Stevenson might have indicated.

Another of the decisions to be taken is what questions to ask. One question too many can be fatal to a defence. It is one of the reasons why, although barristers may be sued for ill-formed advice they give out of court, they cannot be sued for mistakes made on their feet in court. There is the famous story of Billy Rees-Davies cross-examining with vigour and being bombarded by a waterfall of notes from his client in the dock. 'May I read this billet-doux?' he asked. 'Perhaps it's a Billy don't,' replied the judge, Alan King-Hamilton.

One of the nicest stories of a mistake by a counsel is attributed to the late Sir Arthur Irvine, who, when cross-examining, asked one question too many. He was defending in a pre-breathalyser, drink-driving case in the days when it was possible to have this heard by a jury, and when a jury in the absence of the defendant being found in a pool of vomit slumped over the steering wheel would try to find a way to acquit. Here is what is said to have been his cross-examination of the arresting officer.

Q: You stopped the car and asked my client his name?

A: Yes, sir.
Q: Which he gave perfectly properly?
A: Yes, sir.
Q: And his address?
A: Yes, sir.
Q: And occupation?
A: Yes, sir.
Q: And you asked him to get out of the car?
A: Yes, sir.
Q: And he did this perfectly properly?
A: Yes, sir.
Q: So, from the time you stopped him he had behaved in no way which could cause criticism?
A: No, sir.
Q: And then he got into the back of the police car?
A: Yes, sir.
Q: Again perfectly properly?
A: Yes, sir.

So now Irvine had laid a very solid foundation for his client's argument that he was not drunk. The sheer repetitiveness of the questions and answers is impressive. Then . . .

Q: He sat down in the back of the car next to a lady in a fur coat?
A: No, sir. That was police dog Giles.

Then there is the question of putting the client's character in issue. The jury does not have to know of previous convictions unless the defence either tells them about it or makes such allegations against the prosecution and witnesses that leave is given for them to be cross-examined. Nevertheless there is still the worry that the jury will speculate about the convictions unless they are told what they are. If one defendant says, 'I am of good character', or 'I have only one conviction for shoplifting a long time ago', what will the jury think of a defendant whose counsel fails to ask that question?

The prosecution case closed on Thursday afternoon 30 January 1969, and by now it was clear that Platts-Mills was in very serious difficulties over a vital decision. Would his client give evidence? Before the 1993 Act, it was not uncommon for this to happen. There are good reasons why a defendant should not give evidence. In her story, Mrs X says that nothing can go wrong if you are telling the truth, but even the most honest witness can often be made to look bad by an expert cross-examiner. Even if a defendant intends to give evidence, he can still develop a panic at the last minute and refuse. It is also certain that Platts-Mills in making his opening speech intended to play out – again a perfectly legitimate and not an uncommon thing – time until the court rose at 4 pm, and then with his junior and instructing solicitor have a long and hard session in the cells with his client, yet again explaining the pros and cons of giving evidence in the case. When a decision had been taken, particularly if Kray had decided not to give evidence, it would be standard practice with a wavering defendant for him to be asked to sign counsel's brief or at least a piece of paper saying that all options – sworn evidence, an unsworn statement, total silence – had been explained to him, that he understood his choices, and such-and-such was his decision. The benefit of playing out time was not only that more time was available to discuss the case but also that the jury did not know the indecision which was present in the defendant's mind.

It was quite clear to those experienced in trial observation that when Platts-Mills began his opening speech to the jury, a decision had not been taken and that he was, as best he could, keeping both options open. He made a good stab at blaming the prosecution for the fact that his client might opt to make a statement from the dock.

What I say is this – that we treat the giving of evidence on oath in this court as a precious coin, and these witnesses have debased that coin and dishonoured it, so that Ronald Kray will say, 'I am not going in that box where they stood.' He might as well say his words spoken from the dock here unsworn was just as good as that coin that they have so gravely tarnished by their stories. So you may well hear Ronald Kray give his evidence from the dock where he sits. It would be the less courageous course, because he can't be cross-examined by my learned friends for the Crown. It is for him to decide, but you may think it would take considerable courage after the course the Crown witnesses have tried to force upon this court – I mean those of whom I spoke, not the responsible ones – you may think it would take considerable courage, which he may not possess.

He then went on to outline the defence which Ronald Kray would be putting up, when he was interrupted by the judge.

Stevenson: When you use the phrase that you did just now, 'My client will tell you', it appears to me that doubts were expressed earlier whether he was going to give evidence or not. Do you mean your client is going to give evidence or do you mean he is not?

Platts-Mills: I would have preferred your Lordship had not asked me that question. [Translated this means, 'I simply don't know.']

Stevenson: Well, I am quite unable to reconcile the two statements you made.

Platts-Mills: My Lord, it is a question that will arise only between my client and his legal advisers.

Stevenson: But when you say 'My client will tell you', if you say you don't mean that phrase, that is a different matter.

Platts-Mills: I apprehend if he does not give evidence on oath he will give evidence from the dock.

Stevenson: He cannot give evidence from the dock; he can make a statement. That is a very different thing from giving evidence.

Platts-Mills: If that be the case, I am sorry.

Stevenson: What I have in mind is this. You are of course entitled to open to the jury everything of which you intend to call in evidence; you are not entitled to open matters which you do not intend to make the subject of evidence and when you use a phrase like 'My client will tell you', it suggests I would have thought that he was going into the witness box and that is, as I say, inconsistent with what you earlier said.

Platts-Mills: No, my Lord, not inconsistent with the possibility that he make an unsworn statement from the dock because he would still be telling the jury. My Lord, I am not sure whether your Lordship shrugs his shoulders in dissatisfaction with my answer, but, my Lord, surely this is, as I understand it, the most sacred privilege we have in law.

Stevenson: I am not attempting to invade any privilege, as well you know; I am only trying to get the position clear.

Platts-Mills: My Lord, I am greatly helped by your Lordship. I am not sure that it has helped me to get the position clear but, my Lord, I can only do the best, like so many cases, with the material we have. I am not in a position to answer your Lordship's question.

Stevenson: I see, very well.

Platts-Mills: I am not saying whether I know or not. I am not in a position to say whether I know or not. That is a thing I would have hoped would not have been asked. I invite your Lordship to assume that I have the practice in mind.

Whatever can be said in criticism of Platts-Mills, it can never be said he lacked courage. But these repeated exchanges which he could not win must have sapped him and cannot have helped his defence or the jury's attitude to his client.

The application for leave to appeal was heard in the middle of July, after the Twins had been acquitted of the murder of Frank Mitchell. Nowadays, this would seem to be an amazingly short time in which an appeal would come up for hearing. An appeal to the Court of Appeal (Criminal Division) is in two parts. First, the court must give leave to appeal. This is done after the defendant submits a written application setting out what he says went wrong in the trial. The application is usually considered by a single judge without hearing any oral arguments. If he refuses the application, the defendant may renew it to the full court of three. Generally, unless he or his family can raise the money, the defendant will not be represented. If, on the other hand, the single judge grants leave to appeal, the defendant is usually given legal aid and a barrister to appear for him. In cases such as the Krays, the application bypasses the single judge and effectively becomes the appeal. If the application is granted, the court treats it as the appeal itself.

The first ground of appeal was that because charges can be joined together in an indictment if they are founded on the same facts or form part of a series, the two murders, Cornell and McVitie, should not have been heard together because two does not make a series. The second was that Tony Barry's defence of duress was such as to prejudice the trial against the other defendants, and that since Reggie Kray had not given evidence, the judge was wrong in dealing with his counsel's closing speech to the jury in his summing up. There were other grounds of a more technical nature. The hearing lasted for six days and, as might have been predicted, the applications for leave to appeal were dismissed.

The ruling was that two offences could constitute a series if there was a sufficient nexus. The Court of Appeal thought there was.

These two cases did exhibit such features, the murders having many unusual factors in common. Thus each was committed in cold blood and without obvious motive: each bore the stamp of a gangleader asserting his authority by killing in the presence of witnesses whose silence could be assured by that authority. Neither killing would have been possible except on the basis that members of the 'Firm' would rally round to clear up the traces and secure the silence of those who might give them away. All these factors made it desirable in the public interest that these two unusual cases should be examined together, and this was also in the interests of one of the defendants, namely Anthony Barry. Finally, the interest of the Press in this affair was so great that, if the two murders had been tried separately, the publicity attending the first trial would have made a fair trial of the remaining charges impossible.

It is difficult to follow this last remark. After all, the second Kray trial, relating to the escape and alleged murder of Frank Mitchell, took place almost immediately after the verdicts in the Cornell and McVitie cases. This time, Mr Justice Lawton took over from Melford Stevenson and he permitted the jury to answer questions about the newspaper reports they had read on the first trial. A number of jurors were stood down, and eventually the Twins and others were acquitted of the murder of Mitchell.

Now, the situation would not arise. Section 4 of the Contempt of Court Act 1981 permits a trial judge to impose a blanket blackout of reporting of a trial which is split into several parts. It is only at the final conclusion that the press may report the proceedings.

The next question for the court was the defence of Anthony Barry in the McVitie murder. McVitie had been killed principally by Reggie Kray at a party in Evering Road, Stoke Newington. The case against Barry was that he had brought the gun with which Reggie Kray attempted and failed to kill McVitie before stabbing him. Barry claimed that he lived in such fear of the Krays that a message from a Ronald Hart, one of the Firm, that if he would not take the gun the Twins would come to the club themselves, meant he was himself in danger. He also gave evidence and obtained evidence from prosecution witnesses of threats to him and others and violence by the Firm at his Regency Club. Of course, this cut-throat defence had been exactly what the prosecution wanted and what the other defendants feared. Was the evidence admissible or should the judge have excluded it?

Platts-Mills maintained that it was all inadmissible. In a defence of duress the law was that the person putting up that defence should have had no other alternative available. For example, a man might be the driver of a getaway car if he has a gun pointed to his head. Platts-Mills claimed that there was a viable alternative open to Barry. Instead of going to Evering Road with the gun, he could have called at Stoke Newington police station. Paul Wrightson, who appeared for Reggie, accepted that there was a defence if Barry's will had been so broken by threats and fear that he could no longer exercise his own judgment. What he said was wrong was that evidence had been allowed of events prior to 1966 which were not proved to have come to Barry's notice and, highly technically, that a witness called to prove that Barry knew of an incident went on to give evidence that the incident had actually happened. This Mr Wrightson said was inadmissible.

The Court of Appeal did not accept the arguments. The judges considered that Barry had a viable defence that he was so terrified he no longer was an independent actor. They also took the view that so far as the evidence, by the one witness of which Mr Wrightson complained, was concerned it did not give rise to a miscarriage of justice.

Wrightson's other major complaint was that the judge when summing up had not told the jury what Reggie Kray's defence had been. The court would have none of this either. After all, Reggie Kray had not given evidence. He had made a statement from the dock, shown the jury his hands to contradict a piece of evidence given by Superintendent Read, and read out a letter and a poem.

> When the defence call evidence, a failure to put the case derived from the evidence will almost always be fatal to the conviction; but it is well established that the judge need not repeat all the argument of counsel, and, when no evidence is called, the defence necessarily consists of argument. If we had any fears that the judge's omission to refer to counsel's argument in this case had made the conviction unsafe, we should unquestionably have given leave to appeal, but, when the uncontradicted evidence is looked at as a whole, it seems inevitable that the jury should have found an intent to assist in his brother's escape was at least in part the motive behind Reginald Kray's actions.

Ian Barrie's grounds of appeal were slightly different from the others. They were that the prejudice against him resulting from the evidence in the McVitie case, which was nothing to do with him at all, was such that there should have been a separate trial of the Cornell killing. The Court of Appeal rejected this. The arguments against severance far outweighed the disadvantage to Barrie. The evidence, they said, rested mainly on the testimony of the barmaid and the damaging admissions he had made to Henry

Mooney on his arrest. Their Lordships did not think that a separate trial would have produced a different result.

Afterwards, in the comfort of the Garrick Club, Melford Stevenson was overheard to remark that the Twins had said only two true things throughout the trial: the first was that the prosecutor was a fat slob and the second was that he, Stevenson, had been biased.

In his memoirs published in 1994,[6] the Appeal Court judge, Sir Robin Dunn, wrote in a passage in which he described Melford Stevenson as the worst judge since the war, that Stevenson had said Ronnie Kray was a nicer man than the QC defending him. This brought the wrath of the judiciary down on Dunn's head. Sir Frederick Lawton in *The Times* suggested that Stevenson's trouble was that he could not always control his temper. 'He was extremely witty and would say things that were not really in his own interest or in the interest of Justice.' John Platts-Mills, with a great deal of charity, wrote:

While defending Ronnie Kray at the Old Bailey in 1969, I found him to be a most kindly and thoughtful client. I told Melford out of court that Ronnie was probably a nicer chap than I was. I am not surprised to learn that Melford cribbed this remark and made it his own.

[6]*Sword and Wig.*

Contrary to general belief, I had a most friendly relationship with Melford. The only unkindness that I can lay at his door, and this was a gross injustice, was trying the Kray twins for the murders of Cornell and McVitie together when there was no common feature except that the victims had both died.

My judgment of the case was that if Melford had tried the murders fairly, both Twins might well have got off.[7]

He forbore to point out that in 1975, when defending in an IRA bombing case, he had been 'fined' one-third of his fees by Stevenson for allegedly indulging in mud-slinging tactics at the police. The cut was restored on appeal after representations by the Bar Council.[8]

It might be thought that, with their conviction, the Twins would disappear from public view. Apart from a riot organised in 1969 by Frankie Fraser against the conditions and régime at Parkhurst Prison and Charles Richardson's failure to return from home leave, the lower-profile Richardsons effectively did fall from public sight. But the Krays never did. Stevenson's view may have been that the public deserved a rest, but, by and large, it was neither the public's wish nor that of the press. They were

[7]*The Times*, 8 November 1994.
[8]See Appendix – Melford Stevenson.

good copy. They were keen to keep, or rather, be kept in touch.

To try to understand the Kray phenomenon both pre- and post-conviction, one has to look at the social change and the rise of a genuine working-class culture which had swept across England in the twenty-five years since the war.

Until the 1950s and 1960s there had been very little in the way working-class culture influenced its social superiors. As a general rule, rather like blacks in the United States, they were portrayed as figures of fun even when they were the heroes – George Formby is a good example and Norman Wisdom is another. Even when Gracie Fields leads the striking factory workers in *Sing As We Go*, she has been a traditional comical character throughout the film.

Now, there was evidence that the public was beginning to pay more attention to the lives and thoughts of the working classes, not as figures of fun but as people who actually lived, breathed, bled and occasionally thought. We were coming to the time of the rise of the working-class novelist such as John Braine, David Storey and Alan Sillitoe, the working-class playwrights such as Arnold Wesker and the so-called kitchen sink dramas such as *The L-Shaped Room*, made into a most successful film, in which for almost the first time unmarried mothers, gays and black men were treated as having souls.

In retrospect, it is quite apparent that the Kray

Twins were not particularly successful villains in the sense that they ended their criminal careers as such with almost nothing to show for it. The fact that Reggie Kray is now a very rich man is due entirely to the industry which has grown up during his and his brother's period of imprisonment rather than to an accumulation and retention of wealth during his active years. At their trial, the judge, seeking to make an order for costs, enquired what assets they had, and asked Superintendent Read what the police had been able to trace.

> **Read**: My Lord, the only information that I am possessed of at the moment is that the Kray brothers, and by that I mean the Kray twins, do in fact own a house in Bildeston in Essex.
> **Ronald Kray**: It's my mother's house, not my house.
> **Read**: Which I understand is valued at £11,000, which is in fact in the name of their mother, Mrs Violet Kray. Apart from that, I have not been able to trace anything at all, so far as assets are concerned, to them.

This was by no means surprising. At that time few, if any, of the known traditional gangland leaders had managed to retire with their loot and senses intact. Long prison sentences ruined the control of people such as Jimmy Spinks from West Ham. The Sabini brothers, who had ruled the racecourses, had been destroyed by their internment during the war. Derby Sabini, who had once been the lord and master of on-course betting over half the country, had, by the end of his life, been reduced to being a small-time bookmaker operating with the consent of his successors on the free course. In turn, Jack Spot had been ruined by the publicity following his knife-fight with Albert Dimes and the subsequent destruction, by his enemies, of his drinking clubs. He had taken work as a meat packer. Billy Hill, his former friend and co-owner of Soho, is the only one who immediately springs to mind as a man who put his money away successfully. Of course there were others, such as Bert Wilkins and Bert Marsh, who had had the sense to invest in properties and nightclubs. After the charges arising over the death of Massimino Monte Colombo at Wandsworth greyhound track had been dismissed, they also had the great sense to disappear from the limelight as swiftly as they had entered it.[9]

Before Hill and Spot, few traditional criminals tried to rise above their primordial station and mix with their betters. There is no evidence at all that Derby Sabini ever eschewed his collar-stud and cap

[9]Spinks was sentenced to five years as the leader of the battle of Lewes racecourse in which anti-Sabini forces attacked their bookmakers [Ted Greeno, *War on the Underworld*, John Long, 1960]. The Sabinis were interned under the notorious Section 18B [James Morton, *Gangland 2*]. Dimes and Spot battled it out in Frith Street in the celebrated 'fight that never was'. Spot was acquitted after perjured evidence by a retired clergyman who 'happened to be passing'. No evidence was offered against Dimes [R. Murphy, *Smash and Grab*]. The Marsh–Wilkins trial, in which they were defended by Norman Birkett, followed a fight over control of betting pitches [James Morton, *Gangland*].

to put on a black tie and go out nightclubbing with café society. Certainly the out-of-town gangs such as the men who ran the pitching rings in Sheffield or the Rowlands who controlled Welsh betting in and around Cardiff in the twenties never tried to rise socially. The Scots fighting gangs of the pre-war period would not even have considered it.

For their part, by and large, the middle classes allowed the underworld to play by themselves unless and until it impinged on their world. In truth, it rarely did. After all, the racecourse battle at Lewes did not take place in the members' enclosure but on the course. If the upper classes went out slumming down the East End – something the middle classes would not do – just as Harlem became the place to visit after a night on the town in New York, it was on their terms. They might well pay exorbitant amounts for after-hours fake champagne, but that was a price they were willing to pay for arm's-length excitement. When tourists went to Paris in the 1920s, it was to see a sanitised version of Apaches at work in faked bar-room fights which left the punters with the frisson of a dangerous experience they had, through their own skill and, as the stories were retold, bravely, survived. There was still the master–servant relationship. The upper classes might be being cheated by the working-class criminals, but it was on their terms. Drugs, however, cut across classes, and such dealers as Brilliant Chang and Eddie Manning did mix with their socially superior clients, but they were rare exceptions. Sometimes things could not be helped. Atholl Oakley, the professional wrestler, inherited a baronetcy and consequently became one of the few men in the ring genuinely to be able to claim the title they often carried. But, by and large, the social standings remained.

To an extent Spot and to a greater extent Hill changed the public's perception of the underworld. Perhaps it is better to say that the newspaper reporters of the day, particularly Duncan Webb, changed the perspective. Suddenly, the readers of the Sunday papers were treated to the lives of the great villains. If one paper had Hill's version of the Gospel, then another had to sign up Spot to trot out his *bonnes pensées*. Indeed this rivalry to have their names in print led to Spot's undoing. Hill also had the advantage of the reflections from the meretricious glitter of the doings of Sir Bernard and Lady Docker.

The publicity which Spot sought was his undoing and, although he was, at his death, a very wealthy man, it did not help Hill that much either. He failed to land in Australia, to where he had intended to emigrate. Ray 'The Gunner' Kelly, one of the city's leading detectives, went out to meet him when the ship sailed through Sydney Heads. It is recorded that he spent over an hour in Hill's cabin and 'persuaded him not to come ashore'. Instead, Kelly gave the press conference to the waiting, and no doubt disappointed, crowd of journalists and cameramen.[10] He lived for a time in Tangier but he ended his life an old and mostly forgotten man, cared for by a friend with whom he had been in prison many years earlier.

In a way, involvement with newspapers by criminals has consistently proved to be their undoing. Sabini sued over allegations, failed to appear at court and was made bankrupt. Spot was sued for an assault on Duncan Webb and he too was made bankrupt. Ronnie Kray achieved a muffled apology – something of which he was keen to make capital at his trial – over the celebrated photograph with Lord Boothby who garnered £40,000 from the Mirror Group, but reporters and editors have long memories and thick cuttings files.

The truly successful criminals and criminal families have eschewed publicity. Not for them the purchase of a football team or their pictures in the papers attending first nights with fading film stars and former heavyweight boxers on their arms. In September 1995 the *Independent* wrote of a family 'worse than Krays', citing their misdeeds as including murder, drug dealing, protection and extortion. The family of four – three brothers and a brother-in-law – have been around for most of the last decade, but their name would mean nothing to the general public.[11] By and large the Richardsons

---

[10]David Hickie, *The Prince and the Premier*, North Ryde, Australia, Angus and Robertson, p. 297.
[11]Chris Blackhurst in the *Independent*.

were unknown to all but the *cognoscenti* when the unfortunate fracas at Mr Smith's Club in Peckham destroyed them. Had that fight not taken place, it is possible that, like others after them, Charles and Eddie Richardson would have gone on to have seats on the Stock Exchange and publicly-quoted companies.

But the Kray Twins – their elder brother, Charles, never craved the limelight as they did – were something else. They carried self-publicity to an art-form, and the general public of the decade responded. They were fortunate in their timing. There was not only the interest in working-class drama, but the East End, so much of which had been destroyed in the war and so much of which still remained slumland, was beginning its rebirth. Joan Littlewood had taken over the Theatre Royal in Stratford and had quickly established a reputation for being one of the most talented theatrical producers of the time. In their birthplace they were also fortunate. The East End has always had more of a cachet than South-East London. There are countless books celebrating the East London way of life in speech and photograph. I cannot recall a single one extolling life in Catford. Perhaps there might have been, had Jack the Ripper operated there.

The Twins were also fortunate in the people who surrounded them and those such as David Bailey who photographed them. It may be he, more than anyone else, who contributed to their entry into *soi-disant* society. As it was, they busied themselves promoting their image much as the Richardsons' Frank Fraser has done, in somewhat different circumstances, over the past year. The ill-fated wedding of Reggie Kray to Frances Shea was covered by the national broadsheets. Cal McCrystal, who had been personally invited and who covered the event for the *Sunday Times*, recalls Ronnie marching down the aisle to tell the congregation, whom he did not think were putting sufficient into their efforts, 'Sing, fuck you, sing.' Gems of this sort made the slumming so much fun and so rewarding. David Bailey took photographs for the press whilst the talented journalist Francis Wyndham held his flash-gun.

Their entry into society had been through the charity circuit. Although it is said that much of the proceeds stayed in their own pockets, they had raised money for East End charities and, more to the point, let it be known they had. Fund-raisers were beginning to ensure their names were on the guest lists and through that and the louche clubs they owned they were meeting at least the second division of society. It was the era of the nightclub. Esmeralda's Barn, which they acquired, was one of the places for café society to visit. Another, not theirs, was the Blue Angel owned by Max Setty, the brother of car dealer and fraudsman Stanley, who was cut up and thrown into the Essex marshes by Donald Hume. The Nash brothers, the predecessors in title of the Krays, had an interest in the Bagatelle. Bert

Wilkins owned the Nightingale in Berkeley Square, and there were others. Society was interested in going to these slightly seedy clubs which provided dinner, dancing and certainly in the case of the Blue Angel, which resurrected the career of the 1930s star Hutch, sometimes a very good cabaret. The Twins took to squiring fading actresses, such as Judy Garland, about town and retired boxers, such as Joe Louis, around the provinces. It all made for good publicity.

That they received such an amount of coverage in the *Sunday Times*, which until then had not covered crimes and had an almost Methodist attitude, was in no way naïve behaviour by the editor. The traditional route to information on villainy was through the police, but now, with such journalists as McCrystal and Peta Fordham, the wife of barrister Wilfrid, providing an entry to a long-term study of the underworld, it suited the paper to give publicity to the brothers to obtain the real story behind their activities. The Twins were like children when, on the occasion they visited the *Sunday Times* to see McCrystal, he cast about for a room in which to interview them and disingenuously told them he was taking them to Lord Snowden's room. 'They were tickled out of their trousers,' he recalls. 'The Krays didn't have any idea of our plans.'

After a period of relative quiet during the first few years of their sentence, the Twins and the media ensured that the brothers were not forgotten.

Back in 1967, before their trial, they had engaged the attention of the writer John Pearson, who had previously written the biography of Ian Fleming, creator of James Bond. He had begun his research into his justly celebrated book *The Profession of Violence*, published in 1972.[12] It was destined to become, and remains, both a best-seller and the definitive work on the brothers, even though it now appears that a good deal of the colour of the 'background' was especially arranged by them for his benefit. Indeed so taken was he with them that at the time when they were charged with fraud – before the murders were laid at their door – he offered to stand bail for them, something against which Nipper Read strongly advised him.

There things remained for some years. Old news-paper-cutting libraries produce a respectable number of references to their activities in prison but it was not until the late 1980s that public attention refocused on the Twins. In 1986 John Dickson wrote his version of events, *Murder without Conviction*. It was followed by a number of books – written by Reggie Kray, Charles Kray, Chris and Tony Lambrianou, Albert Donoghue, and retired policemen such as John du Rose, Frank Cater, Nipper Read and Gilbert Kelland.

Meanwhile, one of the most positive boosts to the industry had come from the film *The Krays*, starring

[12]It was not the first. Brian McConnell's *The Evil Firm* had been rushed out by Mayflower immediately after the trial.

and featuring Martin and Gary Kemp from Spandau Ballet. The film was said to have made the Twins £370,000. Public attention had also been drawn to them by the highly publicised wedding in Broadmoor of Ronnie Kray to Kate Howard, a former kissogram girl, in a prison ceremony in 1989. His best man, Charlie Smith, a double murderer, shared a room with him in Broadmoor; in turn Smith married Kate Howard's sister. Kate Kray went on to write *Murder, Madness and Marriage*, and Ronnie divorced her in May 1994. In his petition he claimed she had committed adultery, breached marital confidences and the book had demeaned him, thereby causing him to be ridiculed and distressed. The offending chapter had been entitled 'Sex and all that'. It was not the first time he had married. His first marriage in 1985 to Elaine Mildener had ended in divorce four years later.

By the early 1990s Krayology, the word of which Melford Stevenson had so strongly disapproved two and a bit decades earlier, had reached new heights. In 1992 the *Sun* ran a competition asking to see people with Kray tattoos. Chris Masterman had a handsome one of the Twins and Cornell on his thigh. He had paid a modest £200 for the artwork. It was said he wanted to add the likenesses of Violet and Charlie Kray. A Lee Daniels had Reggie sign his tattoo and then had the signature tattooed on. In 1993 there were supporters' parties, T-shirts, records, a limited photo album available for £250 and a limited edition painting at a cost of £199. A computer game was said to be in production. Ronnie was receiving fifty letters a week. In the October of that year there was a march and rally calling for their release. Even acts which might seem to some as smacking of bad behaviour were greeted with applause. When in the summer of 1993 it was reported that Ronnie Kray had 'tried to strangle Lee Kiernender', it was soon reported that the victim had been a pest to other prisoners. By keeping discipline in Broadmoor, he had mirrored exactly the favoured image of keeping crime off the streets of East London.

Just what are the reasons behind the intense interest in the Twins? They were by no means the longest-serving murderers. Amongst others, Joey Martin, convicted in 1965 of the murder of a milkman, has served longer than the Twins. It is not even as if there is any suggestion that they were innocent and the subject of a miscarriage of justice. Their guilt has long been forgotten by the public. A whole generation has grown up of people who were not born when the Krays ran the East End. Why then is there so much interest in their every movement, down to reporting that Ronnie smoked 140 cigarettes a day? 'My theory,' says their early chronicler Cal McCrystal, 'is that they came back into fashion in the same way as the Moors Murderers came back a few years ago with an orchestrated campaign for their release which was taken up on a wider base. The legend has become more interesting than the actualities. The film fuelled the legend to disproportionate proportions.'

The sociologist and writer Professor Dick Hobbs, who was himself brought up in the East End, has a slightly different view. He sees nostalgia as a key word: 'They represent a comfortable time of full employment and a sense of community. The ways up for the working classes in the 1960s were pop music, football, hairdressing and crime. The criminals who were more upwardly mobile were rewarded by the community. I remember their being featured by the *East London Advertiser* every week handing out trophies to boxers at the Repton. I think the revival started with the photographs of them at their mother's burial. That sold newspapers, and it was then that the mini-industry started. Now their violence has been played down in this country. They are seen as the helpers of old age pensioners.'

One argument is that the sheer fantasy of their activities is what has attracted us. Jack the Ripper becomes a gangster when he shoots Cornell and walks away. A giant disappears. There is the undoubted love for their mother. Perhaps, however, the real interest for their abiding fame is that the Krays were twins. Folklore, history and romantic literature is full of stories of twins – often separated ones or a good and bad twin. In academic circles there has long been discussion of heredity studies, and in British criminal history, with the exception of two girls who were convicted of arson, they are unique, and examples of twins who were such high-profile criminals are not exactly common worldwide. The Krays have at least provided a firm basis for such an in-depth heredity study.

It is unlikely that the industry will die when Reginald Kray is released, although as he will be on licence he will, undoubtedly, be subject to restrictions on his activities. For example, it is unlikely that he will be permitted to appear on the lucrative lecture circuit. Instead, he will probably have to retire to the house in a Swansea district on which he was said to have spent £500,000 in March 1995. Whether he will agree that, in the end, crime did pay is another matter.

Appendix

Tommy Butler

The legendary Tommy Butler was one of the last 'stars' of the Metropolitan Police before a policy decision was taken to do away with the system of high profiling officers on the Murder Squad. He followed in the long tradition of Dew (who was the officer in the Crippen case); Wensley (who dealt with the London gangs of the pre-First World War era); Leeson; through to the celebrated Fabian of the Yard, about whom a successful television series was made, and later officers such as Commander Ernest Millen. He achieved his legendary status in the force by his hunting down of the Great Train Robbers, delaying his retirement until he had accounted for all but a handful. Nipper Read, who took over the Kray case after Butler, described him in the days when he worked under him as a junior officer in Paddington:

Tommy Butler, who later led the London end

of the Great Train Robbery investigation and who had a great reputation as a detective, was also there as the senior first-class sergeant. People had enormous affection for Tommy because, on the face of it, he was such a lovely man. He had a good sense of humour and a nice attitude. The police and detection were his only obsessions. As a detective, he was good, but he was also most frustrating. He was always helpful if your report was ill defined or directed. In the old-fashioned way he would say 'what a lot of bollocks', but he would then sit down and go through it with you sentence by sentence, helping you put it in order. But in one way Tommy Butler was the worst detective I've ever come across. He was so secretive. He was a great investigator and plotted things up beautifully, but really opening up and having a conference, saying, 'Listen, chaps, this is what it's all about', would have been as alien as cutting his throat. He was obsessed by security. He would never tell his men what was happening where or when. He would say 'Come with me' rather than 'Come with me, I'm going to interrogate three blokes they've got at Paddington Station.' If he was going to organise a raid he would assemble his forces in the police station at, say, 6 a.m., but it would be not until they arrived at the actual house or premises they were told where they were going.

Sometimes, over the years, I have wondered whether it was just I who thought this a failing, but I have asked around and all have been in agreement that this was his own fault. Occasionally he would join his team for a drink, but it was only occasionally. He was a very private man and no one ever really was close to him. Unmarried, he lived with his mother, but home was really the CID office, and when those of us who could tried to slope off at half-past six or seven in an evening, Tommy, a workaholic, would say derisorily 'Another early night then?' He spent every evening typing in his room upstairs at Paddington. Downstairs we could hear the tapping of the machine. No one knew what he was doing. It may have been he was rewriting poorly compiled reports by the rest of us, but this can't have been every night. The only other thing I can think of is that he was putting together a diary with a view to compiling his memoirs. But none was ever published. (L. Read and J. Morton, *Nipper*, pp. 49–50.)

One of the officers in the Cornell enquiry describes him: 'He was one of the lads to a degree, but he knew when not to be one of the lads. He was very good at man management. Even if no one spoke, you knew he was in charge. His reputation went before him. He didn't really have a lot to say about either himself or his intentions.'

Charlie Clark

Charlie 'Nobby' Clark was a long-standing friend of the Krays who had once been a high-class cat-burglar. He was also an informer. In the early hours of 10 March 1989 Clark, now known as Bateman, was found stabbed to death at his home in Beaufoy Terrace, Dover. He was then seventy-one, and after having had a leg amputated, spent most of his time sitting looking out of the window of his home. In July 1990 nineteen-year-old Shane Keeler was sentenced to life imprisonment for his murder. Keeler, who had been in care since the age of five and was suffering from an abnormality of the mind, had pleaded guilty to manslaughter on the grounds of diminished responsibility, but the plea had not been accepted. He had broken into Clark's home and, when discovered, had stabbed him in the neck. He made off with £5, which he spent at the docks on video games and a cup of tea.

George Cornell

George Cornell, also known as George Myers, had a long criminal record beginning on 30 October 1944 when at Thames Magistrates' Court he was discharged for stealing chickens. He would have been seventeen at the time. From then on there was a steady string, including a three-year bind-over for garage-breaking in September 1945; fifteen months for unlawful wounding in February 1952; shopbreaking in 1953 for which he received twelve months; three years at the Old Bailey in 1954 for wounding; and in December 1961 at Lewes Assizes, nine months for robbery, false imprisonment and wounding.

He had been a member of the old Watney Street mob of dockers. He had married a girl from South London and had crossed the river, teaming up with the Richardsons and working in Eddie Richardson and Frank Fraser's Atlantic Machines, an organisation which put slot machines in clubs throughout the country. He had apparently been in the Twins' bad books for some time. One story is that they had sent a Glasgow hardman to kill him. The man had followed Cornell for some weeks but had only succeeded in stabbing him in the bottom before he returned to Scotland.

Cornell's death occurred at a time when the Twins were fearful that the Richardsons were becoming too powerful. Some accounts of the era have the Kray Firm put on alert with men assigned to take out their opposite numbers. There are a number of reasons given for Cornell's death. The first is that he was on the wrong side of the river and on the wrong territory. He was also said to have insulted Ronnie Kray at the Astor or the Stork Club – accounts vary – calling him a fat poof. Frank Fraser, in his memoirs, suggests that Cornell had not only refused the Krays access to what was a lucrative but one-off blue-movie racket, but had done so in unnecessarily harsh terms. In *Our Story*, Ronnie Kray says the killing was because of the insult in the Astor and also in revenge for the killing of a small-time gangster, Dickie Hart – 'Richard Hart had to be avenged. No one could kill a member of the Kray gang and expect to get away with it' – in a fight at Mr Smith's and the Witchdoctors' Club in Catford in which the Richardsons battled with other South-East London families. Kray says that Cornell, 'the snake who slithered away through the grass', was the only one who escaped, but there is no evidence that he was, in fact, at Mr Smith's that night. There is not much evidence either that Dickie Hart was a paid-up member of the Kray organisation.

Henry Mooney, in charge of the investigation into the Cornell killing, has a view that the killing resulted directly from Cornell's visit to his friend Jimmy Andrews who had been shot, apparently by Kray members, the previous week and was then in an East London hospital. Andrews later died from gangrene. Mooney believes that Cornell's specific brief was to find out who had shot Andrews, a Richardson friend.

George Dixon

After the conviction of the Krays, there were fears

amongst the police that other families or gangs would attempt to take over their interests. One of these was the Dixon brothers. The so-called leader of the Dixons was a publican, the 5 ft 2in Phil Jacobs, known locally as Little Caesar, whose houses were the Bridge House in Canning Town, the Royal Oak in Tooley Street and the Plough and Harrow in Leytonstone, which George Dixon minded. The Dixons had stood up for him when, shortly before their arrest, the Krays had tried to muscle in on his pubs. Commander Wickstead, who had been detailed by Sir Robert Mark to stamp out protection rackets, believed the Dixons were expanding their own empire under Jacobs' guidance, specialising in protection and long-firm fraud.

Jacobs had left school at the age of fourteen and had worked in various restaurants before he went for his National Service. Unlike the Krays and the Richardsons, he must have rather enjoyed it. He became a Leading Aircraftsman. He married in November 1965 with only 10 shillings to his name. His wife's parents bought them the Ship in Aylward Street and from then on, with hard work, he prospered. By the time of his arrest he had a Rolls-Royce with a personalised number plate.

George Dixon had already been acquitted at the Old Bailey, along with Connie Whitehead, of causing grievous bodily harm to a club owner. The allegation had been that injuries had been caused after he had refused the offer to have his club looked after. Wickstead's breakthrough in his enquiries came when a complaint was made to West Ham police station by one of the Dixons' brothers-in-law, Micky Flynn. He was immediately taken round to see Wickstead, who wrote admiringly: 'To say he was big was a little like saying that Rockefeller was rich or that Capone was bad. He was huge, one of the most formidable men I'd ever seen.'

According to Flynn, he was one of the enforcers for the Dixons but now he had left his wife, Lynne, he had consequently fallen out with the brothers. They, he said, had retaliated with a bit of nastiness directed towards his, Flynn's, sisters. One had had her arm broken, another had been threatened.

A friend of the Dixons, and a participant observer in these matters, has it the other way around:

'He'd given his wife a beating and Brian Dixon went round to sort things out.'

Translated, this must mean 'sort *him* out'. Despite his size, Flynn, the Dixons maintain, ran for cover.

Wickstead sees him in a more heroic light, maintaining that he would have visited each Dixon brother in turn and dealt with him.

'But, you see, I didn't know how far I'd go,' he told the Commander. 'So I changed my mind. I wasn't going inside for the likes of them.'

It would not have suited Wickstead to have the Dixons as victims.

'If the Dixons had then made a complaint, we would have had to charge him; and with his almost inhuman strength, it might not have stopped at grievous bodily harm. It could so easily have been manslaughter or even murder.'

When it came to it, no charge was brought over the alleged breaking of Flynn's sister's arm.

It was the familiar pattern of an enquiry. Once one witness came forward it was easier for others, and following a raid on the Greyhound in Bethnal Green run by a man, Osborne, in March 1971 when some fifty cases of gin were found, Wickstead had another witness. He was willing to give evidence about a fight between Michael Young and his cousin Mickey Bailey, which he said had been the usual prelude to a demand for money for protection. The fight was witnessed by two off-duty police officers, who were told not to interfere. Instead, they withdrew and compiled notes of the incident.

Next forward was a long-time criminal, Bernard Stringer, who recalled Bailey attacking him in the Court Club in Inverness Terrace. The arrests came at 5.30 a.m. on 25 August 1971. Wickstead borrowed twenty-nine officers from the Flying Squad and, as a result, nearly came to disaster. His team was briefed at 4 p.m., and dispersed. Someone leaked the story to the *Evening Standard* who, by the time of the raid, had its early headline prepared, 'Yard swoops on London gangsters'.

He learned his lesson. In the future, he used only his own squad and the special patrol group. 'We used to get locked in a gymnasium from the time of the briefing until we left for the raid,' one officer recalls.

The Dixon trial began on 12 April and continued until 4 July. Much of the time had been spent challenging the evidence of the police. There had been no written statements of admission, and much of the police evidence consisted of verbal admissions. There was also the now fashionable cross-over from the dock to the witness box as some defendants gave evidence against their former friends in return for no evidence being offered against them. Of the defendants who were left, Lambert Jacobs and Brian Dixon were acquitted; Phillip Jacobs, Leon Carelton and George Dixon received twelve years. Alan went down for nine and Michael Young and Michael Bailey, who had had the fight in The Greyhound, received five each.

Monty Sherbourne, defending in the case, had called it a 'storm in a teacup', but the judge, Mr Justice O'Connor, had this to say: 'You have mounted a campaign of vilification during the trial against police officers in the hope of saving your skins. Such activity on your part cannot operate on my mind to increase the sentences I have to pass on you. On the other hand, it does show the nature of your guilt. And it removes entirely such compassion as I would have been willing to show.'

When George Dixon was released, he took a pub in partnership with his father-in-law, then bought a run-down hotel in Hastings, did it up and sold it well.

With the proceeds he purchased a caravan park at Frinton and then went into the motor trade.

On his release, Alan Dixon first had a wine bar and then expanded into the entertainment business. Both brothers have become successful businessmen. For a full account of the case, see Bert Wickstead, *Gangbuster*.

The Kray Twins

The Kray Twins were in their first serious bit of trouble in 1950 – a fight outside Barrie's Dance Hall in the Narrow Way, Hackney. One man who gave evidence against them was Dennis Stafford, and they went to Borstal for GBH.[1]

There are so many stories about the Kray Twins that it is now difficult to sort fact from fiction. One story is that they were used as minders at the spring bank holiday meeting at Epsom Races in 1955. Jack Spot and Billy Hill, who ran London at the time, were feuding – a quarrel which would come to a head in the August of that year with a battle

---

[1]Stafford had a long criminal career mainly as a long-firm fraudsman and later in the celebrated Stafford-Luvaglio case in which Angus Sibbett, the manager of a gambling club in Newcastle, was killed. Both Stafford and Luvaglio were convicted and a long campaign began to clear their names. Eventually, when they were paroled Stafford said in a newspaper interview that, in fact, he but not Luvaglio had killed Sibbett. He later retracted this, saying he had confessed only for the money. He resumed his life as a conman.

between Spot and Billy Hill's man Albert Dimes in Soho. Spot was said to be afraid that his grip on the bookmakers' pitches on the Downs, the free course, would be taken from him. Because he was the boss, he had the No. 1 pitch and he collected rent from the others. So the story goes, Billy Hill had Frankie Fraser with him, and another wildman, Billy Blythe, would later be convicted along with Fraser of slashing Spot outside his home off the Edgware Road. At the spring meeting, Spot believed he needed some help, and he went down to the Twins' billiard hall, the Regal in Eric Street at Mile End, just by the tube station. They always maintained they didn't like Spot but that day he found them a good bookmaker to mind. It seems all they had to do was to stand by his pitch and take their percentage at the end of the racing. Not hard work, unless Fraser and the others made a move.

According to John Pearson, the Krays did not take their work that day too seriously. When one of the Saffron Hill Italian Mob offered them the advice that they were stark raving mad to show up as Spot's minders, they laughed and offered him a drink. 'For the rest of that day the Twins kept up their show of insolent indifference against the best-known gangsters in the country. They drank, they entertained their friends, they roared with laughter, they ignored the racing and the betting. Finally Ronnie yawned and rolled off to sleep. When the day ended they collected what was owed them, and without bothering to thank Spot, drove off in their van.'[2]

The difficulty with that story is that, according to his criminal record, Fraser was in prison at the time. In any event, they had already been working as minders first for Jack Spot in his spieler, the Aldgate Fruit Exchange, which despite its name was in Covent Garden, and then making a book with Teddy Machin, one of Spot's men, at Marks Tey races. At that time, meetings about pitches and how they should be allocated were run by Albert Dimes at the Central Club in Clerkenwell; another story which has gained credence was that at one meeting a shot was fired at bookmaker Tommy Falco, after which the Krays had five shillings in the pound from the pitch takings. The Twins also had a foothold in the West End, minding for a half-share the Stragglers Club at Cambridge Circus with Billy Jones and a Kray man, the former boxer Bobby Ramsey who'd been with Billy Hill in South Africa and who now lived off Arbour Square. So in a way, even from the start of their career, they'd had a foot in two camps.

The Kray Twins (Ronnie was the elder) were born in 1933 in Stean Street, London E2. They had an older and loyal brother, Charlie, who was involved by them in their activities rather than himself being a leader; a grandfather, Cannonball Lee, who was once

[2]John Pearson, *The Profession of Violence*, Grafton Books 1985, p. 96.

a well-known flyweight boxer; a father who did a lot of totting and selling bits and pieces of antiques; and their mother, Violet, to whom they were devoted.

All three of the brothers were keen boxers but the only one to show serious promise was Reggie, a lightweight. He was never beaten in his professional career. Ronnie, as a welterweight, won four of his six bouts between July and December 1951. It ended with his being disqualified against Doug Sherlock at the National Sporting Club and then a points defeat by Bill Sliney at the Royal Albert Hall on 11 December. That was the night when all three brothers boxed on the same bill. Reggie, who had one more bout, had boxed Sliney twice. He beat him both times on points. Charlie Kray didn't box too much although his career went on for nearly two years. He lost all three of his contests. He had not been in the ring for some time when he got knocked out in the third round at the Albert Hall by Lew Lazar out of Aldgate, who went on to be a British champion.

The Twins began their club-owning career with the Regal in Eric Street, which by all accounts they simply commandeered. After that they took over the Green Dragon, and later Reggie opened what was their best club, the Double R Club. It was probably financed in part by their profits from other clubs and by poncing from local villains, in other words demanding a share of proceeds from a burglary or robbery in the East End. There was one story that they got £2,000 from a boy who'd done Attenborough's the jewellers in Bethnal Green Road. But who can tell what's true? Certainly the Twins weren't thieves in the proper sense of the word.

There is little doubt that the Twins always had their ears to the ground. It is often not a complete secret when a good job is to go off. For one thing, others, not involved, liked to be in a position to put up an alibi and with the Twins' information service they were in a position to know what good jobs such as major break-ins, hi-jackings of lorries and sometimes, but not usually, bank raids were to take place. When a job had gone off, members of the Firm were sent to see the men who'd done it and then to invite them over for a drink with the Twins. There would be a chat and an assessment of what had been taken, and then the Twins would ask for a cut. Even members of the Firm had to pay. If they did a bit of business on the side, they were still expected to pay up. As for thefts, the going rate paid by a receiver was one third of the value of the goods. The Krays would ask for a third of a third, which wasn't bad for doing nothing.

The Twins also knew villains who were stealing cheque books by office-creeping and then flew kites[3] to get equipment to set up a gymnasium over the Regal Club, itself just a drinker. It was here the Firm was born, helped by the loyalty derived from former prisoners whose families had been looked after by the Krays whilst they themselves were away.

[3]In criminal slang, 'office-creeping' is burglary and 'to fly a kite' is to proffer a stolen or forged cheque.

At this time in social history the Kray Twins were the friends of, and probably subservient to, the Nash brothers from North London who themselves had interests in a variety of enterprises and endeavours.

The trouble arose from the Twins' connection with Bobbie Ramsey, part-owner of The Stragglers, as well as a long-running feud with the Irish fighting gang from the docks, the Watney Streeters. In fact, George Cornell was a Watney Streeter for a time before he married Olive and went to live across the river. So the story goes, one of the Streeters at the time, Charlie, had a small scam going with local post-office drivers who would readdress parcels to places where he could collect them. Ronnie wanted 50 per cent of the profits. Charlie was dilatory with payments and was listed by Ronnie as someone with whom he would soon have to deal severely. The opportunity came when Charlie had a fight with Billy Jones, another part-owner of The Stragglers. In return, the next night, Bobby Ramsey, as Jones' partner, sought out Charlie and beat him up. Two nights later, Charlie, this time with a complement from the Watney Street gang, beat Ramsey unconscious outside the Artichoke pub in the East End.

Although strictly not involved, Ronnie apparently wanted to make an example of Charlie and to shoot him, but both Ramsey and Jones argued against this. Instead it was agreed that a severe beating would be handed out to the Watney Street collection in the Britannia public house on Watney Street territory.

Ramsey and Jones went with him, backed by a dozen others. They found the Britannia empty except for a boy, Terry Martin, who was playing gin rummy. The Watney Street gang had escaped through the back entrance. Martin was made to suffer for this display of cowardliness. He was dragged out of the pub, slashed with a bayonet and kicked about the head.

Instead of going home, Ronnie decided to look for the Watney Streeters. Driven by Ramsey, he was found with a revolver when the police stopped the car in Stepney around midnight. In the car there was a crowbar and a machete. Ronnie explained the bloodstains on his shirt by saying he had had a nosebleed. There must have been some attempt to buy off Martin, but it failed and Reggie was also charged, but he got off. He told the jury that the bloodstains on his jacket might have come from boxers in the gym. On 5 November 1958 the Recorder of London sentenced Ronnie to three years' imprisonment. Ramsey received five years and Jones three. The Stragglers was shut down shortly afterwards.[4] 'But it didn't really matter . . . I bought an empty shop in the Bow Road and turned it into

[4]Ronnie's father, Charles Kray senior, wrote to the Court of Appeal after the attack on Terry Martin on 28 August 1958. 'It is my firm belief that he was intimidated into this brawl; more out of curiosity than any intentions of committing any violence of which he was innocent. If you will at least believe me, sir, they are the most respectful and good-natured lads anybody could wish to meet, so kind to my wife and I and everybody in their thoughts and actions and only do good to everybody, and with my guidance and my wife and son Charles [the eldest brother] they will make good.'

a club. I called it the Double R – a sort of tribute to Ron. Above the club we built a very snazzy gym and I got Henry Cooper to open it.'[5]

The Double R may have been the jewel in the crown but even then there were numerous other interests, each paying money: a drinking club in Stratford, secondhand car businesses, and the celebrated illegal drinking club next door to Bow Road police station.

What was seen, not least by Reggie Kray, as a crucial moment in their career was the hanging of Ronnie Marwood in 1960. He maintains that many of the subsequent problems he had with the law stemmed from the case. Ronnie Marwood, a friend of the Nash brothers, had been involved in a fight in the Holloway Road in December 1959 and had stabbed a police officer, Raymond Summers, who was trying to break up the fight. Everyone else was arrested, but Ronnie Marwood was hidden out. Reggie says it was by him but it may well have been on the authority of the Nash brothers. In early January 1960, Marwood surrendered himself to a police station. He was put on trial at the Old Bailey and was hanged in the spring. There was a terrible fuss about it, with fighting outside the prison on the morning of his death. When the newsreels showed pictures of it in the cinemas, the police were booed. The police were unpopular because, about the same time, another boy had been stabbed to death and his killer had been reprieved. The Homicide Act 1957 had provided the death penalty for the killing of a policeman – you had to hang unless there was a reprieve from the Home Secretary.

Whatever did happen, the police soon closed down the Double R, and in John Pearson's book Reggie maintains that every club he and Ronnie owned after that was persecuted, 'and all because we tried to help someone out'.

By the early 1960s, although Reggie claims that he disliked the protection business, feeling it was none too glamorous, he was looking after the remainder of Billy Hill's interests. The Twins had broken with Jack Spot who, after his slashing and a series of highly publicised trials, was now more or less in retirement, as was Hill who had temporarily gone abroad. Nash interests had been badly damaged, first following a fight at the Pen Club which had resulted in the death of Selwyn Cooney, and a later swoop by officers on members of the family in Paddington. Reggie was, he says, also looking after Peter Rachman's interests in Notting Hill. Rachman, who joined the Earl of Sandwich and Lord Cardigan in giving his name to the English language, had an empire built from prostitution and getting high rents from slum properties, using a collection of wrestlers and strongmen as minders.

Sometimes, it seems, people came to the Krays rather than their going looking for things to protect.

Albert Donoghue explained: 'The Krays would know the right guys who would open a club and approach them. Anyone opening a club would go to them. Young guys only respect someone who is a name, otherwise the doorman is a target. It makes sense. I worked the Green Dragon in Aldgate. I got paid and there was £40 to the Twins over and above my wages. People who came to the club knew who I was and why I was there.

'Then another time I was approached when I was working in an after-hours drinker opposite Stratford Place – the owner of a mini-cab firm down the East End was having scrub calls, you know, you get called out and then there's no one there. Now it can only be people you've interfered with yourself. The fellow asks me to be the manager. Sixty/forty per cent. I'd had a few drinks and I said "my way" and he said "yes". I couldn't believe it. I made a few calls and said if it didn't stop I'd be round, and it did.'[6]

But according to the Twins' cousin, Ronnie Hart, another who was to turn against them when the going became rough in 1967, from that percentage Donoghue had to pay a share from his interest in Advance Mini Cabs of £10 per week, rain or shine, to the Twins.

The list of clubs in and around North and East London and the West End from which the Twins, at one time or another during their reign, were 'on

[6]James Morton, *Gangland* (London, Little, Brown, 1992).

a pension' is staggering. Benny's in Commercial Road was a spieler run by a cab driver and paid £15 a week. The owner of Dodgers in Brick Lane paid £15 and a further £15 for a betting shop. The Stowe Club opposite the dog track in Walthamstow was another. The Krays had invested around £200 to get it started and they took £30 a week plus the wages of the man they had there minding both the premises and their interests. That £30 went straight to their mother Violet for her housekeeping. The Green Dragon in Whitechapel Road paid £40 protection and when another blackjack table went into the basement, a further £10 a week was levied. It was later turned into a betting shop and the payment remained the same. The Little Dragon next door paid £25 a week, and they were not too proud to receive £10 from the Two Aces, a spieler in the Whitechapel Road. Terry O'Brien's club in Cambridge Circus was taken over by them.

In Soho, the Twins, through their collectors, tapped Bernie Silver for £60 a week from his clubs the Gigi in Frith Street, the New Life and the New Mill off Shaftesbury Avenue. This pension went three ways between the Twins, Freddie Foreman and the Nashes. In return Johnny Nash gave the Twins a share of his pension from the Olympic Club in Camden Town as well as from the celebrated haunts, the Astor and the Bagatelle off Regent Street, an arrangement which left the Twins with the lion's share of the take.

In Chelsea there was the La Monde Club in the King's Road and out at Kingston the Cambridge Rooms over the top of the Earl of Cambridge public house on the Kingston bypass. It was here, in one of their well-publicised acts of charity, that a racehorse was auctioned and bought by their friend the actor Ronald Fraser. Then there was a share of the monies Freddie Foreman received from the tables at the Starlight Rooms off Oxford Street. Run by two men named Boot and Barry, the club had been opened after they had quarrelled with the Richardsons. They had gone to the Krays for help and had been installed in the Starlight as managers.

Of the more famous clubs, the Colony in Berkeley Square paid £100 a week and the Casanova, off New Oxford Street, half that sum. But there were occasional reverses. When John Bloom, the Rolls Razor washing-machine king whose empire collapsed in the 1960s, opened the Phone Booth Club in Baker Street, a fringe member of the Firm, Eric Mason, an old-time heavy – reputed to be the last man to receive a flogging in prison – was sent round to ask for a 'pension'. He was thrown out and barred from the club. Later Ronnie Hart was dispatched along with Mason to explain the position. Mason could not be barred but the pension would be scrubbed. If Bloom stepped out of line again he 'would go' and his club along with him. The owner of the Monmouth Club in Monmouth Street, Smithfield was less successful in repelling boarders. He received a beating for his troubles and later paid over a percentage.

The money from all subscribers to the Firm was collected on a Friday by Donoghue, Ronnie Hart, Scotch Jack Dickson and Ian Barrie. It was known as the milk round and the collectors were treated just like the milkman making his weekly call. From time to time the collectors would be given a small gift such as drink or another £10 for themselves. Scotch Jack Dickson and Ian Barrie kept the money from Benny's and the Dodgers as their own wages.

Back in the suburbs there was £10 a week from a scrap metal merchant in Hackney, and the same from another in Poplar. The Twins took £15 of the £30 collected by George Dixon from the Plough in Leytonstone. A Greek-run casino, the Silver Spinner in Stoke Newington, provided a share of its profits and in Leicester, just before the arrest of the Twins in May 1967, Rayners Club paid out over a half-share of the takings in return for a £500 investment.

In 1960, they acquired Esmeralda's Barn in Wilton Place off Knightsbridge. Once it had been a fashionable nightclub, but it had declined into producing strip shows. With gambling legalised by the Gaming Act 1959 it has applied for and been granted a licence for gambling. The acquisition was brought about by the simple expedient of frightening the controlling shareholder, Stefan de Fay into signing away his shares to them for £1,000. They had heard of the vulnerability of de Fay from Peter Rachman and, with implied threats being heeded, the club was theirs within six hours. De Fay stayed on the board of directors for the next two years but drew no salary. In the heyday of the club the Twins cleared £40,000 a year. They now had Lord Effingham on the board with the princely retainer of £10 a week or the sum taken from the Two Aces in the Whitechapel Road. His son was a close friend of Ronnie. The day-to-day running of the club and the Twins' financial affairs were now firmly in the hands of an adroit long-firm fraudsman, Leslie Payne.

All went well until Reggie went to prison in Wandsworth. Ronnie, not the brighter of the brothers, became lonely and frustrated. As John Pearson says, it was not sufficient for him to sit in a smart dinner jacket and watch his tables make him money. He started to take an active interest in the club. Indiscriminately he began to grant long lines of credit and when the punter could not pay, Ronnie took to threatening him. The serious players now began to drift away to find other clubs. A lesbian-orientated discotheque was started in the basement. The club continued its decline until 1963 when it went bust with debts of £4,000.

Apart from those few convictions, by 1964 the Twins did not really have much of a prison record. It never seemed as if the police wanted to do, or were capable of doing, anything about them. They even had their illegal drinking club next to Bow Road police station. As is often the case it was the press which precipitated matters. There was, it was said, in existence some film of a peer and a gangster. The Commissioner of Police, Sir Joseph Simpson, issued a statement denying a witch-hunt against titled homosexuals. The man who took the photographs obtained an injunction in the High Court to prevent the pictures being printed by the Mirror Group of Newspapers.

On 13 July the *Daily Mirror* ran an editorial: 'This gang is so rich, powerful and ruthless that the police are unable to crack down on it. Victims are too terrified to go to the police. Witnesses are too scared to tell their story in court. The police, who know what is happening but cannot pin any evidence on the villains, are powerless.'

The next day Sir Joseph made a statement that he had asked senior officers for 'some enlightenment' on reports that enquiries were being made into allegations of a relationship between a homosexual peer and East End gangsters.

On 16 July the *Daily Mirror* led with the story 'The picture we dare not print', and described it as one of a 'well-known member of the House of Lords seated on a sofa with a gangster who leads the biggest protection racket London has ever known'.

When it came to it, the picture, which appeared a week later in the German magazine *Stern*, turned out to be a totally innocent one. It was Lord Boothby, who was also something of a television pundit, and Ronnie Kray sitting on a sofa. With the fuss that was made it had been thought that at least the pair would have been naked.

Boothby issued a statement: 'I am not a homosexual. I have not been to a Mayfair party of any kind for more than 20 years. I have met the man alleged to be King of the Underworld only three times, on business matters; and then by appointment in my flat, at his request, and in the company of other people.'[7] He received £40,000 in damages. Ronnie got an apology from the *Mirror* but no damages. But, as John Pearson says, the apology kept the *Mirror* away from launching an investigation into him and Reggie.

Then came questions in the House of Commons concerning extortion from club owners and what action was being taken by the Home Secretary; the police began to make active enquiries into the Krays' affairs. A young Detective Inspector, Leonard 'Nipper' Read at Commercial Street police station was asked if there was any reason why he should not conduct a detailed investigation into the Twins' business and personal interests. To his annoyance Read thought it was being suggested that he might be in their pockets.

In his autobiography Read discusses why the police had previously made no serious attempt to

[7]It is now quite apparent that the raffish Boothby was bisexual. He was the lover of Dorothy Macmillan, wife of Harold. Their relationship lasted nearly thirty years but the stories of his homosexual exploits are too frequent and too well documented to be ignored.

break the Krays' hold on the East End: 'Over the previous years the Krays had been taken on by the police but not concentrated on. Before Gerrard formed my squad, the CID had never taken their actions personally and I think they should have done. If ever there was a shooting and the overwhelming level of opinion amongst detectives was that it was down to the Krays, the attitude had been that you went along to see them first and they said "No, we got an alibi". Then you would go and look for the evidence. It should have been the other way round. This is what appalled me even before I started the first enquiry. You'd talk to CID officers and they'd say "Oh this is down to the Krays", and you'd say "Well what are you doing about it?" And the answer was they were doing nothing about it. They never sort of took up the cudgels. They never got keen enough or personally involved enough to want to have a go. That was the sort of thing that surprised me.'[8]

However, despite his efforts, Read could not obtain any hard evidence. People were simply afraid to talk. What he did hear was that the main source of the Firm came from long-firm frauds. These are neither new nor difficult things to organise. Many people, and not only those in the East End, have benefited from one of them even if they did not know at the time they were doing so. The basic version is that a warehouse or shop is taken by a front man

[8]Leonard Read and James Morton *Nipper*, (London, Macdonald, 1991)

who has no previous convictions. Goods are bought on credit and then sold perfectly properly through the shop. The supplier receives his or her money. More business is done with more and more suppliers until there is one big bang, a massive amount of goods are obtained on credit, knocked out at prices often below the purchase price in a great 'liquidation sale' – that's where the local housewives benefited – and the premises are closed. The beauty of a well-organised LF is that goods are bought from the wholesalers over a telephone by a 'blower-man' so identification of the purchaser is rare. Managers of the shops knocking out the stuff are changed weekly or fortnightly. In those days it was difficult if not impossible for the police to find out who was really running the show. In the 1960s a properly run small LF could expect to realise a profit of between £100,000 and £150,000, which was enormous money.

Then, according to his book, Read had a piece of luck. He heard through an officer at Paddington that a club owner, Hew McCowan, had been pressured to pay protection money for the Hideaway Club in Gerrard Street, which he had just opened in partnership with Gilbert France, who also owned the restaurant Chez Victor in Wardour Street. As with many of these clubs, it was difficult to find out just who owns what. The Hideaway had previously been the Bon Soir, owned by France in partnership with Frankie Fraser and Albert Dimes. The Bon Soir, managed by a young man, Sydney Vaughan, had been in dispute with France and the club had closed in early autumn 1965. Now France had met McCowan at Vaughan's 21st birthday party and an agreement had been signed giving Vaughan *carte blanche* to run the premises. For this he had to pay Gerrard Enterprises, France's company, £150 a week. McCowan employed Vaughan as his agent and manager and spent some £4,000 on refurbishing the club, which opened for business on 16 December.

McCowan had already met the Twins through both Johnny Francis and their financial adviser Leslie Payne, who would later turn into one of the police's best witnesses. They had tried to get McCowan to put some money into a housing project in Eastern Nigeria. This was what had led to the photographs getting into the hands of the *Mirror*.

McCowan had foolishly mentioned that he was thinking of opening a club and it was arranged he should meet the Twins in the Grave Maurice. According to his statement, Reggie had maintained it was essential that McCowan have two of his men installed in the club to prevent trouble. Initially a figure of 25 per cent was suggested which was to rise to 50 per cent. A table for ten was reserved for the Twins' party on the opening night, but no one showed. Three days later a writer friend of the Krays, 'Mad' Teddy Smith, did appear, very drunk, caused trouble and did a minor amount of damage in the reception area before being bounced out by the waiters[9]. When McCowan next saw the Krays it was pointed out this sort of thing would not have happened had their men been there to prevent it. An agreement was reached that now 20 per cent would be payable. McCowan asked for, and was told he would receive, a written agreement. He telephoned the police.

Once he had taken statements, Read liked the way McCowan stuck to his version of events and, even more, he liked the way Vaughan gave his account. He would have liked to have had sight of the agreement but what he had was better than nothing. Read thought he had enough for arrests.

The Krays were kept in custody until their trial at the Old Bailey the next year, despite a question in the House of Lords from their old friend Lord Boothby, who wanted to know if it was the intention of the Government to imprison the Krays without trial indefinitely. Meanwhile, Read hoped that with the Twins out of harm's way, people would come forward. He was wrong, and now his case began to fall apart. Sydney Vaughan went to the Twins' home at Fort Vallance to retract his statement before a local vicar. McCowan was offered money not to give evidence, but refused.

[9]Smith, who had written a play for radio and was a part-time driver for the Twins, disappeared in the 1960s and was thought to have been killed in a quarrel over a boy in Steeple Bay, Kent. His body was never found, and no charges were brought.

The first trial got stopped on the second day with McCowan still in the witness box. Manny Fryde of Sampsons (the solicitors who handled the Krays' cases) said he had a witness who had overheard a juryman discussing the case with a police officer. The witness turned out to be a man who had been questioned about the sale of the shares in Esmeralda's Barn but the juryman was stood down and the case proceeded with eleven jurors. Vaughan maintained that the only reason he had made his original statement was because McCowan had threatened to withdraw his financial support. After three and a half hours the jury announced it couldn't reach an agreement and at the retrial things went worse for the Crown. The defence had found out that McCowan had spent some time in a psychiatric hospital, and that didn't help. This time, the jury took less than ten minutes to acquit.

That same day the Twins purchased the Hideaway Club from McCowan and called it the El Morocco. With the defeat of Nipper, for the foreseeable future the Krays now had a licence to do what they wanted in both the East and West End.

A month after the case, on 20 April 1965, Reggie married a young girl, Frances Shea. It was not a success and she committed suicide on the night of 6 June 1967. At her funeral Albert Donoghue was ordered to make a list for future reference of those who had not sent flowers. Reggie was really distraught and, according to what we now know,

Ronnie was beginning to show increasing signs of mental instability. Another list was compiled, this time of those by whom he felt threatened. All his energies were being channelled into revenge and retribution.

The Richardson brothers, Eddie and Charlie, were the masters of South London until 1965. Along with the notorious Frankie Fraser, Eddie Richardson was convicted of an affray at Mr Smith's Club in Catford which resulted in the death of a Kray friend, Richard Hart. After the arrest of Richardson and Fraser, members of the underworld came forward to say that they had been tortured by Eddie and Charlie Richardson and Fraser. Charlie Richardson was later arrested and at their trial in 1966 he received twenty-five years imprisonment. Eddie and Fraser, who were already serving five years for their part in the affray, received ten apiece.

The Krays were fearful that the Richardsons were becoming too powerful and that George Cornell had joined forces with them, making them even more powerful. According to some versions of Gangland history, the Richardsons had refused to join a cross-London alliance and had possibly interfered with a Mafia-linked deal the Krays were putting together.

They became convinced that the Richardsons were going to try to take over their empire, and they weren't having it. As Nipper Read says: 'There was a natural dividing line – the Thames. Soho had for years been something of an Open City. There was plenty of pickings for everybody. Each firm had the clubs which they protected. There was no need to muscle in on someone else's club.'

Now with the Cornell–Fraser–Richardson alliance the Twins began to feel threatened. Whilst Fraser had been in prison following the Spot affair, they had assiduously courted him through his sister Eva Brindle, taking her to see him on visiting days. When he had been released, the Twins had thrown a big coming-home party for him, but he had not been seduced by them. Instead Fraser, always interested in gaming machines, had taken over a chain of machines once owned by the Twins. Cornell took a close interest in the pornography market in both the West End and in Essex. The Twins believed they were on the edge of a big deal with the American Mafia and the Richardsons could interfere with it. At one meeting with a Mafioso chief visiting from New York, the Richardsons had been present and had made sarcastic remarks. Ronnie also feared that the uneasy truce between themselves and the Richardsons would end.

A meeting was called at the Astor nightclub off Berkeley Square for a discussion between the Twins, Ian Barrie and Ron Hart, Charlie and Eddie Richardson, Frankie Fraser and George Cornell. The meeting became heated because the Richardsons apparently wanted a substantial interest in the Kray–Mafia business arrangements. Some people say it was then that George Cornell called Ronnie a big fat poof and told him to bugger off when he asked to be cut in to the blue film racket. It was not an insult that could be accepted lightly. Ronnie had already slashed little Johnny Cardew from an Islington family for saying, perfectly pleasantly, that he thought Ronnie seemed to be putting on weight. To be called a poof in front of his friends was far too much. There was a discussion about instant retribution but it was put off, and instead Ronnie had Cornell's movements monitored.

Shortly after, there was another confrontation. This time it was in Al Burnett's Stork Club in Swallow Street, Piccadilly, and this time it was between Ronnie and Frankie Fraser. As a result the Krays called a meeting with some South-East London rivals of the Richardsons and another smaller North London faction. The old talk of an alliance was revived. It was agreed that a defence union should be formed. The Firm was put on war alert. 'We were each given a name,' recalls Donoghue, 'Ronnie Hart and I had to look after Brian Mottram if it came to it. We were all given the names and addresses of clubs, pubs, girlfriends, where our people could be found. Freddie Foreman had a spy in the Richardson scrapyard. If we went South to see Freddie it was like we were going into Indian country. We would go in a hired car with a gun so, if we got a pull, it wasn't our car and we could say we knew nothing about it. Going south of the river was like going abroad.'

Still the Krays did not believe they were strong enough without help. To counter the ferocity of Frankie Fraser they wanted someone just as fearless on their side. The person they chose was Frank Mitchell. There was only one problem – he was serving a sentence in Dartmoor Prison.

In the meantime they began wearing bullet-proof vests, and a member of the Firm was deputed to be their personal bodyguard to leave any public house or club first and survey the street. Although they felt themselves in need of protection, they did not carry weapons and were becoming increasingly reluctant to allow members of the Firm to carry them either. Wednesday nights were those when the Krays went visiting around the various local pubs. Before these evening visits, members of the Firm would go to the pub or club and hide weapons in lavatory cisterns. They were right to be careful. Shots were fired at the windows of the Widows, the name for the Lion pub in Tapp Street where the Krays used to drink. A few days later a mini-cab owner who resembled Ronnie was knocked down by a car which mounted the pavement.

There had long been a liaison with gangs in Scotland and they got a Glasgow hardman to deal with Cornell. He followed him for some weeks but according to legend succeeded only in stabbing him in the bottom when they met in a basement drinking club before he went back to Scotland. Cornell was shot dead on 9 March 1965 just two days after the Catford fight.

There are conflicting versions of just why Mr Smith's Club in Catford was turned into an English version of the OK Corral. One puts the blame firmly at the Krays' door. It is said that it was not just a battle for the right to protect the club, but that a trap had been sprung for the South London team, with the setter a former running mate of the Richardsons who had switched sides. The Twins' version is that the Richardsons expected the Firm to be in Mr Smith's that night. In fact only one associate of the Twins was there, Richard Hart, who was shot dead; Eddie Richardson, Frank Fraser and a number of the other participants were arrested shortly followed by Charlie Richardson.

Donoghue believes it was then that the Twins began to lose touch with reality. Ronnie was on massive doses of tranquillisers and Reggie, still besotted with the dead Frances, now believed she had been re-born as a robin he had seen in the cemetery. Ronnie was also putting pressure on his twin to 'do his one'. That one was Jack 'The Hat' McVitie.

It is not clear why, with all the Richardsons out of the way, the Twins actually felt they had to get the 'Mad Axe-man' Frank Mitchell away from Dartmoor. There was now no Frankie Fraser about whom to worry. Frank Mitchell was strong as an ox and had just about the brains of one. He'd had a dreadful career. When he was eight he was sent to the first in a series of special schools, then it was Borstal at seventeen, and prison three months later. That was when he had a flogging for an assault on a prison officer. In 1955 he had been sent to Rampton after being certified as a mental defective. In January 1957 he escaped and, whilst on the run and doing a burglary, hit the occupier over the head with an iron bar. He got nine years for this but it wasn't long before he escaped from Broadmoor and attacked another householder and his wife. On his arrest he said, 'I want to prove I am sane and know what I am doing.' This time he received ten years' imprisonment, and after he'd been in the Hull Prison riots in 1962, he was birched and transferred to Dartmoor.

He seemed to get on well with the Governor and, as his behaviour improved, he was removed from the escape list. In May 1964 he was allowed to work outside the prison walls on the quarry party, a small and well-supervised group. In September of that year he was transferred to the honour party, a more loosely supervised group. The Twins were looking after him from the outside and he did more or less what he liked. Instead of working, he would spend the afternoons in a local pub. Once he even took a taxi to Tavistock, where he bought a budgerigar. Girls were sent down by the Twins to help pass his afternoons.

For the Krays, Mitchell became a special 'away'. They were perhaps no longer as popular in the East End as they had been. Some members of the Firm were now disrespectfully referring to them as Gert and Daisy, after Ethel and Doris Walters, the cockney music-hall act. They'd fallen out with their financial adviser, Leslie Payne. The Mitchell release was really a show of strength. If they got him out, it showed the public how they cared for people and what they could do as well. There was also something personal because on one occasion Mitchell had also protected Reggie Kray against a screw in prison.

They worked at things two ways. What Mitchell wanted was a date for his release, and the plan was evolved that he would escape from a working party on the Moor and then a campaign would begin to bring pressure on the Government. To this end, the Twins' friendly MPs such as the noted homosexual Tom Driberg could be relied on for help. On 12 December 1966 Mitchell went to work at Bagga Tor. The weather was too bad to work, and so the party stayed in a hut playing cards. At 3.30 he asked if he could go and feed some ponies. At 4.20, when the prison officers took the remainder of the party to the bus pick-up point, there was no sign of Mitchell. Twenty minutes later the local police were notified, but by now Mitchell was on his way to London. When the hue and cry really went up, he was in Whitechapel.

When, the next morning, his clothing was found

in a lay-by some thirty miles from Tavistock, it was 'assumed he had made good his escape'. It was the talk of the East End. The next and really the last thing the outside world heard of Mitchell was from the newspapers. He wrote to *The Times* and the *Daily Mirror*. Each letter (which was written for him) asking for a release date had a thumbprint impression to confirm its authenticity. At first the Home Secretary agreed to meet with Mitchell but then he changed his mind to imposing the precondition of his surrender. The letters stopped. Again, it was well known in Barking Road who had helped Mitchell in his escape but, once again, no one was talking to the police.

For a few days Mitchell lived in relative comfort. A nightclub hostess, Liza from Winston's in the West End, was produced to provide him with sex, and what is rather sad is that he fell in love with her. What he had done, however, was to exchange one prison cell for another. Without his surrender he wasn't going to get a release date, and if he did give himself up it would mean a loss of privileges, probably loss of remission and further time to be served. He began to say he would never be captured alive. Once he started to say things like this he became more and more of a liability. It was shortly before Christmas, and he wanted to go and see his mother and sister at the family house in Bow and was told a meeting would be arranged, but nothing came of it. He began to rave about going to look for the Twins both at Vallance Road and 'all around the clubs'.

On Christmas Eve, he was told by Albert Donoghue that he was being moved to a new address in Kent. He protested at being separated from Liza but was told she would be following on. That was the last time anyone can really say they saw him, but, like the Lord Lucan case, there were reports that he had been seen all over the world. At the trial of the Krays for the murder of Mitchell, Albert Donoghue gave evidence that the Axe-man had been shot just as the van left the Barking Road, by Freddie Foreman and Alf Gerard, a more or less freelance hitman who died in 1981 in Brighton. The Firm had a series of codes: 'the dog has won' meant a successful operation had been carried out. 'The dog has lost' meant the reverse. According to the nightclub hostess, Liza, Donoghue returned to the flat and said, 'The dog is dead.'

The third of the murders for which the Krays eventually stood trial was that of Jack 'The Hat' McVitie, a long-time friend of the family. He disappeared in the autumn of 1967. Apparently he had fallen from favour for a number of reasons.

Tony Lambrianou, one of the lesser lights of the Kray Firm, who wrote a book on his experiences, described McVitie and his murder. 'Reggie didn't do society such a bad turn. Jack The Hat was a known heavy man. He was six feet two and hard as nails. He done a lot of imprisonment in his time. He'd been through the school and he'd hurt a few people along the way.

'His stock in trade was crime, and he made money

out of it. He was an active robber and he cared little for anyone and he was capable of anything . . . He was on drink and pills and he was unpredictable . . . Even having a social drink, he could suddenly turn vicious for no reason.

'He didn't have a care in the world. He didn't give a monkey for anything, but he should have done. That was his downfall. The Twins only tried to help him: they put lots of work his way. But he started making errors, and he brought trouble on himself.'[10]

The work had included taking over part of a drug-vending operation and spying on the Nash brothers. McVitie was related to Joey Pyle, then Johnny Nash's right-hand man. After McVitie's death, the story was put about that he had died when gelignite in his car had blown up accidently. It was a story to appease Pyle and the Nash brothers.

McVitie was apparently always a bit of a loose cannon. At one time he had a £25-a-week pension. He worked as a freelance robber and when asked to donate half the proceeds to the Firm's funds, he refused. He was expelled. Later, after a beating, he was reinstated as a fringe member if nothing more. Not long after, McVitie also took to criticising the Twins in public. He swindled the Twins and then went about boasting what he'd done. He had been given money to kill the financial adviser Leslie Payne and, half-drunk and on pills, he'd gone to Payne's

[10]Tony Lambrianou, *Inside the Firm*, (London, Smith Gryphon, 1991).

house with Billy Exley, an ex-boxer member of the Firm. Mrs Payne had opened the door and told them her husband was out. McVitie had simply turned away and had pocketed the advance fee.

He was murdered at a party at Evering Road in the home of 'Blonde' Carol Skinner. She had been sent across the road to a friend of hers for the evening. Tony Barry of the Regency Club had been ordered to tell the Krays when McVitie showed up at the club and to bring to the Evering Road party a gun kept at the Regency. There were advantages in this. The more people who were participants as opposed to mere observers, the more compromised they were and so the less likely to tell the police.

The Lambrianou brothers brought McVitie to the flat and immediately Reggie put the gun to his head. The gun failed to discharge. McVitie began to struggle and to try to escape. Finally Reggie plunged a knife deep into his face and stomach. He commented, 'I did not regret it at the time and I don't regret it now. I have never felt a moment's remorse.'[11]

McVitie's body was placed in a candlewick bedspread and taken to South London by Charlie Kray for disposal – something arranged by Freddie Foreman, who, although from South London, was a long-time friend of the Twins. Exactly where the body ended up is impossible to say. Nipper

[11] R & R Kray, *Our Story* (London, Pan Macmillan, 1989).

Read fancied the idea that it had returned to East London and had been put in the furnaces of the local swimming baths. There's a story that he was sent to a friendly undertaker and buried in a double coffin. He may have been buried somewhere in the country but according to Lambrianou, the car in which he was taken to South London ended as an Oxo cube in a scrapyard. 'Jack himself is about three miles away from where the car went into scrap, and fifty miles from where we left him. His body will never be found. He and his hat were put in a grave which had been pre-dug, and covered with a layer of soil. A funeral took place the next day, and the grave was filled. So he did get a decent burial.'

In the autumn of 1967 Nipper Read was appointed to the Murder Squad with the special brief of forming a squad to bring down the Krays. He had learned from his earlier mistakes, and this time it was a case of 'softly softly catchee monkey'. Read went to see Leslie Payne who, like Billy Exley, had split away from the Twins. Payne was afraid that a rather more professional attempt would be made to kill him. Read obtained an indemnity for him against all crimes except those of violence, provided he admitted to them and made a long statement saying what he knew about the Firm. Now Read was able to obtain evidence from others on the fringes, promising that he would not use the statements unless and until arrests had been made. Once more he was looking at fraud: the Krays' involvements with long-firm frauds, some GBHs and their dealings in stolen bonds, rather than at murder.

Meanwhile at the beginning of 1968 the Krays were moving once more into the international market. They met Angelo Bruno of the Philadelphia family, who was looking at casino interests in the West End. The Krays promised him a trouble-free life running those interests. They had successfully disposed of a batch of bonds, part of a number stolen in an armed raid on the Royal Bank of Canada in Montreal. Now their trade in stolen securities was expanding. They had also met up with an American, Alan Bruce Cooper who took them into Europe and the stolen jewellery market in Belgium.

Nipper Read had had Cooper under surveillance for some time when he learned that a man, Paul Elvey, was being sent to Glasgow to collect a briefcase. There had long been a two-way trade in villains passing between Glasgow and London, and there had long been a similar trade of information and assistance between the respective police forces. Elvey was arrested and the briefcase found to contain dynamite, something readily available from the mines around Glasgow. Interviewed by Read, he passed on a story of assassination attempts on Soho stripclub owner George Caruana and others, both in the street and at the Old Bailey. Amazingly, when his premises were searched there was the physical evidence to back it up. Cooper was arrested and at once said he was being run by John du Rose, Read's superior officer, as an informer and possibly *agent provocateur*.

Read knew that once Cooper disappeared from the streets, the Krays would suspect something was up. Apparently he had a stomach ulcer, and Read placed him in a Harley Street nursing home from where he telephoned the Twins. Read hoped the Twins would come and make damaging admissions. Instead they sent one of their henchmen along with Joey Kauffman, a Jewish-Sicilian small-time Mafioso who was dealing in stolen bonds.

On 8 May, after an evening out at the Astor, the Krays went back to their flat and Kauffman to his suite at the Mayfair. The next day around 200 officers, Read's men, swooped on over twenty members of the Firm. Initially they were charged with conspiracy to murder persons unknown. These arose from the statements of Elvey and Cooper,[12] and had nothing to do with Mitchell, McVitie or Cornell.

The swoop on 9 May had included both the Twins' friend Freddie Foreman and their brother Charles. Now, as the police chipped away at the edges of the Firm, several, including Billy Exley, offered to give evidence.

With the Twins and senior members of the Firm on remand in custody, Read was to make further progress in obtaining statements from men who

[12]Those charges were later dismissed.

might consider turning Queen's Evidence, and also other witnesses like Mrs X

Prince Monolulu

Prince Monolulu's real name was Peter McKay, but it is difficult to know what else is true about this great and engaging self-publicist. He was probably born around 1880 in the Virgin Islands, which was then under Danish sovereignty, and he could speak the language fluently. He was said to have won £35,000 at the Derby in 1935. The Aga Khan, whose horse Barham, ridden by Freddie Fox, was the winner, was not pleased with Monolulu because he vaulted the rails and tried to assist in leading in the winner. The Prince lost all his winnings the next day. Apparently his catchphrase was born when the revivalist preacher, Gipsy Smith, vying for the attention of the crowds, called, 'I've got heaven,' Prince Monolulu called back, 'And I've gotta horse.' The crowd sided with Monolulu, and the war-cry stuck.

According to one of his versions of his life – and there were several – he first went to America in 1900, where he worked in a kitchen and later sold patent medicines for a barker. He arrived in England two years later.

He was a part-time dentist as well, pulling teeth in a tent with a gramophone full on to drown the cries of his patients. Certainly at the beginning of the war he sold gas-mask carriers. He also said he had worked as a lion-tamer. When he was broke, he sold peanuts in Germany. He claimed he had a small part in a Marx brothers film, and he appeared in *Wings of the Morning*, the first British film in Technicolour, and Joseph Losey's *The Criminal*. He probably also appeared in a number of British comedies when characters such as those played by Ian Carmichael decide to have a day at the races.

In 1931 he married Nellie Amelia Adkind, described by the newspapers in the fashion of the time as 'a white woman'. He probably married six times in all and his last wife, he said, was a Yugoslav baroness. In 1961 he went to Moscow on a peace mission. 'Horse racing will stop all wars, because as soon as a man backs a winner he becomes a capitalist,' he said.

He died in February 1965 and was cremated at Golders Green crematorium. Few of the racing fraternity attended.

There was an interesting story about the 1935 Derby. Fox on Barham was boxed in at the top of the hill, and Harry Wragg wearing the Aga Khan's second colours on Thrift, which eventually finished fourth, responded to a cry and pulled out to let the first horse through. A Stewards' Enquiry followed, and Wragg was cautioned and reminded of the rule that 'Every horse which runs in a race shall run on his merits, whether his owner runs another horse in the race or not.' In future, said the stewards, offenders would be dealt with severely. It was not thought that Thrift would have beaten Barham but that he would undoubtedly have been second.

Charles de Silva

Sri Lankan-born Charles de Silva, said to have the looks of Omar Sharif, was probably the finest British con-man of his era. It is certain that he sold a fishing fleet, sight unseen, to a farmer travelling between Hull and King's Cross. He was under the thumb of Charles Mitchell, an associate of the Krays, who took most of de Silva's earnings. It is probable that for a time, at least, they protected de Silva from him. It is thought that he committed suicide rather than face a further term of imprisonment – he had already served a seven-year term – but the author Derek Raymond, who worked with de Silva, believed he may have been murdered and the death arranged to look like suicide (*The Hidden Files*, London, Little, Brown, 1992).

Royston James Smith

Royston James Smith had a varied life. He was a dwarf, born to a gypsy family, and was thought to be deaf and dumb until the age of seven. His adult life was divided between being a midget wrestler in

England and Europe, when he appeared as Fuzzy Kaye, a number of spells on the variety stage in pantomime and ice shows, and as a member of the Morton Fraser Harmonica Gang and the owner of a number of West End clubs. During this time he met the Krays and a number of other prominent Soho personalities, including Tony Mella, former boxer and club owner, whom he claimed to have striped – by cuts vertically and horizontally – across his backside in a quarrel over a club Smith was running for dwarfs, and which Mella believed would damage his trade. Mella was eventually shot by his close friend Alf Melvin, who in turn committed suicide. Smith did indeed marry a showgirl, but the marriage did not last and he was found in the late 1980s sleeping rough on the Embankment. His biography, *Little Legs, Muscleman of Soho*, was written in 1989 by George Tremlett (Unwin Hyman).

Justice Melford Stevenson

Melford Stevenson died on Boxing Day 1985; he had been retired for a while, and by this time was blind. He was a vicar's son and had been educated at Dulwich; twice married, he had a daughter from his first marriage and a son and daughter from the second. He stood as Conservative candidate for Maldon in 1945 and was defeated by Tom Driberg. He opened his campaign by announcing that he wanted a clean fight and would therefore not be 'alluding to the alleged homosexuality of his Labour opponent, Tom Driberg'. He did not change his attitude. In 1957 he called the Sexual Offences Act, passed that year and which legalised homosexuality between consenting adults, a 'Buggers' Charter'. Described by Lord Devlin as 'the last of the great eccentrics', he once described a television interview with Diana Dors as addressing the rear of the Graf Zeppelin.

MURDER WITHOUT CONVICTION: INSIDE THE WORLD OF THE KRAYS

To my wife, who showed such understanding when I told her I would like to write my account of the events that took place between 1964 and 1968

Contents

Author's Note

I would like to thank Tony Peake for having confidence in this book from the beginning.

1

To London

This is a true story about what happened to two young men, who in 1964 left their homes in Edinburgh and travelled down to London. They hoped to start a new life in the big city but ended up getting involved with the most violent gang in the East End. They were a bit like flies which got caught in a spider's web: once in it was difficult to get out. I was one of those young men who got caught inextricably.

But first we must go back to the very beginning. I was born in the docklands of Leith, Edinburgh – one of a family of eight. I left school at fourteen and started to work for a local engineering firm. On reaching my eighteenth birthday, however, I began to seek adventure and volunteered to join the Royal Marines. I trained for two years at the Commando School in Lympstone, Devon, where we were prepared for active service. Amongst other things, this entailed learning how to use small arms and doing a course in judo. Then I joined up with 45 Commando and was shipped out to Malaya to fight the terrorists. Following that, I volunteered to join HMS *Newcastle* to fight in the Korean War. I travelled the world with the *Newcastle* and received three campaign medals: one for Malaya, one for Korea and a United Nations medal.

I came out of the Marines in 1955, and went back home to my family in Scotland. I tried to settle down to civilian life and didn't have much trouble finding a job – first as a 'rigger' for the Scottish Gas Board (setting up equipment for the engineers), then working with heavy machinery on a conveyor-type system for a local engineering company – but the routine was monotonous. I even tried going out on the trawlers, but it was no good; I just felt that after twelve years of service, and travelling half-way round the world, Scotland was small and uninteresting.

Years passed. I had spent a few of my leaves from the Marines in London and by 1964 I had begun to toy with the idea of going there to try my luck. One evening while I was chewing these thoughts over in my mind, I met a couple of my old pre-service-days friends and we all went out for a drink. They had somebody with them whom I had never met before and they introduced him to me as Ian. He was roughly five feet ten inches tall (taller than me), slim built with dark brown curly hair. One side of his face was scarred due to petrol blowing up in his face when he was in the army but this didn't stop women finding him attractive. He was a quiet-spoken man, but he looked tough and we got on well together. He could obviously handle himself. He told me he worked for Salvesons Shipping Company in Leith. He was a deckhand on a factory ship which went out to sea and waited for the smaller boats to bring in their catch of whales, which they gutted before fetching them back to the docks.

Ian and I had a lot in common: we were both batchelors and we had both been out with the fishing boats. We became pals and often went out drinking together. After some months had passed I told him that I had been thinking of leaving Scotland and going down to London. He told me that he had been thinking the very same thing. He, too, was bored with the slow pace and wondered whether maybe London would provide us with what we restlessly felt was lacking in our lives.

So we decided to leave Scotland. We made arrangements

to quit our jobs and told our respective families of our decision to start a new life in London. I was thirty-four years old. We said our goodbyes, promised to keep in touch and got the train to King's Cross Station.

We arrived full of high hopes and got off to a good start: on the first morning we found accommodation in a boarding house in York Road, in the heart of King's Cross. Dominated by two railway stations (King's Cross and St Pancras) the area was drab and rather depressing and populated in those days by the Irish and Scots who came to London in order to find work and better themselves. After Edinburgh, with its clean and elegant streets and gardens, and its historic castle teeming with tourists in the summer, King's Cross came as quite a blow.

Two weeks later we decided to move on to a slightly smarter part of town – Stoke Newington in North London. Before the war it had obviously been quite a smart area, consisting of large houses and wide tree-lined streets. By the '60s, however, it was well on the way to decline and was rapidly becoming cosmopolitan and full of bedsits. A sign saying 'Rooms Vacant' in a shop window led to us moving into two furnished rooms over a window cleaning company. In exchange for the room we worked as window cleaners. After a couple of months my landlord – who knew I could drive – offered me a job as a driving instructor.

Once we had started earning money we began frequenting the local card clubs. I was not only a good card player but also a lucky one, and with Ian backing my play we won enough money to supplement what we earned.

After we had been in London about four months one of our colleagues at work told us about a card club he knew in the East End. He often played there and we thought it worth a game or two. It was situated above some shops in Brick Lane. We could see this was a very old part of London, and it was also very shabby: the streets we narrow and full of cottage-style houses, some of which were hopelessly overcrowded and little more than slums. The people who lived there included a lot of immigrants (in the 1900s it had been a haven for Poles and Russians), and over the years it had become the heart of the dress- and coat-making industry. As we walked through the back streets I couldn't help thinking of Jack the Ripper who had stalked these same streets in the 1880s.

To reach the club we had to walk up a very dark and narrow staircase. It was one of several illegal gaming clubs in the East End at the time: it was privately owned and un-licensed and you had to pay to enter. A man stood at the door to warn players of a possible raid by police. Inside you were served with tea and snacks and the most popular games were rummy and kalooki (a form of rummy played with thirteen cards). As we entered, the men (many of whom seemed to be businessmen) all stopped playing and looked over to us. I saw them grab their money off the table and shove it in their pockets. Later on we were told that they thought we were 'the law' doing the rounds – apparently it was illegal to have money on the tables.

The manager came over to us. He looked extremely ner-vous but was very friendly. 'Can I help you?' he asked. 'I am sorry, but this is a private club and only members are per-mitted to play. Someone must sign you in, they are the rules.'

We didn't think it likely that anybody would sign us in, so we said 'OK', and made for the door. At that point, a short man in his fifties came over to us, smoking a cigar al-most as big as himself. 'I am his partner,' he said, pointing to the manager. 'Anything I can do for you?'

I told him that we had come down from Scotland a few months ago. 'And we don't know anybody in London.'

He told us the rules of the club and said: 'Now that you ᵉ here, would you both like some tea?' Before we had a chance to answer he shouted over to an old, Polish gent. 'Alphonse! Two teas over here.'

After talking to us for about fifteen minutes about the East End, he called the manager over and whispered something to him. Then he said: 'I will sign you both in. I am Billy Kray, what's your names?' He indicated a members' book, and we introduced ourselves and got signed in.

We had never heard the name Kray before. But after a few meetings with our new friend we heard from the other card players about the Kray twins. Apparently, they had an interest in the back-street gaming clubs and Billy looked after the firm's interest in the club in Brick Lane. Being a keen gambler, he tended, however, to gamble with the money from the club that should have gone to the twins. Billy was their uncle.

We went out most evenings with Billy after that, and found him to be a rather heavy drinker, but he was a very generous man and we regarded him as a good friend. He was noisy but likeable. We also went quite regularly to his club, having no other social life at that time. One evening at about eight o'clock, we met Billy as usual in the club.

'Do you fancy coming for a drink?' he asked. 'I would like you to meet my two nephews, Ronnie and Reggie.'

We looked at each other and said almost together, 'Why not?'

Had we known then what we were getting into, we might not have agreed quite so readily.

Ian couldn't drive, and I hadn't yet bought a car, so we all got into Billy's old banger and drove the couple of miles to Whitechapel, where Billy parked the car in a side street and we walked to the Grave Maurice, a pub in the High Street.

It was very dimly lit inside, and when I looked around I felt as though I had walked right onto a film set with Al Capone and his gang. There were small groups of men talking and drinking, some were standing at the bar, and some were seated at small tables. All appeared to be wearing £100 suits.

There was one man sitting at a table apart from all the others. He was dark-haired, smartly dressed in suit and tie and stockily built, and was talking very earnestly to a rather elderly looking man, whom I learned later was a lawyer from Fleet Street. Billy turned to us and, indicating the younger of the two men at the table, said: 'That dark young man is my nephew, Ronnie.'

As we looked across the bar, Ronnie peered up over his glasses. He looked serious and commanding. He glanced at us and at his uncle, then he called over to one of the men standing at the bar and told him to get Billy, Ian and myself a drink. We assumed, quite wrongly, that he had been expecting us.

Up to this point, the rest of the 'firm', as we were told to call them, had been standing and watching us in a not very welcoming way. I looked at one of them in particular, who had a scar down the right side of his face. I thought to myself, 'My God, he does look terrible.' I was to find out much later that he was paying the firm for protection for his club, and tonight was paying-in night for him.

After Ronnie offered us drinks the men relaxed. Then Reggie came over to us. We both knew who he was immediately because of his striking likeness to Ronnie, though he was slightly slimmer and better looking. He smiled and shook hands with us, and I felt that he was friendlier, more relaxed and more sociable than his brother. He was just as smartly dressed and he smoked just as heavily. Billy introduced us, calling us his friends.

At first, Reggie didn't seem too sure of us and we just exchanged small talk for a time. But after a while he seemed to loosen up and told Ian and me that he had quite a few friends from Glasgow (the penny didn't seem to drop that we were from Edinburgh). He pointed to a big, eighteen-stone man, who apparently always sat near the door of the pub. 'He's from Glasgow,' he said. 'He's a big fat slob who will not go on a diet.' Reggie said this jokingly because 'Big Pat' was a friendly guy and likeable.

Reggie then told us that he and his brother had interests in gaming clubs in both the East and West Ends of London. Pointing to his uncle he added: 'The one he is in belongs to us, he's an old drunken bastard but we look after him, right Billy?' Billy nodded, but made no reply. Reggie laughed as he told us that Billy frequently 'lost' some of the money from the club.

He then went on to explain to us that there had been quite a bit of bother in the past with a few Glasgow gangsters coming down to London, trying to muscle in on the firm's interests. 'They have never been back, they got well sorted out,' he said, leaving it to our imagination as to what 'sorted out' entailed.

I quickly said: 'The first club we have ever been in is the one where your uncle works.'

Reggie called for some more drinks, and then he said: 'See you later.' He turned away from us and started roaming around the bar, talking to various members of the firm. He had an unusual habit of putting his hands on people's shoulders while he was speaking to them. He obviously enjoyed feeling he could command and control other people.

Ian and I were left alone at the bar for a time. I looked around me and thought that it looked like some sort of secret society, with men coming into the pub and 'Big Pat' acknowledging them with a nod at the door. He certainly seemed to know them all. 'What do you think of this pub?' I asked.

'I am not sure I like the fucking atmosphere here,' he replied. 'Shall we have it away?'

Just then Ronnie called over a member of the firm and whispered something to him. The man went outside for a few minutes and when he came back into the bar he nodded to Ronnie, who then said his goodbyes to the elderly man he had been speaking to. (We learned later that it was a recognized routine for someone to go outside to check that there were no police around before an 'influential' person left the pub after a meeting with the firm.)

Ronnie got up from his table and came over to where Ian and I were still standing. He stared directly at us with penetrating eyes but he did not shake hands with us. Instead, he turned to his uncle. 'You are fucking drunk again,' he said, smiling sarcastically. Before Billy could answer Ronnie went on impatiently, 'Why didn't you tell me first, that you were bringing some people here tonight?'

Billy mumbled that we were good pals of his and that he thought it would be OK. He was clearly nervous in Ronnie's company.

Apparently Ronnie objected to anybody bringing strangers into his company without asking him first. He didn't forget that Billy had disobeyed the rules, because the following evening when we went to the card club, Billy told us that he must forfeit one month's wages out of what the twins were paying him to look after their interests in the club. Ronnie's temper was, we could tell, something to be reckoned with.

2

Joining the Firm

In the course of the next few weeks we were invited back to the pub for drinks, but we were always accompanied by Billy. We started getting on first-name terms with some of the firm and after the pub closed we were sometimes invited to go to various night spots in the West End. This was a new world to us – wining and dining and being paid for by the firm.

One evening Ian and I were at the club playing cards when the 'phone rang. The manager came over to where we were sitting and whispered to Ian: 'Ronnie Kray wants to see you both in the pub to have a few drinks and a chat. He wants you to go early, before the others come in. Don't take Billy, go on your own.'

Ian came round to my side of the table and repeated the message to me.

We played a few more games of cards, and when we got up and went to get our jackets the manager said: 'You had better get there early, because it puts Ronnie in a lousy mood if he is kept waiting.'

It was about 7.30 so we got over to the pub fast.

Ronnie was already there when we arrived, and 'Big Pat' was in his usual place by the door. As we walked into the bar Pat said: 'Ron is in the Gents; he will be with you in a minute.'

We both stood at the bar and Pat called to the barman, 'Give them a drink.'

Just then Ronnie came into the bar. 'Come over here boys,' he called, 'I want to have a chat with you.'

He sat down at the same table he had used on the night we had first seen him. This, we were told later, was the 'meeting table', and only he ever used it, the reason being that he could always see the door. He would look up every time the door opened so he always knew who was in the pub whenever he was there.

He was in a very good mood and I reckoned it was due to the fact that he had a good-looking boy of about nineteen sitting with him. It was common knowledge that he liked to have young men around him. The boy's name was David and Ronnie asked him if he would mind sitting at the bar while he had a chat with Ian and myself.

He asked exactly the same questions that his brother Reggie had asked the first time we met – about villains in Scotland and whether we knew any. (The only villains I knew about were the ones whose names appeared in the daily papers – but I didn't tell him that.) He also seemed interested to know what we did for a living.

'I work for an Irish family,' I told him. 'They have a place in Stoke Newington and I do a lot of driving for them. They are very good to us. Ian works at window cleaning and sometimes he does a bit of work on their cars for them. It suits us because they let us live there and they don't take any dig money from us.'

'That all sounds fucking boring,' Ronnie said. 'How would you both like to be with the firm?'

We stared at him in amazement. This was the last thing we had expected. After all, we had only known the brothers for a short time and up until now we had been very green about London's underworld – all it consisted of, as far as we knew, was illegal gaming clubs. We were just two young

10

workers getting our wages every week and living well.

'What would we be doing?' asked Ian.

'Just what you are doing now,' Ronnie replied. 'Drinking, and going with me wherever I have to go. I need men who can handle themselves. We have a lot of interests in clubs all over London, and sometimes we run into a bit of bother. You both look as though you can handle a bit of aggro.'

Things were starting to look interesting, so we agreed.

Just then Reggie came into the bar with his minder, who sat down at the door next to Pat. Reggie walked over to our table and Ronnie greeted him with: 'Where the fuck have you been? You were supposed to be here early to talk to these two,' indicating us.

'I had to see someone,' Reggie muttered. Then he called the barman to fetch some more drinks.

At the same time the door opened and two men walked into the pub. As they approached a table to sit down, Pat was on his feet making signs to the twins that the two men were the law. They sat not far from where we were sitting, and Reggie shouted for the barman to give them a drink. It didn't seem to worry them that every so often a couple of cops showed up in the various pubs that they used.

'They are from the nick in Lime Street,' Reggie said.

After we had all got our drinks, the two police officers shouted over: 'Cheers for the drink, Reg.'

Ronnie put his glass up to his lips and said, 'Cheers.' Then he muttered 'Pigs'. He called over to the young man who was still sitting at the bar on his own. 'Are you all right, David?' The boy nodded. With a weird smile on his face Ronnie said, 'What do you think of him?' We just smiled back but we made no comment.

The pub started filling up with more members of the firm and I noticed that the two cops had quietly left. The talk became general and then Ian and I were left alone while the

11

'firm' talked 'business'. Getting involved was a very slow process. At this stage we were just drinking with them.

It was about two weeks later that we met the twins' older brother, Charles. He was slightly taller than the twins and very smartly dressed when he came into the pub one evening with his wife. I noticed that she stayed at the far end of the bar, but Charlie came over to Ronnie and Reggie, who were again sitting at the meeting table. We were introduced to him by Reggie and he seemed to be a very friendly type of man. 'What are you drinking?' he asked, looking first at Ian and then at me. Charlie was not, as far as we could tell, involved in the firm. He told us he had his own business in the clothing trade.

It seemed to us as though everybody had plenty of money. Every night was a party night, and money kept coming out of pockets as though it were burning a hole in them. Just a few weeks ago Ian and myself had been working hard each week for what it seemed each and every one of them was spending on drink every night. No matter how hard we worked, our money was peanuts compared to what we saw the firm handling.

On one such night, Ronnie called Ian over and asked him to go to the Gents cloakroom with him. Everybody looked up from their drinks to see where they were going, because that was where he took someone for a private talk or argument, and any of the firm who were in the bar suddenly went quiet. Ian looked apprehensive as he left me and walked over to the Gents. I wondered if something had gone wrong. To my relief, a few minutes later they came out joking with each other.

Ian walked over to me and said: 'Ronnie has just given me a oner [£100]. He wants me to go get a new suit.

'What have you got to do for him?' I asked.

'Nothing! He just wants me to look a bit smart and be with him all the time.'

By this time we had left our previous jobs and had found ourselves furnished flats. Things had been easy up until now. We were getting money handed out regularly to us from Ronnie – he was more inclined to do that than Reggie. But we were doing nothing for it. But that £100 new suit was to cost Ian dearly. He had always been a very quiet person and had never ever got into any trouble. He had been a seaman like his uncles before him. Suddenly he was Ronnie Kray's right-hand man: from now on he had to accompany Ronnie whenever he went to important meetings. This arrangement was not popular with all of the firm. After all, he was still a stranger to most of them. Later I found out that Ronnie enjoyed playing one against the other and for this reason he was always changing his right-hand man as the mood took him.

Weeks passed and we were now members (by which I mean we were paid wages – which varied from week to week) of the best-known gang in London. Surprisingly perhaps the firm consisted of a hardcore of only about twenty men. There were many more on the fringe but they weren't really involved. People were led to believe that the firm could call on numerous men. I can tell you that wasn't really true.

One evening when I was in the club playing cards, Billy came over to me and said: 'Reggie wants to see you round at the house.'

'OK,' I said, and left straight away.

When I got to the house in Vallance Road, where the twins' parents lived, Reggie said, 'How would you like a new set of wheels? We have two cars that have just arrived at one of our car showrooms in Walthamstow.'

He arranged for another member of the firm to drive us over to the showroom and it was about 7.30 when we got there. A man came over to us, whom I took to be the manager. 'Hello, Reggie. What can I do for you?'

'I have been told that you have got two new cars from Canada,' Reggie answered.

'That's right,' the man replied, 'but they are sold. They are being picked up tomorrow.'

'Too fucking bad,' said Reggie. 'We want them and we want them now. It's about time you did us a favour, you have done nothing for us for a long time.'

The man was starting to look worried. 'They have cost me a lot of money,' he complained. 'If you take them, I will be out of pocket. Can't you take one of the cars that are on the front?'

'No,' snapped Reggie. 'I want the ones that I came over for.'

Reggie and the poor, scared-looking man went into the office. I could hear heated exchanges coming from it and Reggie came out in ten minutes with the two sets of car keys. It wasn't too long before I found out that the firm had nothing to do with the car showroom at all, they just collected protection money from the owner. It was one of the many places that their weekly income was coming from.

Then the three of us each drove a car back to Vallance Road. When Ronnie came out to have a look at them he said to me: 'You'd better keep the one you are driving, and take me and Ian around in it.'

I thought to myself: 'Great, a brand new car just to drive him about in.' But from that moment on I was like a doctor on call twenty-four hours a day, for although Ronnie had picked Ian as his right-hand man of the moment Ian could not drive.

We were now really in a gangsters' world, and if we had wanted to get out, we should have done so before, because we definitely had no chance now. We were two small cogs in a big wheel, and it soon got around the East End that Ronnie and Reggie had got themselves two hard men from Scotland to back them up. I sensed this immediately when

14

people's attitudes changed from being relaxed and friendly to being respectful because they knew I was now a member of the firm. I would rather they had just stayed friendly.

The two cars didn't last long. Reggie had only had his car about three days when he went up to the West End on a drinking spree. Coming back he wrapped it round a lamp-post. He and his two companions just got out and walked away. That was the end of one car. I knew it wouldn't be too long before he wanted the other car and, sure enough, he took the other car away from me and the same thing happened. After that, I decided to buy my own car.

Shortly after then money started to get tight. Suddenly it seemed as if the firm could no longer afford to throw it around as they usually did. In the normal way, members of the firm were sent to the gaming clubs to collect protection money the clubs paid on the understanding that they would not get trouble from outsiders.

One evening there was a meeting called in one of the pubs that we frequented. We were told that there were too many people on the firm doing nothing, or getting money and not declaring it to the rest of the firm. We decided that evening, amongst ourselves, that it was about time we looked up some of the small-time crooks who were doing well, see whether we could 'blag' (by which I mean take but not steal) some cash off them. These 'crooks' were men who made a living out of stealing and paid the firm to leave them alone.

Ronnie also told us that he would be setting up a big deal in the next few days but he said he wouldn't be telling us anything about it yet. 'If it does come off,' he said confidentially, 'we will be made.' Then he added: 'Be careful. I have heard that the "Old Bill" have been making enquiries about us.'

3

The Tangiers Affair

Most of us were loyal to the twins, mainly through fear of ending up on a marble slab, which is why we went on various assignments for them without question. One such assignment started for me only a couple of nights after we had the pep talk about getting more money in – Ronnie's 'big deal'.

One evening I was in the club as usual when the 'phone rang. The manager answered, and was only on it for about a minute. Then he put the receiver down and came over to me and whispered: 'Ronnie wants you round at the house right away.'

I played out my hand and got up from the table. 'Sorry, mates,' I said, 'but I've got to go.'

I put on my jacket, and I reckon they all must have known who had 'phoned. On my way out I told the manager: 'If Ian comes in, tell him to wait, I will be back later.'

When I got to Vallance Road, where Ronnie lived most of the time, he told me that we were going to the West End on some business. Had it been anyone but him, I would have asked what part of the West End and what for, but it was better to keep quiet until he was ready to tell me. So I drove to my flat and got into a suit, shirt and tie, and was back within the hour. I tooted the car horn and Ronnie came out of the house, immaculately dressed. As he got into the car he said: 'Make for Hyde Park.' Then, as we drove away, he said: 'We have a meeting with an American. His name is Alan, but we call him the Yank.'

It seemed that he had already been of great service to the firm in the past, by supplying them with guns. As we approached Hyde Park Corner Ronnie repeated what he had said to the firm a few days before about being on a good earner. I drove in silence thinking to myself: 'How many times have I heard that? He talks about these big deals and nothing materializes.'

He also told me to keep my mouth shut because none of the firm was to know about this meeting – which wasn't at all unusual. Then he told me to park the car round the back of the hotel. When we got out of the car we instinctively looked around us to make sure that we were not being followed by 'Old Bill'.

We walked into the foyer of the Hilton Hotel, which was teeming with activity, probably due to the fact there was a private boxing match on that evening. The Yank was already there waiting for us. He was a rather small man, aged about thirty-five, also smartly dressed. He led us up a short, wide staircase to the first floor and into a cocktail lounge, where he made for a table in a far corner which was very secluded. Before anything was said, he beckoned to the waiter and ordered drinks. Then he put forward the proposition.

The general idea was that he would go to Tangiers to have a meeting with three important black Africans from the Congo. They would part with a large sum of money, as a down payment to the firm to supply men and arms needed in order to get a high-ranking official freed from detention. The Yank then opened his briefcase and showed us various sketches of the different types of armoury they required, and he said very convincingly that he could pull off a big con and earn a lot of money. All he wanted to do was use the firm's name and take a cut of the down payment. 'You've got to hand it to him,' I thought. 'He is a real good talker.'

It seemed feasible enough and we were all for it, until he said that he would go to Tangiers in a few days' time on his own. He hadn't bargained for Ronnie's temper. Before he gave the Yank any answer, Ronnie called the waiter over to set up more drinks. Then he looked all around the bar, making sure that there were no police or photographers about. Then he exploded.

'Not fucking likely,' he said, staring right at the Yank, 'I will send someone with you from the firm.' His voice started to rise: 'How do we know that you won't use our good name to set them up, get the money and disappear?'

'Christ! You should know me by now,' the Yank replied. 'I have done a lot for you in the past, and we have always done all right.' He paused for a moment, then had a thought. 'What if I take someone with me? He could look after your interests. You can trust me on this one. There should be plenty in it for everybody.'

He suggested taking one of his own men with him.

Ronnie laughed sarcastically. 'You have got to be joking,' he said. 'He could go back to the States with you.'

The Yank didn't know what to say next. We just sat looking at each other and Ronnie kept looking round the bar. He beckoned the waiter over. 'Same again please.' I could see he was getting very uptight, and when he was in this frame of mind he was very difficult to talk to.

'I have a better idea,' he said suddenly. Before he told us what it was, he asked me if I had my passport handy.

'Yes,' I replied, 'it is at home.'

The Yank opened his mouth to say something.

'Just hang on a minute before you speak,' said Ronnie, 'this is my plan.' He pointed to me. 'He will be going with you.'

How the hell was I going to get out of going to Tangiers

with the Yank? He was a bit too devious for me, and if he did double-cross the firm, he would just disappear and I would be left to face the music. However, I knew that there was no way I could get out of it. The Yank had no option, either, but to agree to our terms. By this time he could see that he couldn't argue with Ronnie when his mind was made up. He was a gun exporter and he had a large office near to where MI5's offices are situated, and he was no fool.

However, it was obvious to me that he wasn't very satisfied with these arrangements when it was left to us to make our plans for the trip. While we did this, Ronnie went through his usual routine of ordering more drinks and looking round the cocktail lounge suspiciously over his glasses. It was about ten o'clock before our arrangements were all completed and we got up to leave.

When we were driving back to the East End, Ronnie said: 'Don't let that bastard out of your sight. It all sounds good but I am not one hundred per cent sure of him. Don't let anyone on the firm know you are going abroad. Don't even tell Ian, at the moment this is between us, the Yank and yourself.'

The firm had changed its meeting-place to another pub, The Lion in Tapp Street, Bethnal Green. We used to call it Marge's or the widow's pub, after the landlady whom we all got on well with. She was a lovely lady: a slim and tall redhead in her early fifties and always very well dressed. She was like a second mother to the twins. The pub was just round the corner from the house in Vallance Road. When we arrived we could see by the number of cars outside that the firm was there, even though it was just after closing time. This was nothing unusual. When we walked in, everybody looked at us and I thought to myself: 'I bet they have all been wondering where we have been.' We went straight upstairs without speaking to any of them and walked into one of the private rooms where we had meetings.

Reggie had followed us up. 'Well! How did you get on with him?'

It was common knowledge that Reggie did not care much for the Yank. He was always very suspicious of him, and was often heard to say that he thought he was working for the police.

The three of us talked about the meeting that had taken place that evening in the hotel when, out of the blue Ronnie started shouting at Reggie: 'Here's me trying to do a deal and get some money for the firm, but all you do is drink and criticize everything I try to do!'

The twins seemed to spend a lot of time arguing but I noticed it was normally Ronnie who took the lead. He took the lead in everything to do with the firm. He really did have the ability to command and once he had made up his mind to do something he was not to be deterred – unlike Reggie, who could normally be talked out of things.

Ronnie was silent for a minute, and I butted in: 'You'd better keep your voices down or you will have Marge coming up wondering what all the noise is about.'

As I spoke, there was a tap on the door. I opened it and Marge, the landlady, was standing there. She asked me if we would like any drinks sent up and told me that the men in the bar downstairs could hear us. She was a very nice woman and let us have the run of the pub allowing us to drink in a private room after hours.

Things had now quietened down and Reggie turned to me and asked if everything had gone off all right at the meeting.

'It all looks very interesting to me,' I commented. 'The Yank seems to know what he is talking about. Ronnie wants me to go to Tangiers too.'

Reggie told me to be very careful of the Yank. 'You will need some readies,' he said.

Ronnie got up off his seat and, putting his arm around my shoulder, said: 'Go and see Fat Wally at the club and tell him I said you needed expense money.'

I nodded in agreement and left them to talk while I went downstairs to have a quick drink before I left to see Fat Wally. Ian bought me a drink and everybody wanted to know what the shouting had been about upstairs. None of them would have dared to come up and interfere when there were arguments.

Time was getting on – it was about midnight. I whispered to Ian: 'I have got to go. I can't tell you anything, but I will see you in a few days' time.'

I shouted goodnight and walked out of the pub and drove to the club where Wally worked. As I drove the short distance, Reggie's last words to me were still ringing in my ears. 'Look after yourself in Tangiers and make sure the Yank doesn't drop you in it.'

For the next few days I stayed away from the firm, mainly because I didn't want to be questioned about where I was going. On the Wednesday morning I went to the Yank's house in Bayswater, where I had previously arranged to meet him. He lived in a big, imposing-looking house and he invited me in while he 'phoned for a taxi. He asked me how long I had been with the firm, but I was in no mood for his questions, remembering what Reggie had said. The taxi then arrived to take us straight to Heathrow Airport. On the way, he suggested that we get on the plane separately, and he said we should not communicate with each other until we got to Gibraltar. I thought to myself: 'What's all this cloak and dagger stuff in aid of?'

When we touched down at Gibraltar, we got a taxi to take us to a hotel facing the sea front. It was a very cheap and dingy-looking building with about forty bedrooms, but it was very busy. We settled in and I said: 'I'm going to have a drink. I will see you at breakfast.'

I had the evening to myself and as I roamed about my mind went back to the last time I was there – when I was in the Marines on a ship going to Korea. It was back in the fifties. We had docked at Gibraltar, and some of us had been given shore leave. A crowd of us went to a local night spot called the Trocodero. We had the usual serviceman's set-to with the local lads and I remembered the captain reading out a telegram that the mayor had sent to the ship. It said: 'If the Marines fight as well in Korea as they did in my town last night, the war will be over quickly.'

The next morning I woke up with a lousy headache after the night before on drink. We met for breakfast as planned and the Yank told me he had spent the evening in his room reading. After breakfast we made our way to the docks and boarded a ferry to Tangiers. When we arrived, we were met by a tall, thin man with a moustache. I was surprised to see him because I had not been told that we would be met by anybody. It seemed to me that the Yank knew him pretty well.

'Who's he?' I asked the Yank. 'And who does he work for?'

'He's all right,' he answered, 'he will be acting as my interpreter.'

The man took us to another part of the docks and asked us to wait at the quayside. He said he would be back soon and we watched him go on board a yacht which was moored there. After a while, he came off the yacht and we were asked to accompany him on board for a meeting with the same three African officials. By this stage I was feeling very unsure of them, and I was definitely not getting on the yacht. I thought to myself: 'If this is a con, I want my two feet on dry land. If they were to get suspicious while we were at sea, we'd have no chance.'

I said to the Yank: 'I don't think we should go on board. We were supposed to have the meeting at one of the hotels here.'

Thankfully, the Yank agreed to what I had just said. He

explained to the other man that we both thought it would be better to have the meeting at a hotel on the sea front. We made our way back to the hotel, not knowing whether or not they would agree to come. After a few minutes they arrived with the interpreter.

We all sat down in a corner of the bar and had a few drinks. One of the men asked us what the plan was to get the high-ranking person out of detention. I got a strong feeling that the Yank had already had talks with them before this meeting. Looking and listening to them, in my mind I felt that they were not strangers to each other.

The Yank then discussed with them how it could be arranged for some men to come from London and free this person. He made it sound very easy. I just sat back and observed what was being said. Then he picked up his briefcase, which was on the floor beside him, put it on the table and opened it. He took out some papers and handed them to one of the men.

'These are the type of guns that I can supply you with, they would be right for your purpose,' he said. 'We can also arrange for men to come over with them to help you with your cause. You can have them at your disposal any time. We have also got a helicopter standing by, and a pilot who is willing to do this mission for a substantial fee.'

Just then, one of the Africans said something in his own language to the interpreter, who turned to the Yank and said: 'They want to know what the down payment would be.'

After the figure of £75,000 was mentioned, the three Africans started talking among themselves in their own language.

'What about the twins?' one of them asked, 'will they be coming too?'

'Of course they will,' answered the Yank, 'assuming we can make a deal. The plan would not work without them.'

I did believe at this point that the Yank, who had done all the talking, really thought that they would part with the cash. Then one of the men said that there would be a pre-payment when they could see that the helicopter was in Gibraltar. Now I definitely knew that this was one of the many plans to con someone out of their money for we had no access to any helicopters.

The Yank said: 'That will be all right, I can arrange for it to be there whenever you like.'

They then asked for one of the twins to come on the next meeting and a date was made for two weeks later. I knew that the request for one of the twins to go on the next trip was impossible.

We all stood up and shook hands. The Yank and I left the hotel first and the interpreter followed. As we walked to the dock to get a hovercraft back to Gibraltar, he said to us: 'Well, it didn't work. I am sure they didn't believe that you could do all the things you said you could. I don't think you convinced them – I will have to get out of Tangiers now in case they find out I was working with you.'

We shook hands and said goodbye. The two of us made our way back to Gibraltar on the hovercraft.

I said to the Yank: 'I've got a feeling that you're pulling a con. Now I know why Ronnie wanted me here.'

He only made one comment: 'The twins will be very disappointed. But I can only tell them I tried.'

When we landed back in Gibraltar he said: 'I will see you back at the hotel. There are a few things I want to do before we catch the plane back to England.'

'All right,' I replied.

Then I made my way back to the hotel to pack my bag. My orders had been not to let him out of my sight – it could have been a double-cross but there was nothing I could do about it. I knew he couldn't leave the country without me; he would have been too scared of what would happen when he got back to London. I just hoped that Ronnie wouldn't find out.

We nearly missed the plane because the Yank was late getting back to the hotel, and when we got to the airport we went through the same routine of sitting apart and not communicating with each other. When we landed at Heathrow I made a 'phone call and just said: 'I'm back.'

We got a taxi to Bayswater and I asked him if he had a message for the twins. He just said he would be in touch. I then made my way back to Vallance Road. Some of the firm were there and I was taken upstairs.

'Well,' said Reggie. 'How did you get on? Did the Yank get any money?'

I had to tell him that nothing had been handed over and he was never out of my sight.

'Are you sure?' they said.

'Yes,' I replied. 'Nothing was handed over.'

Reggie started shouting. 'I told you that fucking Yank was no good. He has never done a good deal for us yet. I don't know why the fuck you trust him.'

It was now my turn to be nervous. If they ever found out that the Yank was on his own for a few hours, things would be very bad for me. But that was the end as far as I was concerned. The big con that never came off. Whether or not the Yank completed the con, we never found out.

4

The Cornell Shooting

One evening we were all summoned to a meeting in Marge's pub, The Lion. There were two bars there, one of which was frequented by local police. They would be on one side and we would be on the other. Ronnie always told Marge to give them a drink.

He had been drinking very heavily by the time we arrived. Ian and I were the first to walk in, and Ronnie got us a drink. A few seconds later Reggie walked in with two more members of the firm. He didn't look pleased, and went straight over to where Ronnie was standing by the bar.

'What do you want everybody here for?' he demanded.

'I am having a party, that's why,' Ronnie answered.

Nothing more was said. As I stood there I thought to myself: 'Christ, he has started early, it's only seven o'clock.'

By this time the pub was starting to fill up with people, who were mostly strangers to me. Ronnie went over to a couple of them and put his arm round their shoulders and whispered something to them. He then called out to the bar in general that he was going somewhere else for a drink, and he told them to stay where they were until he got back. We all looked at eacn other. Ronnie seemed drunk but it was unusual for him to act so aggressively so early in the evening.

'Who's got a car with them?' Ronnie called out. In fact,

only about three or four members knew how to drive.

When nobody answered he called out for Connie, another member of the firm – a married man who collected protection money. 'Ain't that bastard here yet?' he shouted. 'He's always late getting here when I want him – he's always poncing around with other bastards.'

Then he called out to me: 'Have you got your car parked outside?'

Very reluctantly I said, 'Yes'. There was no point my arguing with him. He was the Al Capone of London and he knew it. When he snapped his fingers everybody jumped.

While all this was going on, Reggie was still in the room upstairs but he came down into the bar and Ronnie went over to him and whispered something. He didn't say where he was going to anybody else in the pub, but he started walking to the door so I followed him to get the car.

He turned around at the door and shouted over to Ian, who was standing at the bar talking, 'You'd better come with me, you can keep me company.'

When we were settled in the car, I asked him where he wanted me to take him.

'Drive round to Vallance Road,' he answered.

When we got there, he got out of the car rather unsteadily. 'Wait here a minute,' he told us.

He went into the house and I said to Ian: 'He is in a fucking bad mood tonight. Where does he want us to go?'

'I don't know,' said Ian. 'You know he never tells anybody anything.'

Ronnie then came out of the house and got back into the car.

Before I started the engine I said: 'Where do you want me to take you?'

'Take me to the Blind Beggar,' he replied.

'Where's that?' I asked. It wasn't one of the pubs we normally frequented.

27

'Drive up to Whitechapel and turn left at the lights, then go up to the next set of lights and go straight over.'

When we got over the lights, he made me do a U-turn to go back again. Then he said: 'When you go over the lights stop at the bank on the corner.'

By doing this we had passed the pub once and now approached it from the opposite direction. I parked the car outside the bank, opposite the Blind Beggar pub.

I asked him what time he wanted me to pick him up, assuming that he was going to drink in that pub all evening.

'I want you to stay here!' he said aggressively. 'I shall only be a short time.'

I told him that I might have to pull away from there as it was still early evening and the traffic on the main road was very heavy. He scowled and kept complaining that nobody was loyal to him.

Just before he got out of the car, he handed a small object, which looked like a gun, to Ian. 'Keep that in your pocket,' he told him, 'just in case I need it.'

It wasn't at all unusual for him to hand over a gun to one of the firm to carry for him. He always said that one day there would be someone wanting to shoot him, and he wanted to be prepared. But Ian's face turned white. As far as I knew he had never held a gun before. As they walked across the road to the pub, I settled down in the car prepared for a long wait. I knew from experience that Ronnie's five minutes could be anything up to an hour. But this time I was wrong. Within five minutes they were out of the pub and walking back to the car. They both got in the back seat and I was told to take them to Marge's pub.

'That was a quick visit,' I thought to myself. As I was driving back the whole area of Whitechapel came alive with the sounds of police sirens blaring, and several police cars passed me at top speed. Ronnie leaned over from the back of the car and, with his hand on my shoulder, said, 'There must have been an accident.' He then started to laugh loudly.

I looked at them both in my mirror. Ian sat there like a stone. He was just staring out of the window and he did not speak a word. I felt at that moment that something was very wrong – they were both acting so strangely. Ian's face was as white as a sheet and Ronnie kept laughing and talking to himself, repeating over and over again: 'I have done it at last, I have done it!'

I was much too concerned about Ian to ask what had happened. So I kept quiet and just drove back to the pub. When I pulled up outside, we all got out of the car without a word. Ronnie rushed right into the pub and hurried upstairs to one of the rooms without speaking to anybody, and Ian and I walked over to the bar and had a couple of drinks.

I whispered to him:

'What happened back there?'

I could see he was in a state of shock. He either couldn't or wouldn't tell me what had happened in the Blind Beggar.

There must have been about thirty or forty people in our bar. I did not know half of them, but I noticed there were a couple of the local police in the other bar.

Before Reggie went upstairs he came over to where Ian and myself were standing. 'Where did you take him?' he asked. He was looking very worried.

'To the Blind Beggar,' I answered.

'Who was in there?' he asked.

'I don't know,' I replied. 'He told me to stay outside.'

Then he turned to Ian: 'What happened?'

Ian took him to one side and whispered something to him. I sensed that there was something wrong because Reggie looked flustered and ran upstairs.

While they were upstairs somebody came into the bar and shouted excitedly: 'There has been a shooting in Whitechapel Road!'

At that moment the people who had been summoned to

the pub for a party must have put two and two together, because they left the pub very discreetly and very quickly. By this time, after a couple of drinks, Ian had got a bit of colour back in his face and he told me that Ronnie had shot someone in the pub that evening.

'Did you shoot anybody?' I asked Ian.

'Of course I didn't,' he answered. 'I just fired the gun in the air, the one he gave me in the car.'

'Did he also have a gun?'

'Yes,' he replied.

'Do yourself a favour,' I told him, 'and go home. I will come over to your place later.'

He shook his head and said, 'I can't.'

Just then Reggie came downstairs. He looked around to see how many had left the bar. He could see that the pub had emptied and by the look on his face I could see that he wasn't pleased. He looked over to the other bar where the local police often drank, but they had gone. He told those of the firm who were still in the bar that Ronnie had shot Cornell. What happened to Cornell could have happened to anybody that night. I did not know the man personally, but others on the firm sometimes had drinks with him. Although he was based in the East End, he was a friend of the Richardson gang, rival villains from South London. About a couple of days earlier, Ronnie had been told that Cornell had been going round making snide remarks about him behind his back. 'A fat pouf' was one of the things he'd been calling him.

When Ronnie came down, he saw that his so-called friends, whom he had invited to a party, had all gone, but he was composed by now and fully in control again. I looked at him and thought, 'How could he be so calm after just shooting someone?'

He called over a man named Charlie and handed him a carrier-bag. 'Take that out and get rid of it. Don't come back here – just go straight home and we will be in touch.'

Charlie was out of the pub in a flash.

The remainder of the firm were told to go to a pub in the High Street in Stoke Newington called the Coach and Horses. This was another one of the firm's meeting-places. The pub was quite a large one and managed by a very nice friend of mine, whom we used to call Blondy Bill and who didn't like the idea of the firm using his place for meetings but, like everyone else, had no option; quite simply, he didn't want any trouble.

On our way over to the pub I said to Ian: 'Now you are in trouble. You have been with Ronnie and he has shot someone. He may even have killed him. What fucking chance have you got to get out of this? If he goes down, you will go down with him. If I was you I'd have it away – you know you will get no help from anybody.'

Ian made no comment. I think he was still too shocked at what had taken place.

When we arrived at the pub plans were already being put in motion to hide Ronnie. Nobody seemed to care about Ian. I could see he was out in the cold after being involved with a shooting done by somebody else. That night Ronnie went into hiding. He was taken to one of the many hide-outs that were available for any emergencies. Now Reggie was in charge.

The next meeting was in the house of a friend of the firm's in Walthamstow. It was over all the newspapers that there had been a shooting and by then most of the people who lived in the East End had guessed that Ronnie had shot Cornell. The firm were feeling very uneasy and talked amongst themselves about what had happened at the Blind Beggar. They thought it was only a matter of time before Ronnie got arrested. A few of them decided that they had had enough of this way of life and took the opportunity of getting out during all the commotion. With Reggie worrying about his

31

brother he never paid much attention to what every member of the firm was doing. I stayed put because of my concern for Ian.

The remaining members of the firm kept in touch with each other, and messages were carried backwards and forwards between the hide-out and the pub where we drank. One evening I was told to get hold of Ian as I was the only one who knew where he lived and had promised him I would tell no one. He lived with his girl-friend, but the twins were worried that if he was seen, he would be picked up by the police. This was something they had to avoid, for Ronnie's protection.

I drove over to his flat in North London and knocked on his door. It seemed a long time before anybody answered. I saw the curtain move and then the door was opened by Ian. I followed him up the stairs.

'You are wanted,' I said. 'I have got to take you over to Walthamstow because they want you to go away, out of London for a few days.'

Ian was a bit apprehensive. 'Wouldn't it be better if I stay where I am? You're the only one who knows where I live.'

I thought for a moment, then I suggested: 'If you don't want to go, I will go back and tell them that I can't find you.'

'No,' he replied, 'I had better come with you. They will see me all right.'

I looked at him. 'I think you had better be on your guard at all times. Just remember that you are an eyewitness against them and don't forget the old saying, "Blood is thicker than water". If you don't want to go I am quite prepared to drive you up to Scotland until Ronnie gets nicked.'

'Don't worry,' Ian replied. 'If I think that anything is going to happen, I will get out quick.'

We got in the car and I dropped him off outside the hide-out. As he got out of the car I said, 'Don't forget what I have told you.'

A few days passed and I heard nothing from Ian, so I went round to see his girl-friend. She was very upset and crying. 'Where's Ian? I haven't seen him for two days. He hasn't been back since he left a note saying he had gone somewhere with you.'

'Are you sure he hasn't been in touch?' I asked.

'Yes,' she answered, 'I wouldn't be here crying if I knew where he was.'

I tried to reassure her, then I left, saying I would be in touch. I drove over to the house in Vallance Road, where Reggie was holding his meetings.

'Where is Ian?' I asked him. 'I have just left his girlfriend. She is very worried and doesn't know where he is. She might go to the police. She loves him – we had better give her some kind of reassurance.'

Reggie nodded. 'You know we are trying to keep this as quiet as possible. We've managed to get them both out of the country for a few days.'

I got a feeling that he didn't completely trust me because he knew that Ian and I were close friends. He told me that he and Ronnie were on their way to the villa of an old-time gangster friend of theirs abroad. He added that Ian had left a message for his girl-friend and that he would be back in a few days' time.

Nothing went right while they were in hiding. The firm could not get their hands on any money – it seemed as though everybody had decided to stay away from the clubs, and money was tight. The managers just kept making excuses. We all kept away from Vallance Road, too, on orders from Reggie, although he did arrange for two of the lesser members of the firm to stay there – one of whom was a married man with a family, who objected to this, but he had no option but to go.

Somebody got in touch with Reggie through the East End grape-vine and told him that the barmaid from the Blind

Beggar could be a threat to Ronnie. He sent a message to the manager and asked him to meet him at another meeting place. The manager was very reluctant to meet him, but he was persuaded.

Reggie told him that he was sorry about what had happened in his pub. He asked if the barmaid was all right. The manager said: 'She will keep her mouth shut. The police interviewed her and she didn't tell them anything.'

Reggie looked relieved. 'Tell her to keep it that way. There will be a few quid sent round to her if she keeps to what she has already told the police.'

We waited, thinking that Ronnie would be arrested at any time, but nothing happened.

When Ronnie came back to the East End his position was even stronger and he really became 'the Godfather'. He started to make himself busy again, and called a meeting.

'Nothing has been done all the time I've been away,' he said, in true Al Capone style. 'The Cornell thing is finished, no bastard will do me for it now.'

However, they did find out later that there were two more witnesses to the shooting; they were two businessmen who called in at the pub on their way to play cards. They were warned off by the firm. Time passed and we all started to forget about the shooting. I felt, though, that the police must be building up a dossier on our activities because the local police were not around drinking in the pubs as much as before. Perhaps they had been told to keep a low profile to prevent the firm getting wise to the fact that the Regional Crime Squad was interested in them.

5

Nobby Scapegoat

Now that the Cornell shooting was forgotten, at least as far as the firm was concerned, and now that Ronnie was fully back in control, a lot of club owners who had not paid their dues when he was in hiding were now too scared to refuse. They realized that the firm was led by two of the most ruthless gangsters in London, who never ever forgot anybody who managed to break away.

One man who did break away, paid a price. He left the firm and started his own business quite successfully. We knew him as Nobby. He was always smartly dressed and smoked big cigars and he never came in contact with the firm unless he was sent for. He was a very good friend of 'big brother Charlie'.

The firm summoned him one evening. 'We need some readies,' he was told. 'We have been checking up on you and we know that you have been doing very well lately. We haven't bothered to ask you before, but now is the time to prove your friendship.'

He was another one of the many who were wary of the twins and it showed on his face. He told them that 'things were bad' and he had 'no cash to spare', but he had a warehouse full of different types of merchandise that would fetch quite a lot of money into the firm if it could arrange for transport to pick it up. The warehouse was in Kent.

I felt sorry for him. Here was a man who was handing over his stock and could do nothing about it. I knew that he would not dare to go to the police, even if he wanted to – he had a wife and children and he was scared of what might happen.

In the days that followed we had to find out if any of the small-time crooks that we could trust had a large van and wanted to earn some ready cash. That was easy, there was one man who always wanted to work for the firm. He was a loner, a bit of a drunk and an occasional drug-user. He was also a small-time crook who had served time in prison and he would be more than willing to do something in order to be one of the firm. His name was Jack McVitie but we all knew him as Jack the Hat. He got the name through always wearing a hat – he was never seen without one.

I was sent to a club in Dalston, North London, run by four brothers. 'Is Jack the Hat in tonight?' I asked when I went into the foyer.

One of the brothers said, 'Yes, he is fucking drunk as usual. He is downstairs.'

I made my way down to the basement bar to see him and told him that the twins wanted him to do a favour. 'It could be a good earner for you. If you are interested I will pick you up tomorrow night and take you to the pub and they will tell you what they want you to do.'

He agreed, and I said: 'I will pick you up at about six-thirty. Make sure you are sober.'

I picked him up at his house in Forest Road, East London, as arranged. I drove him to where he had to meet the firm and when we walked into the pub he got so excited that they had actually sent for him to do a job for them. He was asked if he could get a van and take it to Kent to pick up some merchandise from a warehouse.

'Yeah! Yeah! Of course I can,' he said eagerly. 'What's in it for me?'

'We will pay you £200 to pick it up. Here's fifty for expenses – you will get the rest when the job is done,' they told him. He was handed a piece of paper with the address of where he had to deliver the goods on it.

After all the talking was done and the arrangements made, he wanted to stay in our company, but nobody wanted him to because he was such a big mouth and most of us knew he couldn't care less whom he insulted. I managed to get him to leave with me and I dropped him off at one of his favourite haunts.

I went back and Ronnie called me over to one side. 'I don't trust him,' he said.

'Well, he is the only one you can get to do it on such short notice,' I replied.

'I know. That's why I want you to follow him in your car,' he said. 'Just to make sure he picks up and delivers.'

I went home early that night because Jack the Hat was going to leave at five in the morning. I followed him to Kent and sat in my car, unseen by Jack, until he loaded up. Then he made his way back and I drove a short distance behind him. But he knew my car and he must have got suspicious because he drove so fast he made sure he lost me in the traffic. I made my way back to London and went to the twins' house where I told them that I had lost him. Ronnie almost exploded. 'The bastard has double-crossed us. Who the fuck said we could trust him?'

I tried to calm him down. 'Maybe he has already gone to unload the van at the address you gave him.'

Ronnie turned to a couple of the firm who were there. 'Go round to this address,' he told them, handing them a slip of paper, 'and see whether he has delivered the goods. If he hasn't been there, don't come back until you find out where he is.'

After an hour passed they came back. 'He has been there,' they said, 'but some of the gear was missing.'

Much later we were told through the grape-vine that Jack had stopped off somewhere on the way back to London and sold some of the goods. He never came back for his £200.

Poor Jack the Hat. That was one bad mistake he should never have made. No one ever double-crossed the firm and got away with it. I think we all knew it would only be a matter of time before they did something about it. There was some talk of shooting him in the legs in case it got around how easy it was to double-cross the firm. But they soon stopped looking for Jack the Hat because they knew it wouldn't be too long before he turned up. He was such an idiot. He kept going round the clubs telling people that he had turned the Kray gang over and that they didn't do anything about it.

Soon after this the twins decided to throw a party one evening. It went on into the night and Reggie drank heavily. He got fed up with hearing his brother boasting about the murder of Cornell, that he now assumed he had got away with. All of a sudden Reggie changed the conversation. He said he thought that Nobby had arranged with Jack the Hat to sell some of the gear before it got delivered and was part of the double-cross. I knew that wasn't true – Nobby was not the kind of man to do anything like that. There were other things on Reggie's mind but he was looking for a scapegoat. Nobby was going to be it.

Ronnie was geeing him up: 'Get out and do something to someone,' he said, and Reggie was getting more and more intoxicated. It looked as if we were all in for a bad night. One or two of the firm who were married made excuses to go home. Ronnie kept telling them to stay. No one had the guts to leave when he didn't want them to. They all knew he could and would shoot any one of us just to prove that he was in charge.

By about four in the morning we were all just sitting there. Ian asked Ronnie if he could leave. 'I haven't seen my

38

bird for a few days,' he complained. 'Will you drive me home?' he asked me.

I jumped up off my chair – I was only too pleased to get out of the house – but Reggie looked up and interrupted.

'He'll drop you off,' he said, pointing to one of the firm. 'He's got to go home to his wife.'

My heart sank. 'Why can't I take him? I have got to go that way,' I said to Reggie.

'I may need you later,' he answered.

They both left and the relief was clear on their faces as they walked out of the door.

Reggie went into the hall. When he came back into the room he was holding a gun.

'What the hell are you going to do with that?' I asked, looking at him in amazement. He looked very agitated.

'That bastard keeps telling me that he is doing everything. I'll fucking show him.'

There was more screaming and crying from Reggie, which happened when he got in a rage. This was the sort of thing that we were all used to if they were fighting amongst themselves. Nobody would dare to interfere because they would turn on us if we did.

Reggie got on the 'phone and told the person who answered that he wanted to speak to Wally.

'Fetch your van over,' he told him, then he listened for a moment. 'I don't care if you're bloody busy, get someone else to look after the club.'

He banged the 'phone down on Fat Wally.

It took him about half an hour to get to the house. I opened the door.

'What does he want me for at this time of the morning?' he asked.

I felt so sorry for him – he was shaking like a leaf and he wasn't even a member of the firm.

'I don't know,' I answered. 'You had better ask him.'

Reggie asked Wally if he knew where Nobby lived. 'Yes, I think so,' he replied, not suspecting anything.

'I want you to drive me over there because I want to have a chat with him.'

Wally laughed nervously. 'What, at this time of the morning? He will be in bed. Can't he take you?' he asked, pointing to me. 'I am very busy in the club – I'm the only one looking after it.'

Reggie exploded. 'Who's fucking looking after it right now?' he screamed.

Wally tried to pacify him. 'I told the barman that I was only nipping out for half an hour and the barman said he couldn't handle it any longer than that.'

Ronnie sat through this tirade without saying a word, knowing full well what his brother had in mind.

It was now about five in the morning and I felt that something terrible was going to happen but I was powerless to do anything about it. Now that Wally was there, I said: 'I am going home to get some shut-eye,' but Reggie stopped me in my tracks.

'Hang on a minute,' he said. 'I want you to come with me.'

Knowing that he had the gun, I said, 'You don't need me to have a chat with Nobby. Anyway, it's time we all got some sleep.'

Reggie told Wally to go outside and start the van up. Then he turned to me. 'Go out with him,' he said. 'I will be out in a minute.'

When I got outside in the street I said to Wally: 'What on earth made you tell him where Nobby lived? If you had said that you didn't know his address we wouldn't be going over there now.'

'What does he want to speak to him about at this time of the morning?' asked Wally.

'You ask him,' I replied.

Reggie came out of the house wearing a strange smile. 'I will drive,' he said, so Wally moved over into the passenger seat. 'You just tell me how to get to the house.'

It was very quiet on the streets at that time in the morning, all we passed were some early risers and milk-floats. When we got to the part of London that Nobby lived in, Wally told Reggie to drive down a cul-de-sac and pointed to a block of flats. 'He lives on the first floor,' Wally pointed upwards. 'The one with the blue curtains.'

Reggie turned the van so it faced outwards towards the main road. As he got out of the van, Wally said: 'I'll wait for you here. I'm tired so I will have a kip, because I have been working all night.'

'You had better come with me,' said Reggie, 'you know what door it is.' He looked at me. 'You'd better come too.'

We all got out of the van and walked up the stairs to the first floor.

'Knock on the door,' he told Wally. 'He will come down and open the door if he hears your voice.'

It was then that Wally seemed to realize that he was being used, because he started to sweat. He knocked on the door very softly, but there was no answer. Reggie got impatient and banged hard on the door. After a few minutes a woman's voice called out: 'Who is it? Do you know what time it is?'

'It's Reggie, I want to speak to Nobby.'

She called back: 'He's in bed.'

'Tell him to get up,' Reggie said, 'it's important.'

Just then Nobby appeared shouting: 'I'm coming! I'm coming!'

He opened the door. 'What's wrong? What are you all doing here at this time in the morning? You could have 'phoned if you needed me for anything.'

Reggie's voice was quiet. 'There's nothing wrong, I just want to talk to you.'

We weren't invited in, and Reggie said: 'Tell your wife to go in the kitchen and make a cup of tea.'

The kitchen was situated near the front door so I followed her in. She whispered to me: 'What is he going to do? Is he going to harm my husband?'

I had only met Nobby's wife once before, and I thought that she was a very quiet and timid woman. Nobby never brought her to any of the parties that the firm had. I told her that Reggie was in a strange mood but I didn't think that he would harm his brother's best friend. I told her that I would go outside and see what was happening.

As I walked out of the kitchen to the front door I saw Reggie take the gun out of his pocket and point it at Nobby. Just a split second before he fired I pushed Nobby to the floor. He went down with a bang and his legs went up in the air. The bullet, which would probably have hit him in the chest, ended up in his foot.

Wally was so shocked by this unexpected turn of events, he disappeared down the stairs and into the van. I bent over Nobby and whispered: 'Stay where you are. I'll try to get him out.'

Just then his poor wife came running out of the kitchen. 'You bastard!' she screamed at Reggie. 'You have shot my husband!'

I shouted at Reggie that Nobby was badly hurt and he had better get out of there. I knew that my quick actions had saved Nobby's life that morning.

The shot must have been heard all over the building because lights were going on in the other flats. People were opening their doors and shutting them again. As we walked down the stairs we were seen by men who were leaving for work that day. Reggie was such a well-known face in the East End that he must have been recognized by somebody. Yet nobody 'phoned for the police. If they had, we would surely have been stopped. It was the same as the Cornell shooting – the East End wall of silence went up.

Reggie got into the back of the van and I got in next to Wally, who already had the engine running.

'You had better drive,' Reggie said. 'You know the way out of these flats.'

I could see that Wally was still very nervous: he was driving so fast, it was a miracle that he didn't get stopped for speeding. We could hear Reggie talking to himself but couldn't understand a word. Wally couldn't get back quick enough. We were both relieved when we pulled up at the house. It must have been about seven o'clock in the morning. Wally didn't want to go into the house.

'Can I go home now?' he asked.

To his relief Reggie said: 'Yes, go back to the club and keep your mouth shut!'

I thought to myself, poor Wally, now he was like me; involved with no way out.

Ronnie was in bed when we entered the house but he must have heard us drive up.

'Go and tell Ron that I have shot Nobby,' Reggie said to me.

At that moment Ronnie came into the room from his bedroom and heard what Reggie said.

'You fucking bastard!' he yelled. 'Now you have really got us into trouble!'

There was so much shouting going on between them that it is a wonder the police didn't come to see what the noise was all about. Ronnie then took charge, and got on the 'phone to big brother. Poor Charlie, the only time they called on him was when one of them was in trouble. I am sure he never knew half of what was going on.

'Get round here quick,' he told Charlie. There was a pause while Ronnie listened, then he said: 'Never mind what time it is,' and he hung up.

Charlie arrived shortly after and it seemed obvious to him

which one of them was in trouble by the look on Reggie's face.

'He has shot your mate, Nobby,' Ronnie said. 'That bastard has really done it now.'

Charlie looked shocked. 'What the fuck did you shoot him for? He is a friend of mine.' He was shouting now, 'For what reason?'

'I don't have to tell you why I shot him,' Reggie answered.

Charlie looked at the three of us: 'Some bastard had better tell me,' he said.

He was pacing the floor, so I decided to butt in. 'He's not badly hurt,' I told him. 'He only got hit in the foot,' but I shouldn't have opened my mouth because it started Reggie off.

'It should have been his head. He might be your friend, but he's not mine!' he screamed.

Charlie was very annoyed and said: 'I have known Nobby for a long time. He has always been very loyal to us. I don't care what you do – just leave my friends alone. We had better stop all this arguing and see if the Doc can go round and patch him up.'

'The Doc' had a practice in the East End and he always came out if he was needed.

'By now the police could be there,' Ronnie said.

I spoke up. 'There must have been a lot of people who saw Reggie coming away from the flat.'

Charlie looked straight at me. 'Who took him round to Nobby's place?'

I answered, pointing at Reggie. 'He 'phoned Wally at the club and ordered him to come and pick him up.'

'Did you go with him?' he asked me.

'Yes,' I replied, 'I had no option – he was determined to see Nobby last night, or should I say this morning? Anyway, I'll leave you to it. I'm going home – you know where to get in touch with me.'

I was never told whether the police went round to Nobby, but I assumed they would never have known enough to investigate the matter. Only one good thing came out of all this: the twins never did bother Nobby again.

6

Outside Connections
and Threats

There were some lighter moments in our lives. Parties were always popular with the firm – Reggie, in particular, loved a party. Often we would be in a pub, having a few pints accompanied by our wives and girl-friends, and somebody would shout: 'Let's have a party!'

Somebody else would reply: 'OK! Let's go to my place!'

If it wasn't someone's house it might be a private room in a club, like the Regency Club in Stoke Newington. We would have a whale of a time – eating, drinking and dancing till the small hours. No strangers were ever allowed upstairs at the club if we were having a get-together.

We never had parties in Vallance Road. The twins' parents lived there of course and I suppose that made things more complicated. I knew both of them quite well: the twins' mother, Violet, was always very welcoming to the firm if we went round there individually and used to lay on plenty of tea and sandwiches (the twins loved their mother's cooking). She was a lovely woman and I liked her very much – as did all the firm. She was discreet, too, and always left the room if we were discussing the firm's business. It was obvious that the twins thought the world of her. They got on less well with their father Charles, however. He was a dealer in second-hand gold and, although I always found him a sociable sort of fellow (like Reggie in that respect) and enjoyed the occasional pint with him, the twins didn't see eye to eye with him.

In the way that everyone has a good side to their personality, the twins had one to theirs. It was not unusual, for example, to see Ronnie handing a couple of quid to elderly East Enders who had approached him in the pub saying they were short of cash. If the twins were asked for a donation to charity, they would give freely. They were especially generous to the clubs helping young up-and-coming boxers. Both of them had been keen boxers in their teenage days. In fact, Reggie was still a keep-fit fanatic and used to run regularly round the park next to the house in Vallance Road.

The firm were on very friendly terms with some great stars of the day like Diana Dors and some of the visiting stars from America. Of course, they all knew that we were gangsters, but it seemed to fascinate them being in our company. There was nothing in it for them really, apart from the fact they could say they had been wined and dined by the firm. The twins had entertained the great Judy Garland many times. She really got the red-carpet treatment, being taken to the smartest night clubs in the West End. There was also a singer over here, singing in the popular night spots. His name was Billy Daniels. We all arranged to go to Luton where he was appearing. We had a fabulous night. After his act he came and joined us at our table for the rest of the evening – the twins had met him many times before. Lots of well-known celebrities kept on coming up to speak to him, and I had the pleasure of driving him back to the Astor club, a London night spot to see a midnight cabaret and have a late meal.

Then there was George Raft, the film star. The firm were all fascinated by him. He was not only good looking and immaculately dressed, he was also an excellent host. He used to like being taken around the East End pubs by the twins. He had business interests in a club in London and we went there on many occasions. I could see that Ronnie loved being in his company. He used to say with unaccustomed humour: 'He is only a gangster in his films. I am one for real!'

I was lucky enough to be asked to go to various London pubs with George Raft and Ronnie in the limousine driven by George Raft's chauffeur. Ronnie wanted to show him off. At times I felt like a film actor just walking around with him. These good times soon came to an end, though. He had to go to France, and we thought we would continue to see him when he came back. But unfortunately he was not allowed back into the country because the police believed he was involved with the Mafia. We heard much later that George had died in France. We were very sorry.

Once we were told that we would be going to a mansion house in Saffron Walden, in Essex, one week-end. It was a big place in the country surrounded by acres of woodland and Ronnie had some business to do there. I drove Ron and Ian and the others went in their own cars.

As we drove into the country Ronnie said: 'One day, I will have my own mansion down here and I will only have a few of the faithfuls with me.'

We made no comment – none was needed.

When we arrived, Jeff, the owner of the mansion was there to greet us. I recognized him immediately. He always came to London to see the firm in a white Mercedes and he was always treated like royalty. The other cars arrived just after us and we were all invited in for drinks. There was a lot of small talk, and later, as we walked around the grounds, I asked Ian: 'What does he really do for a living?'

'I don't know, he must have his finger in a lot of pies,' he answered.

Only Ronnie ever stayed at the house. The rest of us, including Reggie, were booked into a local hotel. Over the week-end we all noticed that we were being tailed by plainclothes police, but we didn't know whether they were locals or London police. It did make us cut the week-end short.

When we arrived back in the East End there was a message for Reggie at the pub where we had all arranged to meet. We didn't know what it was, but the following morning he phoned me at the card club and said: 'You will be taking me up West tonight. Be here at about seven o'clock.'

'OK,' I said. Then I went back to where Ian sat drinking tea with Billy. 'It looks like I won't see you tonight,' I said. 'I have got to go to the West End. At times I wish I didn't drive, I seem to always be on call.'

I picked Reggie up as planned and I got the same old story that I had heard many times before on other meetings, about how we were going to make plenty of money. This time we were going to meet two Canadians, who were already known to Reggie. They wanted to put a proposition to the firm. When we drove up to the hotel where the meeting was to take place, I did what I had done many times before, driving round, parking the car away from the hotel, and looking around to make sure we weren't being followed. Every time I went on one of these meetings I got the feeling that I was an extra on a film set making a gangster movie.

We made our way into the hotel and up to the cocktail bar. As we entered a man came over. He was wearing a white raincoat and a trilby hat. He shook hands with us. I asked him how long he had been waiting.

'Oh,' he answered, 'about half an hour.'

As we sat down I noticed a man sitting at the next table, close to us. 'Is he with you?' I asked, indicating the man.

'Yes,' said the man in the trilby, 'but he will stay where he is, he knows all about the business on hand.'

Reggie and I looked at each other and I knew that he was

thinking the same as me – that this was a set-up. I did not like the atmosphere one bit. It seemed strange that the other man did not want to sit at our table. I ordered drinks and the Canadian spoke about forged stamps and plates. After a while he took an envelope out of his raincoat pocket. 'This is what we have been talking about,' he said.

In the envelope were some samples of British saving stamps. He tried very hard to get one of us to handle them, but we wouldn't just in case it was a frame.

He then said: 'They are very good forgeries. You can have a quarter of a million pounds worth for as little as £25,000.'

'Why so cheap?' Reggie asked.

'We have so many of them, we want to move them quickly,' he answered.

Reggie then called the waiter over for more drinks and started the same routine as his brother had when I was with him discussing the Tangiers affair, staring round the bar suspiciously. It was at this point that we suspected that the Canadian had more than one other person with him. We felt that other eyes were on us. I could not make up my mind as to whether they were working for the police, or were Canadian villains. We carried on talking as if we were really interested in what they proposed, but Reggie then asked if he could make another meet, because he had to report back to the rest of the firm.

'It has got to be soon,' the Canadian said. 'We will only be here for a few more days.'

He asked Reggie for a 'phone number where he could get in touch with him.

'That's all right,' Reggie replied, 'we will be back in two days with our answer.'

The Canadian accepted that and we shook hands with him, but the other guy just looked up and nodded, and as we left the cocktail lounge I still had the feeling that we were being observed.

We made our way back to the car and as we drove back to the East End I said to Reggie: 'What are you going to do about this meeting?'

He replied, 'We'll see what Ronnie says.'

We went to the pub where Ronnie was drinking and told him about the meeting with the Canadian, but with all the mistrust that was being felt at this time, we were told to 'leave it out'. The Canadian proposition was just another big waste of time.

Now and then, stories filtered to us on the grape-vine that some Greek villains were moving into the territory that was our domain.

The firm stayed very much on its own territory – the East End and part of the West End – and expected other gangs to do the same. We knew, of course, that other gangs existed – there were, for example, others in East London as well as several Chinese and some South London gangs (of which the Richardsons were the best known). But we had no contact with them, if we could help it.

One night, soon after the Canadian episode, two men with swarthy complexions appeared in one of the pubs that the firm called their own. They walked over to the bar and asked for a drink. One member of the firm must have recognized them from somewhere because he went over to Ronnie and told him they were Greeks from the North London area.

Ronnie got it into his head that they were spying on the firm because suddenly, without any warning, he went straight over to them and started punching them. As usual, some of the firm joined in, and in no time they were a bloody mess. The poor bastards, they were so badly beaten up they had to be taken to the London hospital.

A few weeks later, another Greek came to the pub to meet the firm – but this one made an appointment first. He wanted to make a proposition.

'If I can say that I am working with the firm, I can command a fair amount of money from the Greek gaming clubs who know your reputation. The firm would get a good percentage out of it.' He looked round at us hopefully.

Ronnie took an immense liking to this man. He was tall, handsome, in his early thirties and very well dressed. We met him in our pub a few times, then Ian and I went to North London with him to visit some of the Greek-run clubs that he had spoken of. We got on very friendly terms with him, and were allowed into these clubs which normally only let in Greeks.

A few weeks later, Ian and I got a 'phone call at the card club where we still spent our days. Ronnie wanted to see us right away. We drove over to the house in Vallance Road and he greeted us with: 'The big Greek has died.' We were shocked. We found out that he had suddenly had a heart attack.

'I want you to go round and tell the firm that they have got to go to the funeral,' he said. 'I don't want his crowd to find out he didn't work for us.'

The funeral was like one you would see in a Mafia film. We were all dressed in dark suits. I can remember all the Greek club owners and friends of his on one side, and the East End gangsters like us on the other. But it didn't do the firm any good after that to try to muscle in on their territory. The Greek club owners doubled up their minders in all their gaming clubs, making sure that nobody from the East End moved in, and Ronnie told us to keep out of the clubs in the Greek area. 'We don't need any trouble from that direction,' were the words he used. We had met some nice Greek guys, but after that warning from Ronnie, we dropped them all.

The firm weren't so interested when it came to drug dealing. Rumour went round the firm that there was a factory in the country just outside London that was producing purple hearts. They were very powerful pills and in great demand in the West End of London. Some of us were told that if we wanted to get involved with this, we could make a fortune on the black market.

At one of the meetings that we had in the pub, we were asked what our thoughts were on the subject of selling these drugs to the peddlers in the West End. One or two of the firm were sceptical, they started talking among themselves. This was something new to them. We had all been so used in the past to getting our money from the gaming clubs. Now it seemed the twins wanted us to get involved in something very dangerous.

We had to be very careful when we criticized the twins because we didn't know whether we could trust each other. From experience, we all knew that things had a habit of getting back to them. If they discovered that anybody was talking out of turn there was trouble. I, for one, was not in favour of dealing with drugs.

Ian said: 'What about Jack the Hat? He knows everybody that handles dope in the West End. Why doesn't Reggie get him to show a few samples and take orders?'

'You had better put it to Ronnie,' someone said. 'We all know that Jack the Hat has already double-crossed the firm with that vanload of gear.'

'Maybe you're right,' said Ian. 'I don't think it would be such a good idea after all even to mention it to him.'

Unknown to us, the pills were eventually handed over to a man not connected with the firm. I only found this out some days later, when I was sitting in the lounge of the house in Vallance Road waiting for Ronnie to get dressed to go out. There was a knock at the door and I went to answer it. A man stood there who was a stranger to me. He asked if Ronnie was at home. Just as I was going to call him, he came down the stairs – he looked furious. 'What the fuck are you doing here?' he shouted. 'You had better come in.'

The man followed him into a different room. I shut the street door and went back into the lounge. I heard Ronnie screaming at him. He had brought a small parcel with him and Ronnie called me into the room where they were arguing.

'Get this bastard out of here quick,' he yelled, 'and make sure he puts that parcel down some bloody drain.'

The man started to sweat and shake. He said: 'But Ron, they are duds. I have had experts testing them – look for yourself.'

He opened a bag. It contained hundreds of round purple objects that looked like pills.

'I know nothing about them!' screamed Ronnie.

I gave the man the nod to move out, knowing the kind of mood Ronnie was in. I went outside with him and said: 'Where are you going to dump them?'

He said: 'I will get them off my plate quickly.'

I beckoned him to come round the corner with me where there was a drain. We opened it and I said: 'Put them down there, that way we'll know they are not on the streets.'

He dropped them down the drain and I felt relieved now they were destroyed. 'I think you had better keep out of sight until this thing has blown over. You've put Ronnie in a right bad mood,' I told him.

'OK and thanks,' he said.

I went back into the house where Ronnie was still getting ready. He turned to me and asked, 'Do you really think they were duds?'

I looked at him and replied: 'I know nothing about dope and I don't want to. If the law had followed that geezer here we would have been in a lot of trouble.'

Ronnie nodded and asked, 'Did you see him get rid of them?'

'Yes,' I replied. 'We put them down the drain!'

There was no more talk about purple hearts.

7

Jack the Hat's New Trick

We were changing our meeting-places so often now, it was decided that the firm should have a pub of its own. The one chosen was a very small one off the Bethnal Green Road in Cheshire Street, called The Carpenter's Arms. Situated in a narrow street, surrounded by very old houses and shops, it was very much like all the others: very dark inside, but with only one bar. The twins arranged for a very good friend of their father's to look after it. He was a man who had never been in any trouble, and he looked after the bar very well.

One evening I went round to see a man called Bill who, although he was a member of the firm, was only a very small cog. I told him that the firm was opening a bar of its own. I knew that he was not a well man and could not get a regular job.

'Why don't you go round and try to get the barman's job?' I asked him. 'At least you will get a few quid each week.'

He did as I suggested, and asked for the job. They felt sorry for him and he got it.

One night in the pub, the firm were discussing the various clubs that they were taking money from. They were constantly on the look out for more, it didn't matter whether they had any connection with the firm or not. There was one that we had heard of which had just opened

55

in Stoke Newington and a friend of the owner was drinking in our company – he had been on the firm before my time, way back in 1962. He was talking about this club and saying how well it was doing. Reggie seemed impressed. If it was making money, it might be prepared to pay for protection.

'Go and have a look at it tomorrow,' he told me, 'and take Ian with you.'

Ian and I looked at each other, but we made no comment because we already knew the club. We had been going there pretty regularly and we were both very good friends of Jim, the owner of the club. A few nights later, Reggie asked us if we had been to the new club and how we had got on.

'All right,' I replied, 'the man is only making a living, it's just a small place and not worth bothering about.'

Unknown to me, they sent a couple of the firm to have a look at the club because they didn't believe me. They reported back and said: 'It's a good club. The firm should get a few quid out of it every week.'

Reggie looked at me, his temper rising. 'I thought you said it was no fucking good.'

I told him that the man was a friend of mine and it would not be fair if they tried to blag him. I repeated that he was only making a living. I tried hard to convince him but it was a waste of time. Later on in the pub, while they were still talking about how they could get money from this new club, I thought to myself: 'Christ! Things must be getting bad again.'

Just then, Jim's friend came into the bar and walked over to where we were sitting.

'Did you get a result from the club I was telling you about?' he asked.

This started Reggie off again. 'You know him, go to the club and tell your friend we need £1,000. You can tell him that we will look after his place for him.'

This was something that the man did not expect. He

didn't mind getting Jim involved with the firm, but he didn't want any part of it himself. He had the look of a man who wished he had never opened his mouth. 'Can't you send someone else?' he asked. 'He will know that I have been talking to you about his club if I go and tell him that he has got to give me £1,000 for the firm.'

The twins started screaming and shouting at him, so I said, 'I will go with him.'

They weren't too happy about that because I knew Jim, but I would have said anything to get away from all that noise. They let me go, and when we got outside I said: 'You had no right to get the firm to try to blag money from Jim. You know as well as I do that he can't afford to pay any money for protection.'

He looked worried and said: 'I didn't expect it to go this far.'

We drove to the club in my car and when we walked in I felt like telling Jim about his so-called friend, who had discussed his business with the firm. But I had second thoughts because it would only have caused more bother for us all. However, he must have been tipped off by somebody because when we sat down he came over and offered us a drink. Then he said: 'I can let them have £200, that is all I've got. If that's all right, you can meet me at the Angel Bar tomorrow lunch-time.'

I said: 'Don't worry about it. I will see them in the morning and tell them that you haven't got that kind of money. I will try hard to talk them out of it.'

He was very grateful for any help, so we had another drink with him and left.

The next morning, when I got to the house I was greeted with: 'Well, did you get the grand?'

'The man hasn't got that kind of money,' I said, choosing my words carefully. 'He has put his last few quid into this little drinking club and besides, a lot of our friends use it, you can ask any of them and they will tell you the same.'

I carried on telling them that he was willing to help out and hand over £200. I wished I had not opened my mouth because Ronnie screamed at me: 'Who the fuck does he think he is, offering that kind of money? I spend that on a night out. Go back and tell him that we want what we asked for within the next three weeks.'

I hated the idea of going back and telling Jim that they wouldn't accept the £200. 'They want the full amount in the next few weeks,' I had to tell him.

'Can we leave it at that and I promise I will try and sort something out?' he said.

On one of the meeting nights, Jim's club was brought up again. 'How's that little club doing? Have you had a result yet?'

'It's all right,' I said, but I knew by the look on Ronnie's face that it wasn't the end of it. Just then the door opened and in walked Jack the Hat. I thought to myself, 'You have got to hand it to him. After double-crossing the firm a few weeks ago, in he walks as bold as brass as though nothing had happened.'

'Hello, chaps,' he said brightly, 'how are you all? I haven't seen you for a few weeks. Just thought I would drop in and let you know that I am still about.'

I have never seen so many surprised faces. He was so doped up he couldn't have cared less. He knew that the firm had been looking for him, but he came straight over to the table where we were sitting, rubbing his hands together. 'Sorry I nicked a bit of that gear,' he said happily, 'but I needed the money. I did it on my own and I will make up for it. If you want me to do anything for you, you know you can count on me.'

He was so good with his words he might have been practising before he came into the bar. If anybody deserved an Oscar for a performance, it was him. I thought he had guts

58

that night and we all included him in the drinks that evening. Bad as he was, I couldn't dislike him.

Reggie was getting quite drunk by now and out of the blue he stood up and, turning to Ronnie, said that he was going to the drinking club in North London. As usual, I had to drink with him there. Ronnie pointed to Jack the Hat and whispered to me: 'Take that drunken bastard with you, I don't want him left here with us.'

Jack jumped at the chance to go with us – he really thought that they had forgiven him for the double-cross earlier. 'Where are we going?' he asked.

'We are going to Jim's drinking club,' I said. 'See you there.'

Reggie and I got into my car and there was no conversation on the short drive over. Jack drove his own car. When we arrived at the club and walked in, Jim came over.

'Hello, Reggie, would you like a drink?' he asked.

Reggie looked around and said to me: 'I thought you said this place wasn't taking money.'

'It's not that good,' I answered, 'look around, it's half empty.'

Then Jack walked in. Poor Jim, neither he nor anybody else could have foreseen what was to happen in the next few minutes. The man who had originally told the firm about the club came up. 'Hello, Reg,' he said. 'What are you doing here? Would you like a drink?'

Reggie put his hand on his shoulder and, indicating Jim, said: 'Tell that bastard I want to speak to him.'

Jack the Hat got excited. 'What's the matter, what's the matter? Do you want me to do someone for you?' he shouted.

At that a few people who had been drinking at the bar left their drinks and went out quickly. Jim came over and said apologetically: 'I'm sorry that I couldn't help you with money, but as you can see there's not a lot of business here.

This is only a little sideline that I have.'

Suddenly, out of the blue, Jack started hitting and kicking him. Within a few seconds he was a terrible mess. I grabbed hold of Jack and dragged him out of the bar. When I got him outside, I yelled: 'Who the fuck told you to do that?'

'Nobody, I'm with Reg,' he said, trying to shrug me off.

I kept hold of him. 'He doesn't need you to fight for him. He only came here for a drink.'

Just then we heard a shot from inside the club. I ran back and Jim was lying on the floor, bleeding from the beating up he had just got from Jack and from the bullet that had entered his foot.

'If we tell you to pay up, we are not fooling around. This is just a warning,' said Reggie coldly.

Jim was being helped up by his so-called friend.

'You had better get him home,' I said.

As I spoke, Reggie handed the gun to Jack and told him to get rid of it right away. Then he ordered me to take him to one of the hide-outs that were used at various times when violence erupted. It had happened again. Reggie had shot someone when he was drunk and everybody else was involved by having to do all the dirty work – like disposing of the gun, calling the Doc, and taking Reggie to a hide-out. Twenty-four hours later it was all over the East End that someone had been shot. Everybody knew who had done it but the wall of silence went up again as usual. I thought that the police must surely be told by their informers what was going on, yet they were keeping a very low profile.

A few nights later, when we were all in the pub having a drink, in walked Jim's 'friend'.

'How's your mate?' I called out to him.

'He's all right now,' he answered. 'He says that he has had enough and he is closing down the drinking club.'

'It was all your fault what happened to him,' I cut in. His face reddened, but he carried on speaking.

'He doesn't want any more aggro, but he didn't go to the police, the Doc patched him up all right.'

Later that evening Reggie came into the pub and beckoned to me. I went over to him and he put his hand on my shoulder and whispered: 'Who did I give my gun to that night?'

'Christ,' I replied. 'Can't you remember? You gave it to Jack the Hat. You told him to get rid of it.'

Knowing what type of person Jack was, he got into a bit of a flap. 'You had better go over to his house,' he said, 'and ask him if he got rid of it.'

I had a couple of drinks with the boys and left the pub to drive over to Jack's house. When I got there he told me that he had not been out since the shooting. 'What happened the other night?' he asked. 'Why did Reggie shoot that geezer? I had already done what I was told to do and I gave him a good hiding – there was no need for Reggie to shoot him.'

'Nobody asked you to beat him up,' I said. 'It would never have got out of hand – Reggie only wanted to talk to him.'

Jack looked a bit confused. 'He's fucking mad, just like his brother,' he said.

'I wouldn't go around saying things like that if I were you,' I told him.

Jack knew how dangerous they were, but he said: 'I don't care about them, I can look after myself.'

Just then, his girl-friend came into the room with a cup of tea. She was a big girl and cared a lot about Jack. His past was no secret to her, but she stood by him and always said that one day he would change and settle down.

After she left the room, he said: 'What brought you over here anyway?'

'I came to find out what happened to the gun that you were supposed to get rid of – can you remember? Reggie gave it to you at the club.'

61

'Oh yes,' he said, calmly sipping his tea. 'I smashed it up and put it in the dust-cart. Tell him not to worry, it's gone for ever.'

Knowing him as I did, I somehow found it hard to believe that he had really got rid of the gun. He was far too unreliable – although he might have meant to do it at the time.

'I hear they are going to spring Frank Mitchell to do a job for them,' he said suddenly.

'Who's Mitchell?' I asked perplexedly.

'What!' he asked, looking equally puzzled. 'Don't tell me you don't know him? Everybody in London knows Big Frank.'

Jack went to a cabinet in the corner of the room and poured out a couple of drinks. I took one and he carried on talking. 'I've heard that they have been sending some of the firm down to Dartmoor Prison to see him. If they want me to go on a visit I will be glad to. I know a lot of the cons there.' He went on to boast that he had been inside with Mitchell for a time.

I thought, 'This is very interesting, he is telling me something I don't know.' He mentioned the names of one or two villains that he knew in Dartmoor. Because I was silent he looked at me and, realizing that I had not heard about this from the firm, he changed the subject. He went on to tell me that he and his girl-friend would like to settle down and have a family. I knew he was just dreaming – he couldn't go straight if he tried.

'You will have to keep off the dope first,' I told him.

'Yeah! Yeah! Of course I will,' he answered laughingly.

I looked at my watch and jumped to my feet. 'I have to go now, Jack. I will have to report back to them and reassure them that you have got rid of the gun.'

He laughed again, 'Yeah! Yeah! You tell them it is well out of the way.'

I called out goodbye to his girl-friend and let myself out.

When I got back to the pub, I went over and whispered to Reggie: 'It's all right. Jack has got rid of it.'

He looked relieved. 'Are you sure?' he asked.

'Yes, I don't think he would lie to me,' I told him. He seemed to accept this, but it was a known practice among some members of the firm to tell the twins only what they thought would please them, so as to avoid trouble.

8

'The Mad Axeman' on the Loose

One evening, a few of the firm were having a drink. Everything was quiet in the East End. There had been no arrests for the shootings and no questions asked, and a few of us, discussing it among ourselves, could not understand it. Could the law not touch the twins? Or, as some of us were thinking, were they playing a waiting game? It was now 1966 and I had been with the firm for two years.

In the passing weeks, members of the firm were sent to various prisons all over the country to see certain friends of the twins and find out if they needed anything. There was one man in particular that they gave a lot of attention to. His name was Frank Mitchell, otherwise known to the Underworld as 'The Mad Axeman'. This was the man Jack the Hat had mentioned to me – Big Frank. Frank Mitchell had the reputation for being a violent man and difficult to control. He had spent half his life in prison for robbery with violence. As he admitted to me later, he had also attempted to murder another prisoner. He was called 'The Mad Axeman' because once, when he had escaped from prison, he picked up an axe from an old couple's yard and had supposedly threatened the couple with it. Now he was in his early thirties and being held in Dartmoor Prison.

It was around this time that Ronnie moved for a brief spell into a flat in Finchley, North London. One evening I was at the club playing cards when I received a 'phone call from Ronnie, asking me to go to see him at the flat. As usual, I had to leave in the middle of a game – and that always met with great disapproval from the other players. However, I had got to go. It took me about one and a half hours to get there because it was unfamiliar territory to me and I had to make sure I was not being followed. I drove off the main road into a cul-de-sac where the block of flats was.

I knocked at the door and it was opened by a man that I had never seen before. I hesitated, thinking I was at the wrong flat. But he was expecting me because he said: 'Ronnie is waiting for you.'

I followed him into a lounge where Ronnie was sitting. He stood up and said to me: 'This is Teddy. He is a very old friend of mine.'

Teddy was tall, with dark curly hair; he was about thirty years old and very smartly dressed. By the way they laughed and joked, it appeared they had a lot in common. Teddy also liked to be around young men.

'Is your car in good running order?' Ronnie asked me. 'Do you think it would go on a long journey without breaking down?'

I felt a nagging suspicion about this question. 'I wouldn't want to drive it too far, it is only an 1100,' I told him.

'Pat and Teddy are going down to Dartmoor Prison to see an old friend of mine,' he said. 'Would you mind driving them down in your car?'

'It's only a small car,' I said, thinking about the size of Big Pat, 'and I don't think it would take the distance.'

Luckily this was almost the first time he had asked me to do something, so I took advantage of his good mood, which was so rare, and declined to go. He was quite cheerful about my refusal, which surprised me, and I couldn't believe my good fortune. I was in no mood for driving people backwards and forwards to Dartmoor Prison.

Unknown to the firm, though Jack had hinted at it, Teddy (a very old friend of Ronnie's but not a member of the firm) and another man had already been down to Dartmoor to see Frank Mitchell. It was easy to visit him because he was with an outside party, which meant that he was a trusted prisoner – he was out on the moors working instead of being locked up all day in his cell. He could even go to the local pub for a drink as long as he was back at the right time to be counted.

A few days later Fat Wally came to the club to see me one afternoon. He was looking worried. 'Teddy has just been on the 'phone to me,' he said, 'and he has had a message from Ronnie that I have to give him my car for a few days. Have you got any idea what he wants it for? You know that I can't do without my car – how will I get around?'

I laughed and said: 'Tell him what I told him, that your car is not a very good runner.'

Wally looked doubtful and said: 'You know what he is like, he will do his nut if I tell him that and he finds out I am lying. Can you do me a favour and tell him that for me?'

Wally was understandably scared because the last time they wanted his car he had got involved in Nobby's shootings. I felt a bit sorry for him but I had to say that there was no way I could get in touch with Ronnie unless he wanted me to. Wally then left and went back to his club. Later, Bill, barman at the pub, came to see me.

'I thought you were working in the pub,' I said, surprised at his visit.

'Ronnie has taken me out of it,' he replied. 'He wants me to go to a house in Barking, in Essex, and stay there with someone called Lennie. He sent a message telling me that a friend of his will be coming to stay for a few days and he wants me to keep him company at this Len's place. It's the same old fucking thing, they have put me on a promise for doing this favour.'

I laughed to myself – I had also heard those promises – but he kept on grumbling. 'You know what their promises are like. I thought I might have carried on working in the pub – at least I was getting my wages. I am fed up with this kind of life – they only want to use people.'

Bill was really getting into the swing of it now. 'It's coming up to Christmas,' he complained, 'and I have a lot of things to do. It's all right for them in their gold watches and new suits, I can't remember the last time I could afford a suit.'

I listened to this, and then I had an idea. 'Why don't you ask them for a new suit?' I said, knowing that they had given Ian money to buy one.

He just looked at me and grinned. I felt sorry for him – he was always being used. He sat at the table with his hand on his forehead. 'I suppose I will have to do it for them,' he sighed. Then his face brightened as if he had had an idea: 'Why don't you tell them that you will take my place?'

I nearly choked on my cup of tea. 'How the hell can I go and say that when I am not supposed to know what they want you to do? You shouldn't even have told me about it. You should know better than to tell anybody their plans. Anyway, I will be going to Scotland in a few days' time for Christmas and New Year.'

Bill started again: 'This is definitely the last favour I am doing for them. I don't care – I am getting out before things get any worse.'

'Do you really think you will be able to walk away from all this and live to tell the tale?' I asked, surprised at the way he was talking, but Bill knew that what he said to me wouldn't be repeated.

On one of his visits Frank Mitchell told Teddy that he didn't have a release date. Because of this he was getting very depressed. Teddy told the twins about this and they sent a message back to Frank saying that they would arrange for his escape so that he could write to the papers and state his case. Then, with the newspapers' help, when he got a release date he would go back to prison and serve his sentence.

This was quite a challenge to the twins and, if successful, would prove that they could do anything and get away with it. Presumably everything went according to plan because I was summoned to the flat in Finchley by Ronnie. When I got there, he said: 'I want you to go over to a place in Barking to stay with a friend of mine. Bill is there now and I want you to give him a break so that his wife doesn't get worried.'

'I can't,' I answered. 'I told you a few weeks ago that I was going up to see my family in Scotland for Christmas and the New Year.'

'You will just have to put it off,' he replied.

He told me that he had arranged for Frank Mitchell's escape. 'Teddy will go to Barking with you,' he said. 'He is going to write some letters for Frank to send to the newspapers. He will write and say Frank wants them to know that he is one of the few prisoners who have not got a release date. And he thinks that if he brings it to the notice of the authorities via the newspapers, they may do something about it.'

'It must be terrible,' I said, 'for a man to be locked up without knowing when he will be freed.'

Ronnie nodded. 'He will go back inside after the letters have been printed.' Then he changed the subject. 'I don't want you to take your car to Barking, instead I want you to meet Teddy at Whitechapel station at six o'clock tonight and he will take you over there. Don't tell anybody else where you are going.'

I nodded and left. On my way back to the East End I noticed that the police were out in full force. I presumed that they had been told about Mitchell's escape and would be visiting their informants to see if any of them knew where he was holed up. I knew that their efforts would be fruitless. Hardly anybody knew about Mitchell's escape – and if they did they wouldn't dare inform on the firm.

I met Teddy as arranged and it was the usual cloak-and-dagger stuff, making sure we were not being followed. The flat in Barking was on the ground floor and looked very nice from the outside. When we got to the front door, Teddy gave a special pre-arranged knock. The door was opened immediately by a grey-haired thin man of about fifty-five who was wearing glasses. Teddy had already met him.

'Hello, Len! Everything all right?' He handed him an envelope. 'Ronnie sent this over to you to get some food with. He said that he would pay you off later.'

Up until now, we had been standing in the small hall-way, but as we followed Lennie into the living-room I thought, 'I have heard that one before from a few other people.'

As Lennie and I were introduced, I glanced round and saw Bill sitting at the dining-room table. He looked very surprised to see me there as I had told him I was going up to Scotland. He nodded to Teddy and told him that Frank was in the bedroom. Teddy went to the bedroom door and tapped on it. He called out: 'It's only me, Frank.'

After a couple of seconds, Frank came out. I had never seen him before and was surprised to see such a giant of a man, dressed only in a pair of jeans, who could easily have been taken for Charles Atlas.

Teddy introduced me to Frank and told him: 'He will be staying here to keep you company for a few days. Bill can't stay here all the time – he has a wife and children to look after.'

When we shook hands, it was as if mine was held in a vice, he was so strong. He towered over me. He must have been at least six feet three inches tall and extremely broad, with what I considered were very good looks.

'Have you got any writing paper and envelopes, Len?' Teddy asked. 'We want to start on Frank's letters as soon as possible.'

Lennie had to think for a moment, then he went into the kitchen and we heard him searching through the drawers. He came back into the living-room waving the paper and envelopes. 'That's all I've got,' he said, handing them to Teddy. 'Will that be enough?'

Teddy took them and said: 'That's fine. Will you make a pot of tea before we get started?'

Bill stood up. 'You don't really need me here any more, I think I will have it away,' he said, as Frank and Teddy sat at the table and prepared to write the letters to the papers.

As Bill walked into the bedroom to pick up his few things, I followed him. He was moaning like hell: 'I have been here all fucking night – my wife doesn't even know where I am – she must be getting frantic. They wouldn't even let me 'phone her.' He was rushing around the room wiping everything clean with his handkerchief. I looked at him in amazement, wondering what had gotten into him.

'What the hell are you doing now?' I asked. He carried on with his antics of cleaning the room and answered: 'If Frank gets nicked in this flat, I don't want my fingerprints all over the place.'

'Well,' I said, 'I was told by Teddy that he will give himself up as soon as he gets his release date. That is the only reason they have arranged all this.'

'Huh!' said Bill in a dry voice. 'Just you wait until you have been with him for twenty-four hours, then you will see for yourself whether he has got any intention of giving himself up.'

His words worried me. I hoped it wasn't going to be as difficult as Bill had just indicated getting Frank back to Dartmoor.

Before he left, Bill went into the living-room to see Frank. 'Bye for now, and good luck to you,' he said.

Frank looked up from the table and said to Bill: 'Will I see you again? Are you coming back?'

Bill smiled at him, 'You might – but good luck anyway.'

He said goodbye to us and Len went to the door first to check there was nobody around outside on the stairs. He turned back to Bill and called: 'It's all clear – you can go.'

Teddy had started writing samples of letters for Frank to copy. Frank, being rather illiterate, wrote about twenty copies which were not usable and were subsequently thrown away. Eventually, two hours later and after going through several writing pads – which Lennie was sent out to purchase – he finally got a couple completed, to Teddy's great relief: 'All I am asking for,' he wrote, 'is a date of release. From a young age I have not been free. I am not a murderer, nor a danger to the general public.'

'Do you think this will do?' asked Frank anxiously. 'I don't mind going back to prison, if only they would give me a release date.'

I genuinely think that he would not have minded going back, even if he did have to spend another twenty years behind bars, provided that the authorities could give him some hope that he would eventually be released. Teddy got up from the table and stretched. 'I have got to go now,' he said yawning. 'I think I have been here long enough. After Ronnie has read the letter, I will take them somewhere else, out of this manor, and post them to the *Mirror* and *The Times*.'

Lennie then did the same for Teddy as he had done for Bill. He went outside and made sure the coast was clear – after all, we were harbouring an escaped prisoner from a top-security prison!

The street door was opened by Lennie, so Teddy whispered to Frank: 'I will be seeing you Frank. Good luck.'

The door closed and Teddy was gone, leaving just Lennie and I to look after Frank. Lennie went out into the kitchen to cook us a meal and Frank said excitedly: 'Do you think they will print the letters in the newspapers?'

'Of course they will,' I told him encouragingly. 'I wouldn't be surprised if you don't see your face on TV. After all, it is not often that someone escapes from Dartmoor and gets clean away.'

He started to tell me how easy everything had been with the escape. 'I always knew in advance what days I would be working on the moors. Some of the prison officers let me wander off to feed the wild horses. As long as I was back for counting they didn't bother me. The escape was planned weeks ago.'

He was so grateful to the twins for arranging his escape from prison that he kept telling me that Ronnie was his best pal.

Just then Lennie interrupted as he came into the room with our meals. Frank's meal, in particular, must have contained at least one pound of steak. I looked at his plate stacked high with food and I thought: 'Christ, where does he put it?' The evening passed with us watching Frank doing his exercises. He was a fanatic about building up his body and keeping fit.

9

The Mitchell Episode

The following morning, Bill came into the flat while Frank was bathing and Lennie was out shopping. He came into the living-room and whispered: 'How did you get on last night with Frank?'

'All right,' I whispered back, 'but he keeps telling me that he wants a girl.'

'What girl is going to come here?' asked Bill, looking annoyed. 'It's all over the papers who he is. It's been three days since he was brought here and I am not going to be doing this too long. What chance would he have if the police were tipped off that he was here? No chance, and we would be left holding the bag. We would get no fucking help from anybody.'

I told him to keep his voice down but he carried on: 'It's all right for them [meaning the twins], they have the money to buy their way out of this. I have a family to think of. My wife is scared to be on her own at night. I want to see Ronnie – do you know where he is?'

'Yes, I do,' I replied, 'but do you really think they will let you out now?'

As we were speaking, Frank came out of the bathroom. He was wearing a new shirt that Len had bought him earlier.

'Hello, Frank,' Bill said, smiling at him. 'You look good.'

'I will be seeing Ron later,' I said to Bill. 'I am going to ask him if he will get someone else to take my place here because, as you know, I am supposed to be going to Scotland for Christmas and the New Year. I might as well leave now.'

They said 'Cheerio', and I left them and went over to Finchley. Ronnie answered the door and let me in. He was alone, sitting drinking and listening to records. As I followed him into the lounge, he said over his shoulder: 'You have just missed Teddy. He has gone back over to Barking to help Frank write to a few more newspapers. How is he getting on there? Is he causing any bother?'

He sounded genuinely interested.

'At the moment he's all right,' I said, 'but he wants a bird, and if you don't get him one while he's in this frame of mind, he will go out and get one himself, and we won't be able to stop him.'

Ronnie's whole attitude changed and he jumped up, shouting, 'That ungrateful bastard! Who does he think he is? He will drop us all in it if he starts that bloody caper – I have my own troubles.'

He sat down again and lit a cigarette and told me to pour the drinks that were on the coffee table in front of him. He stared over his glasses broodingly, thinking. It looked as if he was in another world – there was nothing said for about five minutes, but it seemed like an hour. Then he spoke.

'Go back and tell him not to worry, we will arrange for a girl. Tell him to be patient and everything will work out all right for him.'

His attitude had completely changed again. 'Who's looking after him at this moment?' he asked.

'Bill's there just now, but he is not happy with the situation,' I replied. 'I am not due back there until tomorrow. Is there any chance of you getting someone else to take my place? It's a bit nerve-racking being with him. All he does is exercise, and he keeps diving into the bathroom to clean his teeth – he's going to run out of toothbrushes and paste at this rate – I have never known such a clean-teeth fanatic.'

Ronnie gave one of his strange laughs. 'I don't want too many of the firm to know that we have had anything to do with Mitchell's escape, you know what they are for talking in the pubs.' His voice got serious. 'I've heard a whisper that the law has been making enquiries around the East End about the escape and I don't think it is just local coppers. There's one called "Nipper Read" who has been after me for years.'

Ronnie carried on talking. 'Tell Bill it won't be too long before we move Frank to the country, where he will stay on a farm. It's not easy for me being cooped up here, but I am busy trying to make all the arrangements. You will still be able to go to Scotland for your New Year.'

Reggie came in and Ronnie told him: 'He's going back over to the flat in Barking. I have given him a few messages for Mitchell.'

I sat down again, I wanted to hear what Reggie was going to say to Ronnie, but he dismissed me. 'You can go now, we will be in touch.'

When I got back to Barking I was let in by Len, who looked surprised to see me. 'What are you doing here?' he asked. 'You are not supposed to come back here until tomorrow.'

I didn't answer him, I just walked into the living-room. Teddy was already there, sitting at the table with Frank writing more letters. I turned to Bill, who was sitting reading a paper. I told him that he could go home to his wife if he liked, now that I was there – I would stay in his place.

'Did you ask them about a bird?' asked Frank.

'Yes, they are going to arrange it as soon as they can,' I replied, hoping it would be soon.

By this time, Teddy had finished writing the letters. He and Bill left together, leaving Lennie and me with Frank – who was getting very excited at the prospect of a girl coming to stay with him. He kept on walking up and down between the living-room and the street door doing breathing exercises and flexing his muscles. One would have thought he was going on his first date.

It was now about 10.30 in the evening. 'Where is she?' he asked, getting very impatient. 'Are you sure they are sending a bird out? I haven't had a bird for years and I have a lot of time to make up for.'

I couldn't help laughing – he was just like a kid in his excitement.

At about twelve o'clock the 'phone rang twice, then stopped. This was a pre-arranged signal with Len for answering the 'phone. We waited for a few seconds, then the 'phone rang again, as expected. Len picked it up, listened for a moment, then put it down. He spoke to Frank in an excited voice: 'The girl will be coming over here at about two in the morning.'

Frank got up off his chair and said: 'I am going to have a bath and clean my teeth.'

I felt sorry for Lennie. He was rather a nervous person who had his own little business – a second-hand bookstall in the East End. He had never been involved with the firm before though he was a friend of Reggie's. This was his flat and he didn't even have a bed to sleep in. Frank had his bedroom and Bill and I took turns to use the small one – which left Lennie with the settee. He had to be accessible to answer the street door.

Frank came out of the bathroom, and Lennie poured us out a drink to celebrate. To pass the time while we were waiting, we each tried to describe what she would look like. It was funny at the time, because Frank said: 'I hope she will be blonde and tall like me. I have never had sex with a blonde. The last time I had sex with a bird was about a year ago when I was working on an outside party and I met a bird from the local pub. She made arrangements to see me

The twins in their teens. Reggie, pictured on the right, could have had a great future in boxing. Had he stuck with it, he might have enjoyed a different kind of celebrity from the one he enjoys today *(Popperfoto)*

Reggie gives Ronnie a light as they have tea in the family's flat in Old Street in London's East End, where they moved from Vallance Road *(Popperfoto)*

Above left: The Blind Beggar pub in Whitechapel Road, East London. This was the scene of the George Cornell shooting *(Popperfoto) Above right:* The Regency Club in Stoke Newington, North London – one of the firm's favourite haunts. They would often wine and dine here *(Popperfoto) Below:* A typical street in London's East End. Brick Lane, where Ian and I met Billy Kray at a card club, looked much like this in the 1960s *(London Borough of Tower Hamlets)*

Family group outside the Krays' home in Vallance Road, Whitechapel. Ronnie shakes hands with grandfather Jimmy, while Reggie puts his arm round Violet, the twins' adored mother *(Popperfoto)*

Reggie's wedding day, 1965. He and his brother Charles (far left) look on smiling as Ronnie kisses the bride, Frances Shea. A year later she was to commit suicide *(Photo Source)*

'The Mad Axeman', Frank Mitchell. Despite his nickname, I found him to be a gentle giant. He spent most of his short life in various prisons *(Photo Source)*

Evering Road, Stoke Newington. Here, at a party held in the basement flat, Jack McVitie, alias Jack the Hat (inset) met his death *(Popperfoto)*

As the firm's right-hand men, Ian and I accompanied the twins everywhere. Here Ian (left) stands with Reggie outside Bow Street Magistrate's Court where Reggie had been charged with a motoring offence *(Syndication International)*

Reggie knew how to treat ladies and was always the perfect host. He is shown here at a nightspot with Barbara Windsor *(Popperfoto)*

Ronnie and Reggie out on the town with Judy Garland, one of their favourite celebrities *(Photo Source)*

Billy Daniels, the popular American singer, gave me this snapshot of himself when he was over in Britain in 1966. He enjoyed being entertained by the twins when he came to London

The most recent public appearance of the twins. Ronnie (left) smiles, grateful to the authorities for letting him and Reggie (below) attend their mother's funeral in Chingford, Essex, in 1982. Crowds gathered to watch the twins arrive. Both were hand-cuffed to detectives and led away immediately after the service *(Popperfoto)*

and we had sex on the moors. The prison officers were only a mile away – if only they had known they would all have wanted a bit!'

He told us that if he was nice to the prison officers, and kept out of trouble, then he could work on the moors any time he wished. It seemed strange that a man doing a life sentence at Dartmoor Prison could roam about the moors freely. He had, after all, a record of robbery with violence.

It must have been about 2.30 in the morning when we heard somebody coming. Len was at the door very quickly because he didn't want them to knock in case they disturbed the other tenants living in the block. As the girl walked into the room with one of the firm, I looked at Frank's face. He had the look of a man who couldn't believe his luck. She was just the way he had described the girl he wanted: big, blonde and very attractive. She knew right away which one of us was Frank Mitchell, probably from his picture, which had been on television when he escaped.

'Hello, Frank!' she greeted him with a smile. 'My name is Lisa. I have heard a lot about you.'

At that moment Frank fell in love.

The member of the firm who had brought her over to the flat now made his way to the door: 'I will leave you now, Frank,' he said. 'Have a good time and be gentle with her, she is a very good friend of the firm.' He smiled as he said this, and Frank smiled in reply. He certainly wasn't going to need any encouragement and Lisa knew what she was there for.

We all sat down and Len poured us a drink, but we wanted to go to bed. Earlier in the day Frank had asked Len to purchase a box of chocolates for him to give the girl when she arrived. Frank told Lisa that he had a present for her. 'Will you come and get it?' he asked her.

'Yes, all right,' she answered.

He took her hand and led her into the bedroom. At the

door he stopped and, turning back to us, said: 'Goodnight, we will see you in the morning.'

I had to laugh – it was already morning. The bedroom door closed behind them, and Len and I looked at each other and smiled. I spent a very restless night, it was very hard for me to get to sleep. I must have heard Frank get up several times during the night to clean his teeth. I was relieved when morning came and I got up at about 10.30. Len was already in the kitchen cooking our breakfast. By the amount of food he had prepared, one would have thought he was cooking for an army. He took breakfast into the bedroom for Frank and Lisa, and it was about one o'clock when they came out of the room.

'Christ!' she exclaimed, 'He is like a stallion – he hasn't stopped all night.'

She was wearing a black negligée, and I commented, 'You look very nice this morning.'

'Thanks,' she replied, 'but I wouldn't want too many nights like that.'

We all laughed and Frank said to me, 'When you see Ronnie, tell him that I need some money. I want to buy Lisa a Christmas present, she has been so good to me.'

I nodded understandingly. 'OK, Frank,' I said, 'I will give him your message.'

He then decided to take a bath and disappeared into the bathroom leaving Lisa and I alone.

'What do you think of him?' I asked her.

She looked at me thoughtfully and said: 'He is so gentle with me, I have never known anybody to be like that with me before. I would like to know how long I will have to be here with him. When Reggie came to the club where I work, he told me that I would only be here for a couple of nights.'

I also looked thoughtful for a moment, then I said slowly, 'I hope so, Lisa, I have been here too long already.'

Just then, Frank came out of the bathroom wearing jeans

and a string vest. He started to do press-ups and exercises, flexing his muscles. After we all had lunch, they went back into the bedroom and stayed there till early evening, when Teddy came back to the flat to write the last letter to the newspapers. This time even Lisa joined in, trying to tell them what to write. When it was finished, Teddy stood up.

'I won't be coming back here again,' he said, 'I have done what I was asked to do by the twins.'

Frank nodded and shook his hand. 'Will I be seeing you again?' he asked.

Teddy also nodded and said, 'Yes, of course you will.'

I couldn't help but sense something in his voice that didn't sound right.

When Teddy left the flat, Frank said to Lisa: 'That was the man who helped me to escape from Dartmoor Prison. It was so easy,' he continued. 'I was in London before anybody missed me. Ronnie told me that he is taking me to stay in the country – will you come with me, Lisa?'

At that question, Lisa looked surprised and said: 'I thought you were going to give yourself up after you got your letters printed in the papers?'

Frank's voice suddenly rose. 'I am not going back to Dartmoor – the police will have to shoot me before I ever give myself up. I have been inside too long. I want to see my family – I haven't seen them for years.'

He was starting to get rather agitated. To calm him down, Lisa suggested that they go into the bedroom. Later, when they joined us again in the living-room, Frank told Lennie that she was the best thing to happen to him for years. It seemed to me that, although Lisa was not in love with him, she obviously did sincerely care for him.

I went into the kitchen with Lennie. He liked to keep watch on the street by looking out of the kitchen window, which faced that way. He turned as I entered and I could see he had something on his mind.

'They promised me that I would be paid for letting them use my flat and all I have been given is a few quid to buy food for them in the other room.' He glanced at the door to make sure the others couldn't hear him. 'It can't go on much longer. I am bound to be missed at my bookstall. I only agreed to do this for a couple of days because Charlie asked me. I have been there for years and my regulars will miss me. I reckon it's been too long already and it's making me very nervous. I am missing all the Christmas trade and no matter what I get from them now, I will still be out of pocket.'

He broke off because Frank came into the kitchen while we were speaking – but he must have caught the tail end of the conversation.

'What did they say they would give you for looking after me?' he asked Lennie.

Lennie said, 'I was promised £500 for letting you stay here for three days.'

Frank didn't answer. He went into the bedroom, and when he came out he handed Len some money. 'Here, take that,' he told Lennie, 'and we will have a good Christmas.'

This money had been given to Frank by one of the firm, from the twins, on the night of his escape.

'No, I can't take your money,' Lennie said, trying to give the money back to Frank. 'Don't worry,' he continued, 'I will get what they have promised me.'

At that moment there was a knock at the street door. We weren't expecting anybody and we all looked at each other. Frank ran into the living-room and grabbed hold of Lisa. He hurried her into the bedroom. Lennie went to open the door. Bill was standing there and Lennie looked very surprised to see him. 'What are you doing here?' he asked. 'You are not supposed to be here until tomorrow.'

Bill walked into the living-room and said: 'I have come over to make sure that I have not left anything in the flat that will connect me with harbouring Frank.'

Lisa heard Bill's voice and came into the living-room where we were talking. Bill was saying, 'I won't be coming back any more. They got word to me that Frank will be OK with Lisa here.'

Lisa came over to me and whispered: 'I can't stay here forever.'

I said to Lisa: 'Call Frank in, but don't tell him what you just told me.'

I suggested that we all played a game of cards to pass the time away. Bill stayed for a while, but after a couple of hands Frank started getting moody. We didn't know what to do to keep him amused.

He suddenly got up from the table and said: 'Do you want to see how strong I am?'

Just to please him we all said 'yes'. He flexed his muscles and told Bill and I to stand one on either side of him. Then he held our belts and lifted us both up in the air, one in each hand, with all the ease in the world. He was happy again now that he had shown us how strong he was.

At about 11.30 Bill got up. 'I will have to go now,' he said, 'I have a bus to catch. I won't be seeing you here again, Frank, I have heard that you will be going to the country with Ronnie.' He put out his hand to shake hands with Frank, 'Goodbye and good luck.'

Frank shook hands and said warmly: 'Thanks for everything.'

After Bill left the flat, Lisa said, 'I think I will have a bath. Is there any hot water, Lennie?'

'Yes, Lisa, plenty,' he answered.

While Lisa was in the bathroom, Frank started to get frustrated. 'Ronnie promised me he would come and see me,' he complained. 'I have been here for nine days now and not one of the twins has been near me. I had more fucking freedom in Dartmoor. At least I wasn't cooped up – I could get out and see a bit of sunshine.' He was really getting wound up now. 'How long do they think they can keep me here? I want to see Ronnie. He's fucking letting me down – if he doesn't get here fast I will be looking for him. He was supposed to have me out of London days ago.'

During these ravings I just sat, as I couldn't get a word in. I remember thinking about all the promises that the twins had made to other members of the firm, including myself, and had then forgotten to carry them out. I also got a strong feeling that Frank was getting too hot to handle. He was extremely moody and, knowing that he was called the mad axeman, I wondered whether it had been such a good idea getting him out of prison and taking it for granted that he would go back peacefully.

The flat was full of tension. Lennie was not feeling too good – he was letting it show that he was having regrets. After all, it was almost Christmas and he had lost out on trade. I now felt that he would not get the £500 that was promised to him, and I reckoned that he knew it too. As far as he was concerned, it had all been for nothing. I tried to boost his morale. 'Don't worry,' I said. 'They won't let you do this favour for nothing.'

He looked at me and knew I was lying.

Just then, Lisa came out of the bathroom. She was a happy type of girl, but the strain of the past days was beginning to show on her face – even make-up couldn't hide that. She tried to look cheerful. 'Let's all have a Christmas dinner tomorrow! I will cook it and we will see if we can get Bill to come over too.'

I shook my head. 'Bill can't come over, he has a wife and kids and I don't think I will be here – I am hoping to go up North tomorrow for the New Year.' I turned to Frank, who had been sitting silent. 'If you are here over the holiday, Ronnie will send someone else to keep you company.'

Frank jumped angrily to his feet and shouted: 'I don't

need anybody to look after me, I can take care of myself. Fuck the lot of you!'

Lisa started to cry, 'Oh Frank, don't carry on like that, you will spoil Christmas.'

Just then, the 'phone rang twice and stopped. Then it rang again. We all knew it was one of the firm and Lennie answered it. He listened to the voice on the other end and when he put down the receiver he said to Frank, 'Someone is coming to see you.'

Frank jumped up and said excitedly: 'Who is it? Is it Ronnie?' Before Lennie had a chance to reply, he continued: 'I knew he wouldn't let me down. We have been good friends for years and he has always been good to me.'

I sat watching all this and thought how changeable Frank was, one minute he didn't want Ronnie, now he had him back on a pedestal, raving about what a good pal he was. I am sure that if Ronnie had chosen to come over to see Frank and had ordered him to do some diabolical deed for him, he would have jumped at the chance.

10

The Final Escape

It wasn't long before we heard the special knock on the street door. Lennie answered, and in walked Reggie with another member of the firm. I could see that they were both uneasy. It was the first time that either of the twins had been over to the flat to see Frank since his escape.

'Hello, Frank,' Reggie said, as he entered the living-room.

Frank looked pleased to see him and said: 'Thanks for coming to see me, is Ronnie coming over soon?'

Reggie didn't look Frank straight in the eye and he kept his head down as he answered. 'Ronnie is coming over to pick you up tomorrow, and you and him will be spending the New Year in the country.'

I sensed something wrong as I knew that it would be impossible for Ronnie to be here the next evening because he was in hiding at the flat in Finchley. But Reggie had Lisa and Len convinced that Frank was going with Ronnie to stay on the farm, and it sounded good to them. I wasn't so sure, but I kept my thoughts to myself.

'I want to take Lisa with me,' Frank said. 'She has been so good the last few days and I don't want to leave without her.'

During the time that I had known Reggie, I had never known him to let anybody tell him what to do. In different circumstances, he would probably have shouted Frank down, but not this time. He kept his cool and said: 'If Lisa wants to go, then we will arrange for her to come down later.'

Frank interrupted. 'I don't want her to come down later; I want her to come down with me when Ronnie picks me up!'

Lisa just sat, staring at Frank and agreeing with everything he said. Something was wrong here, I knew, but I couldn't put my finger on it. I kept looking at Reggie but his face was expressionless and he was giving nothing away.

'If he is getting picked up tomorrow by Ronnie,' I said, 'I think I will try and catch my train to Scotland. They don't need me here.'

Reggie looked at me coldly and replied: 'Ronnie said that he wants you to stay here until he picks up Frank. We have already told Bill that there is no need for him to come back to the flat.'

Now that all the arrangements had been made, and Frank was convinced that he was going with Ronnie to the country, the atmosphere eased considerably, and Frank started to show Reggie how strong he was. But Reggie wasn't impressed and his impatience showed. All he wanted now was to get out of the flat. He humoured Frank for a few minutes then got up to leave. As he did so, he said: 'I will be down to see you and Ronnie on the farm next week – who knows, we might even get you out of the country.'

Reggie told the man who had come with him to go outside and check that there was nobody about in the street. Then he said goodbye and they both left.

I don't think any of us slept much that night. The four of us had a bit of a party – we felt so pleased for Frank. His excitement seemed to rub off onto all of us. It must have been about four in the morning when Lisa said to Frank: 'I think we had better go to bed now. You have quite a long journey ahead of you tomorrow evening.'

I stood up and said to Frank: 'I will probably be gone in the morning before you get up. There is no need for me to stay here any longer.'

I tried to say goodbye to him, but he kept on asking me to stay until Ronnie came over to pick him up. 'If you stay,' he said pleadingly, 'you might be able to talk him into letting Lisa come with me.'

I looked at him doubtfully and said: 'I don't think my being here will make any difference to Ronnie – no one can tell him what to do – and I don't think I would even try.'

Lisa had been listening to this conversation quietly, then she turned to Frank and said: 'I won't be able to come with you when they pick you up. I have a flat-mate and if I don't show my face she may go to the police and say that I am missing.' Frank started to interrupt but she continued: 'She is bound to know that Reggie came to the club and took me somewhere. I couldn't even 'phone her, I had strict orders from Reggie not to get in touch with anybody. But I do promise, Frank, that when you get settled at Ronnie's friend's mansion, I will ask them if it is possible for me to come down and stay with you for a while.'

Frank looked very upset at Lisa's words. 'Will you marry me later? If everything goes well, even if I have to go back to prison?' he asked her.

'Of course, if that is what you want,' Lisa replied, and I knew she was only trying to humour him.

He seemed to accept her words and cheered up. He went into the bathroom and we could hear him cleaning his teeth yet again. While he was in the bathroom, Lisa, who was looking very worried, said to me: 'How am I going to get out of all this? I can't go with him. I have done everything they have asked me to do. Now that they are coming to take him away tonight I would like to go away and forget I was ever here.'

I tried to keep her calm and said, 'You will have to be like me and stick it out until Ronnie comes to pick him up.'

At last we all got to bed – it was five in the morning. I didn't leave after all – I did as Frank asked, and I stayed. About one hour later, Frank came into my bedroom. I was still sitting on the bed smoking and wondering what they could have planned for Frank. I knew that it was all lies about Ronnie coming over to the flat. He would say anything to keep things going the way he planned.

'What's the matter?' I asked him. 'Can't you sleep either?'

'No, I can't,' he answered. 'If they are going to pick me up tonight, I would like to take a chance and go round to see my family.'

I felt a shock run through me at his words. I had to talk him out of it. 'I don't think that would be a very good idea,' I told him. 'The cops are bound to be looking for you and they would most likely be hanging about where your family lives, ready to pounce, and you will muck up all the plans the twins have made.'

His attitude changed. 'All right, all right,' he said, 'but I still want Lisa to go with me.'

'I will ask them – that's all I can do,' I said. I was starting to get irritated by his persistence, and I was also very tired. 'Why don't you go and have a few more hours in bed with Lisa? The time will pass quicker for you,' I told him.

Just then Lennie came into the room with a cup of tea. 'I can't sleep,' he said, 'so I am going to make some breakfast. Shall I bring some into you and Lisa?' he asked Frank.

'No,' he replied, 'let her sleep, we will have it later,' and he went back to his bedroom.

I told Lennie that I would come into the kitchen and keep him company. He had a concerned look on his face. 'What's going to happen to Frank?' he asked. 'Do you really think they are going to get him out of the country?' He carried on, 'You know as well as I do that he is just like a child –

87

someone would have to be with him at all times. I will be glad when tonight is over, I haven't had any sleep for about ten days.'

'How did you get involved in all this?' I asked.

'Oh,' he replied, 'Charlie knew that I lived alone and he asked me if I could do the firm a favour.'

'Have you had any money from them yet?' I asked.

'Only the few quid for food,' he said. 'I am supposed to get paid off tonight.'

'I wish you luck,' I commented. I knew that he wouldn't get paid for this favour. No one ever did – all they got were promises. Any money that was coming into the firm would be used to keep Ronnie at his hide-out and Frank at his.

The last day seemed to drag. At about three in the afternoon Albert came to the flat. Albert was another member of the firm. He was Irish and stood about six foot tall. He was broad and fair-looking. He and I often used to drink together, and we got on well. Once he and Reggie had had a huge row in a pub which ended up with Albert being shot in the foot by Reggie. After that he had become Reggie's right-hand man for a while – until he fell from favour.

Now he took Frank into the bedroom to tell him the details about where he would be going. They were in there about fifteen minutes – it was obvious to me that he didn't want us to know what he was saying.

Frank came out of the bedroom looking excited. 'He is really coming over here for me tonight, Albert just told me, and he has said that Lisa can come with me.'

I glanced over at Lisa and she still looked scared as he raved on about what his plans were going to be, so I gave her the nod to take him back into the bedroom. When they had closed the door behind them, I turned to Albert. 'He is not really coming over to the flat to see Frank is he?' I asked.

'No,' he replied. 'They have told me just to humour him until he gets picked up tonight.'

'Who is coming for him and where are they going to take him?' I asked – knowing he wouldn't tell me but hoping anyway.

'You know that I can't tell you any details,' he answered. 'If they found out that I had told any of you about their plans I would be in a lot of bother. It's better that you don't keep asking questions – that way you will keep out of trouble with them.'

As he was talking I started to get the same apprehensive feeling that I had got with Reggie the night before. 'I am not a fool, Albert,' I told him. 'I smell a rat. We are all in this very deep and sooner or later we are all going to end up nicked – down to the twins.'

We were both silent for a minute and he handed me a cigarette. Then I remembered something. 'Frank wants to take a chance and go round to see his family. He has been driving me round the bend, and if he wants to go I can't stop him. I don't think anybody else could stop him either.'

'He can't go out,' Albert said. 'If he goes there and gets picked up by the law, we will all be in it up to our necks.'

He asked if there was any drink in the flat – he was getting irritable with me now. I passed him a large scotch and he carried on talking. 'They are depending on you to keep him here. They know you can handle him.'

I poured myself a drink and said, 'I don't know how I got involved in looking after a stranger for ten days. It was only supposed to be for forty-eight hours. I must have been off my head to agree. Roll on tonight. With any luck I should be on my way up North for New Year. When you go back, tell them that I am definitely not going to the country with Frank. I think I have stuck it out long enough. You can tell them to let someone else have a go at looking after him – I feel like a babysitter.'

'It will all be over tonight, and there is nothing else I can tell you,' he said. 'And for your own sake, don't ask any

89

more questions – you know I have already been shot in the foot by Reggie and I sure don't want a bullet in the head – so just leave it out.'

I shut up then because I knew Albert was doing his best not to get me further involved.

He called out to Frank, who was still in the bedroom, 'I am going now, Frank. See you tonight. Be ready at seven – Ronnie doesn't like to be kept waiting.'

Frank came out saying, 'All right, all right. I'll be ready.' His face was flushed with excitement.

As Albert was leaving, I thought he had a strange look on his face that I had not seen before. When the door closed behind him, Lennie, who had been in the kitchen, called out that dinner was ready. At about six o'clock, Frank went into the front bedroom to look out of the window. He was in there for about a minute when he came out shouting: 'There are police outside.' He thought that the place was surrounded, but it was only a couple of uniform police walking past. Frank had almost jumped out of the back window – and this was only an hour before he was to be picked up. When he had calmed down Lisa said, 'You had better get yourself dressed in your new shirt and jeans that Lennie got for you. You want to look smart when Ronnie comes to pick you up.'

Frank nodded in agreement. Although he was a big man, he was very simple-minded. He went to get ready and when he came out of the bedroom he really looked good in his new clothes. While we were all hanging about waiting for the time to pass, the 'phone rang twice and we all knew that they were now on their way. It wasn't a long wait. At five minutes to seven, there was the usual secret knock on the front door. Lennie went to open it and Albert was standing there. He walked into the living-room where we were all waiting. He didn't look at Frank for a while and the atmosphere seemed cool. Then he said: 'It's time, Frank. Ronnie won't be coming in, he is waiting in the van outside.'

Frank looked very disappointed. 'I thought that he was coming over in a car for me,' he said, looking puzzled.

Albert looked a bit tense. 'He thinks it would be better to leave London in the van,' he said, 'then get picked up by car.'

Frank looked pleased at Albert's words and said, 'Yes, what a good idea, he always thinks of everything.'

He turned to Lisa, who was standing in the background not really paying much attention to what they were saying. 'Come on, Lisa, get your things. You might as well come with me now – they must have room in the van for both of us.'

Lisa looked at me for support, with fear in her eyes, and said, 'Not yet, Frank. I will get them to bring me to you later when you get settled in to wherever you are going.'

Albert then interrupted, and smiled at him. 'She will be with you in the next few days, Frank. Don't worry – you know she loves you.'

Frank looked stubborn and I thought he definitely was not going to leave without Lisa. Albert pulled him to one side. 'Come on,' he said, worried now because Frank seemed determined not to leave. 'You don't want to keep Ronnie waiting. You know he has got to get out of London himself. He has been like you, cooped up in a flat in Finchley – and he has been there for weeks.'

While they were talking, Lisa came up to me and whispered: 'I don't want to go. Help me, please.'

I looked at Albert, and I could see he was getting anxious. 'Frank,' he said, 'I will find out where you are going and I will have her with you in twenty-four hours. She must let her flat-mate know where she is going. Please trust me,' he continued. 'Come on, let's go now, he is waiting.'

While they were arguing about Lisa, Lennie went into the bedroom to make sure Frank hadn't left anything behind, and I looked at Lisa reassuringly, but it seemed ages before Frank finally agreed to leave without Lisa. As we were all shaking hands Lennie hurried out of the bedroom to wish him luck. Frank stood for a long time, kissing his new-found love, while we stood by awkwardly.

As he walked out of the door with Albert, he looked very sad. I knew it was because Lisa was staying behind, but we all sighed with relief – it had been a very tense few minutes and we were rather pleased that he had left peacefully without any more fuss. Lennie, Lisa and myself stood look-ing at each other for a couple of minutes when suddenly we heard what sounded like three gunshots.

Lisa was the first to react and she screamed out hysteric-ally: 'They have shot him! Oh God, they have shot him!'

The colour drained from her face, and Lennie and I stood frozen. Then we heard another two shots. Lisa, still hysteri-cal, wanted to open the door and run out into the street to see if her worst fears were confirmed.

I caught hold of her and said, 'Don't go out for Chris-sake! If they have shot him and you see them you will be next. You don't want to be an eyewitness do you?'

Lennie tried to play it down to calm Lisa. 'I don't think it was gunshots,' he said, looking hopeful. 'It sounded more like a car backfiring.'

I looked at him, not quite so hopeful. 'I hope you are right,' I said, 'for all our sakes.'

As we stood there, wondering what had happened out-side, there was a knock on the street door. We weren't ex-pecting anybody, and Lisa started to shake. Before Lennie opened the door, I whispered to Lisa: 'For God's sake, don't go with anybody unless you know them, if they ask you to.'

She was shaking so much that I went over to the drinks cabinet and got her a drink. I put it in her hand and said: 'Here, drink this, it will stop you from shaking.'

I had a quick one myself because by then I was fearing the worst.

Lennie had opened the street door and two members of the firm came in very quickly. They looked at the three of us and the look on their faces confirmed the truth. Something terrible had happened. I wondered then whether somebody outside in the van had shot Frank, so I asked them: 'What has happened to Frank?'

One of them replied: 'Don't ask fucking questions. We have had orders to take the girl to the pub and you have got to stay with Lennie and clean this place up.' His voice was full of panic. 'Make sure that there is nothing left here belonging to Mitchell.'

I nodded, and remembered that Frank had given Lisa a comb. It was a small gift that he had wanted her to have. I thought, 'Poor bastard. He had such high hopes and had been so full of life.' In my mind, I knew they must have shot him – but I just couldn't fathom out why. After all, in the last ten days I had got to know him very well and he seemed to be the type of man who would give himself up without trouble if asked to by Ronnie. The worst that could have happened to Bill, Lennie and myself if Frank had gone back to prison and talked to the police was that we would have been charged with harbouring an escaped prisoner.

Lisa still looked nervous and said: 'I don't want to go to a pub. I can 'phone for a taxi from here and go home. This has all been a terrible nightmare for me and I just want to forget I was ever here.' She was very near to tears now, and it was obvious to me that she was still thinking about Frank and the shots that we all had heard.

'You have got to come with us,' one of them told her. 'There is some money over at the pub for you and they are having a party. Anyway, Reggie wants you there.'

I put my arm round her shoulders and said: 'Don't worry, you will be all right. I will see you over there later.'

Lennie had been looking out of the window, and he came over and said: 'The van's gone.' But there was no comment from the two men.

Lisa asked them to wait a few minutes while she packed some things that she had brought with her. When she came out of the bedroom she said goodbye to Lennie and me.

As they were leaving, one of the men turned to me and said: 'When you have finished here, you have got to come over to the pub.'

I nodded but made no comment.

Lennie and I cleaned up the flat and sat talking about the events of the last ten days. 'Do you think they really shot poor Frank?' asked Lennie.

I thought for a moment. 'I don't know,' I replied. 'It did sound like gunshots to me, but I don't think you should start asking questions. If I were you, I would go back to work on my stall and try to forget all that has happened. But be careful who you talk to. If anybody thinks that you are trying to find out what happened to Frank, you and Lisa could go the same way.' I got up to leave.

'Will I see you again?' he asked.

'No,' I replied, 'I don't think so. But someone will be in touch.'

We shook hands. 'Be lucky,' I said, and left the flat door for the last time.

I never did see Lennie again.

11

Who Killed Frank?

My last orders had been to go to the pub, but I didn't feel like drinking with the firm knowing in my heart that they had Mitchell shot for no reason. 'Poor Frank,' I thought, 'you would have been better off if you had never escaped from Dartmoor Prison.'

It was about 9.30, so I went home to my own flat and I stayed away from the firm for about two days. I knew they wouldn't miss me because it was Christmas and there were a lot of parties going on.

The first member of the firm I saw was Ian. He came round to my flat to see me.

'Where the hell have you been?' he asked. 'You were supposed to come to the pub for the Christmas party – Reggie gave strict orders for all the firm to be there.'

'Fuck the parties! We are all going to do plenty of bird for nothing – or some of us are going to end up dead,' I shouted at Ian. Then I quietened down a bit and poured us both a drink. 'It's nearly New Year and you did say you were coming up to Scotland with me. What's changed your mind?' I said.

He gulped his drink in one swallow. 'I have got a message,' he said, handing me his glass for a refill. 'Ronnie says he doesn't want you to leave London. You are to go over to the flat in Finchley. I had better mark your card – he knows you haven't been available since you left Lennie's and he wants to have a talk with you.'

I started to get on edge. 'I'm not in the mood to go over there,' I said.

'You had better go or they will think you are trying to get out,' he said, 'and you know what he gets like when he is moody.'

I looked Ian straight in the eye and asked: 'Did you know that they shot the Mad Axeman? After getting him out of prison and promising to get him a release date.'

'It wasn't Ronnie,' he said, 'I was with him in the flat when he told Albert to pick him up.'

'Then he must have ordered it,' I remarked, 'because we all heard the shots. Who will be next on the list? It's getting out of hand. Look what's happened in the past year – you get involved in the Cornell shooting; Jimmy from the club in North London got shot in the foot, for nothing; Nobby, Charlie's pal, got shot in the leg; and, before our time, Albert got shot in the foot.'

Ian looked startled when I mentioned Albert getting shot. 'How did you know about Albert?' he asked.

'Oh,' I answered, 'it was mentioned around the firm, but I know now the minor extent to which he was involved with Mitchell's shooting.'

Ian was looking thoughtful, and I carried on talking. 'Who is next on the list? It could be one of us.'

He agreed with everything I was saying. 'Between you and me,' he said, 'we are in very deep now. They are so powerful, they have got people who would do anything for a price.'

He got up to leave, and I told him I would go and have a talk with Ronnie, later.

It was all over the East End that Frank Mitchell had been shot. Everybody was talking about it and the police had been making extensive enquiries – but they had come up against the wall of silence and nobody had been arrested. Before I left to go to Finchley, I decided to write a letter to one of my brothers in Scotland, telling him that if I didn't keep in touch he was to give the sealed envelope inside to the police. The envelope contained some details about the Cornell murder and Frank Mitchell's disappearance that I thought would be useful to them if anything were to happen to me.

I got dressed and drove over to see Ronnie. He answered the door himself, which was very unusual. Normally somebody else opened the street door.

I looked around when I walked in. 'Why are you on your own?' I asked him. 'Where's Teddy?'

Knowing that Teddy had been with Ronnie for the last ten days, I had expected to see him now.

Ronnie gave me one of his weird smiles and, lighting up a cigarette, said: 'He has gone on a trip out of the country and he won't be back for a while.' Then he changed the subject and said, 'Why didn't you go to the Christmas party at the pub? You were told to go after you left Lennie's flat.'

I decided that I also needed a cigarette, and I poured myself a drink – both were always very plentiful. Then I said: 'I wasn't in the mood for any parties. I just fancied having a few drinks with a friend of mine.'

That was the worst thing I could have said. He seemed to explode and go red in the face. 'What friend?' he shouted. 'Do I know him? Where does he come from?'

I had to think fast. I couldn't tell him who he was because he was in the police force and I had known him quite a while.

'No, you don't know him. I used to work for him in his car hire business and I sometimes have a drink with him.

He seemed to accept what I told him.

'Let's have another drink,' I said, and I poured him a gin and tonic, while I had a rum and coke. I could see that he was under some strain because he had been cooped up in that flat for over a month now.

'Did Mitchell leave anything at the flat?' he asked.

'No,' I replied, 'he took everything with him.'

I decided not to tell him about the comb that Lisa had kept, which was a gift from Frank. It would only have created more aggravation.

As we sat there drinking, he said: 'What about the girl? Will she keep her mouth shut if it gets around that Mitchell is down in the country?'

I could see that Ronnie was trying to convince me that Frank was still alive. 'It's all over the East End,' I said, 'that Frank Mitchell was shot dead.'

'We want people to think that,' he commented, 'so that the police will stop looking for him in the East End.' He carried on speaking. 'He is in a safe place and Teddy will be looking after him. They haven't seen anything in the newspapers yet about the letters they wrote.'

I had to be very careful how I asked my next question, but it was on my mind and had to be asked, and this seemed a good time to ask him, while we were on our own.

'Did Albert kill Frank, when he took him out to the van?'

Now that I had started, I had to continue. Before he had a chance to answer I carried on: 'I am only asking because we heard about five gunshots.'

He jumped up and seemed to lose control. 'He's fucking dead!' he shouted. 'We had to get rid of him – he would have got us all into a lot of trouble. We made a mistake getting that bastard out. He told Bill he was going round to Vallance Road – and no bastard goes to my mother's house unless I want him to.' He started to rave on. 'He has cost us about five grand and we have had to put others on promises. I suppose that little bookstall geezer will be looking for his five hundred now that it is all over – we will have to keep an eye on him.'

'I stayed at the flat with Lennie,' I said, 'for a couple of hours after they took Lisa away. He told me that he is going to try to get an exchange on his flat because he doesn't think he can stay there much longer.'

Ronnie butted in when he heard that. 'We will have to find out where he moves to just in case.' Then he repeated what he had said earlier: 'Do you think the girl can be trusted?'

I had no time to make any comment because he carried straight on: 'I never like the idea of getting him a bird – you can't trust them – she will have to be watched at all times.'

I disagreed. 'I don't think you will have to worry about the girl,' I said. 'Albert has been staying with her for the past two days. If he thought that she was going to talk, he would let you know.'

He lit a cigarette and sat staring at me. 'We should have let her go with that bastard Mitchell,' he said slowly. 'She would have been one less to worry about.'

I repeated what I had already said and then changed the subject. 'Is anybody coming over tonight to keep you company?'

I could see that he was getting depressed being cooped up in the flat for so long, and he would be worse now that Teddy had gone and he was alone. I never did see Teddy again. A few members of the firm asked about him in the days that followed, but they all got the same answer: 'He has gone to stay with Mitchell in the country.'

Ronnie poured us a drink and said, 'There is nobody coming over here tonight. Reggie has got things to do and we have been told that there is a tail on him. You had better stay here tonight, he should be over here in the morning.'

This didn't appeal to me at all. It was something I never expected him to ask. I knew it would be a boring evening but I couldn't refuse; he wasn't one for watching TV and the records he listened to were classical and not my scene. I left him sitting and smoking, very deeply in thought, at about one o'clock in the morning – but I couldn't sleep. I kept thinking about what he had said about Teddy being with Mitchell and getting rid of Lisa. If he could shoot someone in cold blood, he could do anything and probably get away with it.

I eventually dozed off, but I was awakened by the smell of gas in my bedroom. There was a gasfire in the room and it had been left with the gas open. I got up and turned it off. I didn't sleep at all after that – my mind was working overtime. Did Ronnie come in and turn it on? Or did I accidentally turn it on? I never found the answer to that.

Nor could I understand why Ronnie was still in hiding. There was no warrant out for his arrest and it was costing the firm quite a lot of money to keep him in the private flat. Ronnie hated being cooped up and not knowing what was going on and I knew that Reggie would not be able to handle things for long on his own as he didn't have the same command as his brother.

I was glad when it was morning and I got up early and cooked breakfast for the two of us. After a couple of hours, Reggie came over with one of the firm. He told us that he had to make a few detours on the way because he was sure the police had someone following him. Ronnie took this quite seriously and said to the minder who had come with Reggie, 'Go out and buy some cigarettes and have a good look round, just to make sure that nobody tailed you over here.'

There were only the three of us in the flat now, and Reggie turned to me, showing his annoyance, and said, 'I haven't seen you about for a few days – where have you been?'

Pointing to Ronnie, I said, 'I have already told him where I've been and what I've been doing.'

They were always so suspicious – they expected us all to

.ccount for every evening spent away from them.

Then I repeated what I had asked Ronnie. 'Is it true what everyone in the East End is saying, that Mitchell is dead?' I wanted to hear it from them both, then I would know that it was true.

Flushing, Reggie looked straight at me and answered: 'Yes. It was a big mistake getting him out of prison, we should have left him there. He has been a big burden to us and has cost us a fortune. We still have to find more money to pay off a few people to keep their mouths shut.'

At these words Ronnie looked furious. 'We are not paying anybody anything. We have paid enough – they can go to hell,' he said, raising his voice. 'Even if I have to give them a little help.' Again, he gave his funny smile.

The minder came back into the flat with the cigarettes and reported: 'There is no one about, I don't think we were followed over here.'

I was getting impatient to leave, so I said: 'You don't need me any more now so I will be going.'

I got up to leave and Ronnie said: 'Yes, go round to the clubs and see if there is a lot of talk about Mitchell. If anybody is making themselves busy asking too many questions you had better let us know. We will be in touch.'

I was glad I didn't have to stay there for another night, but I didn't bother going round the clubs, I just went straight back to my flat. In the evening I went round to my local pub, one that the rest of the firm never used. I had only been in there for about an hour when Jack the Hat walked in. By the look of him I could see that he had already been drinking somewhere else.

'Where is everyone?' he asked in his usual breezy way. 'I haven't seen the twins or any of the firm for days.'

I had to lie to him, knowing what a nuisance he could be when drunk: 'I haven't seen them either. I think they have gone down to the country.'

Jack didn't believe me. 'The bastards are in hiding,' he said aggressively. 'Everybody is saying that they have killed one of my best friends, Big Frank. The dirty bastards – they should be castrated.'

He carried on rambling and his voice was getting so loud I had to tell him to shut up, but he said: 'Frank was a great friend of mine, one day they will get their lot, and no one will miss them.'

I listened to all this because I liked him. Ian and I treated him as a friend even though he was a bit of a drunk.

'I don't know why you and I .. stay with the firm,' he continued. 'If they can do that to one of their friends, they can do it to you.'

There was a lot of truth in what he was saying, but I didn't answer. One day, if he wasn't careful about the way he kept shooting his mouth off, he was going to land himself in big trouble. Unfortunately he wasn't a man to take advice although many people tried to steer him on the right course.

'Do you want to come to the Regency Club with me for a drink?' Jack asked me.

'No, not tonight,' I answered. He was the last person I would go drinking with – he seemed to attract trouble wherever he went. To shake him off I said I had a meeting with the rest of the firm and I stood up to leave.

'I will be in touch,' I said as I left and drove home.

The next afternoon I went round to Bill's house. He was pleased to see me and asked me in. There was no one else in the house so I asked him if he would like to come out and have a quiet drink and a chat. I wanted to find out whether he knew more about Mitchell than I did.

'Yes, I would,' he replied. 'As a matter of fact there are a few things I want to ask you about Big Frank.'

We went to a quiet pub that none of the firm used and after we had got our drinks we sat at a corner table, which was quite secluded, Bill started talking. 'Is it true,' he asked, 'that Big Frank is really dead? I haven't slept for days knowing that I was looking after him only a week ago.'

I didn't have to answer that question because he already knew the answer, but wanted me to confirm it.

'Why did this have to happen?' he asked. 'You know as well as I do that he was harmless. He wouldn't have done anything to get the firm into any trouble. I am telling you this as a friend – if I ever get picked up I am not getting involved with his murder.'

I nodded and said: 'I agree with you, Bill, but do you really think you can walk away from the past few weeks and live to tell the tale?'

I could talk to him like this because we had a mutual trust in each other. He was very worried and looked it.

'Do you know where I can get in touch with Ronnie?' he asked. 'I would like to have a talk with him.'

I knew it was out of the question taking him to Ronnie's flat in Finchley because very few people knew about it, so I said: 'He will be coming out of hiding in the next few days. I don't think you should say anything to him about Mitchell, or ask any questions – it's a very sore point with him at the moment.'

I lit myself a cigarette and Bill refused mine saying that he preferred to roll his own. I continued the conversation: 'I would keep out of the way if I were you. It can't be too long before someone talks to the police. They are not fools, they have been keeping out of our way, and we haven't even seen the local ones who drink where we drink. Let's face it, if all the East End are saying that Frank was killed, then the police must be doing something about it. I will keep in touch with you. Don't worry, I will let you know what's going on.'

Once again Ronnie came out of hiding and things got back to normal, with members of the firm going round the clubs collecting their protection money. There was talk at one of the meetings about building up an arsenal of guns. Word had gone around that there were some people about who wanted revenge over Mitchell's disappearance. Once again, I was sent for by Ronnie, and he said: 'I want you to go over to the cinema in Edmonton. I have made arrangements for the Yank to meet you there and he will give you a parcel. Take it round to Pat's place and tell him to store it.'

I got into my car and drove across London to Edmonton in North London. I got there early, and remembering what Reggie had said a few months before, I had a stroll around making sure there were no police traps. Reggie had never trusted the Yank. When he arrived, he didn't get out of the car but beckoned me to follow him. We drove to a quiet road in Tottenham, where we pulled up. He handed over the parcel, which I put in the boot of my car, and he drove away.

I hadn't been told what was in the parcel, but from the weight of it I presumed it was the guns. I took them round to Big Pat's place as I was asked. He was waiting for me and when he took the parcel in he opened it and stood back, shocked. Then he said: 'For Christ's sake. What are they going to do with them? Is there going to be a war?' He was referring to what was now on show to us. Two 1948 brenguns with ammunition. They were like the ones I had used in the Royal Marine Commandos.

'Don't worry,' I told him, smiling to myself. 'They will never be used. Ronnie just likes to have guns around. You should know, you've been with the firm long enough.'

Pat wasn't so sure, and he said, 'People don't buy guns unless they intend to use them.'

He picked up the parcel, which he had rewrapped, and started to walk across the room. But I stopped him and said: 'I don't want to know where you keep your arsenal. I am going back now to tell them that I have delivered them to you.'

I walked to the door. 'See you later,' I called out, and left. I drove back to the pub and, as I walked in, I saw Reggie and Ronnie talking to some of the firm. Ronnie came straight over to me and, putting his hand on my shoulder, whispered, 'Well, did you see the Yank?'

'Yes,' I replied, 'I have picked the parcel up and delivered it to where you told me.'

I didn't tell him that I had seen what was in it. I just wanted to forget about it and hope the guns were never used. Frank Mitchell was still uppermost in my mind. I knew I wouldn't rest until I found out what really had happened to him. There was only one man who could tell me the truth if I managed to get him in the right frame of mind. That man was Albert.

I decided to ask him one evening when most of the firm had gone to one of the West End night spots. Albert and I met for a drink in a club in North London. After we had settled at the usual corner table I asked him: 'What did happen when you took Mitchell out to that van? Did you have orders to get rid of him?'

He started to look a bit cagey and I said: 'Don't worry, I only want to know for my own satisfaction. I have been hearing so many different stories since the night you walked out of the flat with him.'

I lit up a cigarette and went over to the bar for drinks, leaving Albert to chew over my words. When I got back to the table I carried on speaking. 'You are the only one who holds the key. He was done in, wasn't he? We all heard the shots, even Lisa must have told you when you were sleeping with her. Did you tell them that she was scared now?'

'No,' he replied, 'of course I didn't. I wouldn't want anything to happen to her. She has only done what she was asked and I think she would be frightened to say anything about it.'

No matter how persuasive I was, he didn't intend to tell

me who he thought shot Mitchell. As he got up to go to the Gents, I thought, 'I had better not press it any further just in case it got back that I was quizzing him.'

We didn't discuss Frank any more and after an hour or so, I got up to leave. The following morning I went round to Ian's flat. He looked as though he had a giant-sized hangover.

'Where did you all go last night?' I asked.

'We went to the West End,' he answered, 'and we all had a ball. But they started screaming at each other.'

I got interested. 'What was it about this time?' I asked, knowing that it was the usual thing to happen when they were out drinking together.

Ian replied: 'They were talking about a geezer called Payne. Ronnie told Reggie that he wants him bumped off. He has heard from some associates of his that Payne has been to the law. They seem to be worried about this one.'

'I don't know anything about Payne,' I said. 'I have only heard that he did some deals with the twins before our time. I remember taking Reggie to his solicitor's office in Fleet Street to meet Payne but he didn't show up. Who's got the job of bumping him off?'

Ian laughed as he said, 'They are talking about getting Jack the Hat to do it. They even said that they would let him off with that double-cross on the last job he did for the firm with Nobby's merchandise.'

I couldn't believe this and said so. 'They have got to be joking. Jack's no assassin – he is only a small-time crook. Why should he put himself out on a limb for them? He's not on the firm and if anything went wrong he would be on his own.'

'Well,' said Ian, 'they still want him to do this favour for them.'

I laughed and said, 'I wish them luck.'

We found out later that they eventually tracked down

Jack the Hat and told him that they would forget about the past if he would do them this favour. He agreed immediately because he was eager to get back into their good books. He was taken to the area where Payne lived so that he could 'case the joint'. After he had looked round the area and made mental notes about the house, he got back into the car that had taken him and said: 'After you drop me off, go back and tell them it's as good as done.'

Once again he was given his expenses for the job in advance, but one or two of us knew that he had no intention of shooting anybody for £100. He would agree to anything as long as he had his drinking money, even if it meant double-crossing the twins once again. I didn't care who they asked to do these kind of favours, as long as it wasn't me.

We waited a few days for news that he had done what he was paid to do, because this time the twins were sure he wouldn't let them down. To safeguard themselves they even held parties and meetings to make sure they had alibis for when the event took place. But some of the firm had been right. Jack didn't do the job, but he did spend the money and, true to form, dropped out of sight. The cards were now stacked up against Jack the Hat. Some of us knew that he couldn't possibly get away with it.

12

Some Nosy Parkers
and the Mafia

One evening, Ronnie decided to hold a party in one of his favourite haunts, a pub called the Old Horns in Warner Place, Bethnal Green. He told all the firm to bring their wives or girl-friends along because he had some showbusiness people coming and Reggie wanted to show off his new girl-friend. The guests of honour were two well-known American dancers – the Clark Brothers – who had their own dancing school in Tottenham Court Road, a blind pianist called Lennie Peters, and the well-known London photographer, David Bailey.

Everybody appeared to have forgotten about the shootings that had taken place and it seemed to us that the police were still not bothering with the firm's activities.

There were a lot of photos being taken that night by the firm's photographer, but during the evening I spotted a man standing at the bar alone. He was tall and thin, and he wasn't with the celebrities or the firm. He just kept on clicking away with his camera at all and sundry. I saw one of the firm go over to him to find out who he was. He reached into his pocket and took out a card which he showed, and said he was from a local newspaper, sent to photograph the celebrities that were there.

The member of the firm walked over to where Ronnie was sitting with the Americans. He bent down and whispered something to him. Ronnie looked up, but as this was going on the man suddenly left. Someone ran out of the pub to get the car number, but it was too late. The car was already receding into the distance.

Whispers started going round the pub that he was a plainclothes man taking everybody's photo in the bar. But by now quite a lot of us were getting into the swing of things. The entertainment had been good and the entertainers were getting ready to leave. It looked as though it was going to be a trouble-free night, without anybody getting beaten up or having a bottle put in their face. And well it might have been, but for two strangers who walked in.

They came to the side of the bar where the firm were drinking and gave their order to the barman. The atmosphere suddenly changed and we all sensed trouble. The two dancers had already left and the other celebrities were on their way out. Ronnie had got up from the table where he had been sitting all evening. After saying goodbye to the last of his showbiz friends, he made his way over to the bar and said to the two strangers: 'This part of the bar is private. You will have to go round to the other side of the bar if you want to drink here.'

He was speaking very quietly, but I knew what was going to happen, we all did. After all, hadn't we seen it time and time again?

The two men looked at Ronnie and one of them said: 'We have already bought our drinks and nobody told us we can't drink here.'

It was obvious that they didn't know who Ronnie was or what his capabilities were.

Reggie moved towards his brother, and then it happened. The two strangers were taken by surprise as they were punched and kicked by Ronnie and Reggie, who didn't need any help, but a couple of the firm joined in. There were shouts from Ronnie that the men were spies from South London. The fight lasted for about ten minutes, then the twins stopped as suddenly as they started, and we got the two men, who were by now bleeding quite a lot, into a car and driven to the London Hospital.

Ronnie and Reggie went into the Gents to clean themselves up. As the door closed behind them, Jack the Hat popped his head into the bar. Ian was the first to see him. 'For Christ's sake,' he shouted, 'look who's at the door. If he comes in there will be trouble.'

I made a move towards the door. 'Don't say anything to them,' I said, meaning the twins. 'I will get rid of him.' I went outside to where Jack was standing. He was doped up as usual.

'I want to see the twins,' he said. 'I went round to that geezer Payne's house to shoot him but I think he has the law with him. There's nothing I can do now. I have the gun that they gave me – I want to give it back.' He took the gun out of his pocket. 'See,' he said, waving it about, 'I haven't fired it!'

I couldn't believe this was happening. 'Jack,' I said, 'there has been some bother here tonight and we are expecting the law round at any moment. If you get picked up with that gun you will get nicked, and the twins wouldn't like that. We have got to leave now and I think you should have it away sharpish. I will tell them what you have told me, but not until the morning.'

I knew that I couldn't tell them right now about Jack because the evenings were not the best times to give them bad news, especially after a bout of drinking.

'Go over to the Regency Club and I will try to see you there later,' I told him.

When I went back into the bar, I saw that everything had been cleaned up and the firm was ready to leave. I went over to Ian and said: 'I gave him a tenner to get rid of him,' which, in fact, I *had* done many times in the past.

Reggie came out of the Gents where he had been cleaning the blood off his hands. 'Is everything clear outside?' he asked.

'Yes,' someone answered, 'there doesn't seem to be any Old Bill about.'

I didn't tell him that Jack the Hat had been to the pub to speak to them. Reggie called across to the girl that he had brought with him. She was sitting with the other girl-friends and wives. They all looked slightly dazed at what had happened.

'We are leaving now, come on,' he said to her. Then he said to me, 'Come round to the house at twelve o'clock tomorrow. I have something to tell you.'

When they had left, the rest of the firm followed, but I decided to take my girl-friend to somewhere away from the others. The barman looked relieved to see us all go. If that photographer who we thought was the law hadn't left the pub so hurriedly, he would have had some real action photos.

The next morning I went round to the house as I had been asked. Nothing was said about what had happened the night before in the pub. It was almost as if it had never taken place. Ronnie was waiting for me when I arrived, and he had a grim look on his face.

'We have been told through the grape-vine that a big Irishman has been going around the East End asking a lot of questions about us,' he said, and I must have looked startled because he went on, 'I don't know if it is anything to worry about, but I do want everybody to be on their guard.'

We found out later that it *was* something to worry about because this man was one of the 'top cops' in the police force.

As Ronnie finished speaking, Reggie came into the room where we were sitting and smoking. He was dressed very smartly, as usual, and he was sporting a pair of bruised knuckles from the fracas the night before.

'Ronnie and I are going to Tottenham Court Road,' he told me, 'and we want you to drive us there. We are borrowing the office of those two Yanks to do a bit of business in.'

The Yanks that he referred to were the two dancers from the night before.

'We have a meeting with a couple of members of the Mafia,' Ronnie said. He stood up, ready to leave, and Reggie and I followed suit.

His words came as no surprise to me. There had already been a few meetings with some of the top men from America who I thought had connections with the Mafia (I assumed they were gangsters).

As we left the house we saw two men sitting in a red Ford Cortina. I knew they were going to follow us, but we couldn't be sure whether they were the law or friends of the two men who had been badly beaten up in the pub. The twins didn't agree often, but this time they decided that the two men in the red car were the law. After all, there had been two murders and two shootings, apart from other smaller crimes, so it would seem obvious that the police would be trying to put evidence together.

I was told to drive around and try to lose them, but it wasn't easy. They stuck to us like glue. However, after a while, I managed to shake them off in the heavy East End traffic and drive to the West End. I was instructed to park about two hundred yards from the office and we walked from the car to the building where the meeting was to be held, in what looked to me like a very high-class dancing academy. We were greeted by one of the brothers.

'Hello, Ron. Hello, Reg,' he smiled – but behind the smile was an air of unease. He led us upstairs to a very large office that was thickly carpeted and boasted a cocktail cabinet fully stocked with every kind of drink. It was the glamorous kind of office one would see in Hollywood films. I guessed that this was all to impress the Mafia.

Before they arrived, I was told by Ronnie not to speak but to stand by the door and just observe. After about twenty minutes there was a tap on the door and the American dancer called out: 'Your guests have arrived. If you need me I will be downstairs.' He then showed in two Italian-looking men. It was obvious that he didn't want to know what the meeting was about because he left the room immediately.

As the door closed behind him, both Ronnie and Reggie went over and shook hands with them. I recognised one of them right away – he had been at a flat we borrowed once in Albion Road, Stoke Newington, only a few months before. He turned to me and said, 'How are you? Long time no see.'

I shook hands with him and replied smilingly, 'I'm all right. I see you are still as fat as ever.'

He nodded and laughed. When I first met him I was told that he had been one of the bodyguards of a well-known American singer.

There was nothing very different about this meeting from previous ones. They talked and we listened. We looked like any normal businessmen in our pin-striped suits. The general idea was that the Mafia wanted to move in on London with the backing of various London gangs, and a few of their big shots were of the opinion that the firm could be of use to them. This was not the firm's style – taking orders from people from America. I could never imagine them taking orders from anybody – not even the Mafia. Though the twins agreed to nearly everything that was said.

I gathered that the man doing the talking was the spokesman. He was the one I had met before. He said that he was paving the way for another meeting with someone else who would be coming over to this country soon. We wouldn't be seeing him again because he was going back to the States that night. He pointed to the other man, who was also just observing, and said: 'He has booked a suite at a hotel near Hyde Park where you will be having the meet.'

They all agreed to this other meeting taking place in a few days' time.

The fat man was full of bounce and very jolly, and after the discussion was over, we all relaxed and I poured drinks for everyone. We all shook hands when they got up to leave and, before opening the door, he turned round and said, 'Make sure you go on that meet. I will phone you if I come back to London.'

They left as quietly as they had arrived and we sat down with another drink. Ronnie then said, 'We should go to the next meeting.' He got up and went over to the window.

Reggie didn't look so sure. 'I think it will be a waste of time. It looks like they only want to use our name,' he replied.

As usual, Ronnie had the last word, so it was agreed that we go to the hotel and find out what they really wanted the firm to do.

There was a tap on the door and the American walked in. We all stood up, and Ronnie said: 'Thanks for letting us use your office.'

'That's all right,' he answered, 'that's what friends are for.' He looked relieved, now that we were ready to go.

We left the building and walked to where we had parked the car. We looked around to see if the red Cortina had tracked us down, but there was no sign of it. We drove back to the East End without making any conversation. When we pulled up, we noticed a car parked across the road. This time we felt sure that it was the police and that there was a twenty-four-hour tail on us.

About a week later we went on the meet to see the men from America at the hotel where they were staying near Hyde Park. I was beginning to feel quite at home there now as there had been so many meets in it in the past. We were met in the foyer by the fat man's friend, whom we had been with a week earlier. He took us up in the lift to a suite on the tenth floor, which consisted of a sitting-room, bedroom and bathroom. It must have cost a fortune, I thought, to stay in a place like this. There was a man waiting.

I looked at the two men, who were looking at us at the same time. They looked like the Mafia I had seen in films, but these were for real with their dark suits and gold rings, and I reckoned that they were carrying guns. We all stood looking at each other for what seemed like minutes, but were only seconds.

Just then, another man appeared from out of the bedroom. He looked as though he had just finished shaving – he was only wearing a string vest and trousers. He looked pleased to see us and as he walked over to where we were standing, he put out both his hands and said, 'Which one is Ronnie?'

After all the introductions were made, he 'phoned down to room service and ordered tea and sandwiches.

As he put the 'phone down, he said: 'Christ, it's so easy to get into this goddamn country.' He proceeded to tell us how he had dressed up as first officer on board a cargo ship and docked in at Southampton. 'But I will be catching a plane back,' he grinned. 'That boat was too damn slow.'

The waiter tapped at the door and came in with the teas. Maybe I was getting over-suspicious, but even he looked out of place. I was sure he was the law – it seemed to me that he wasn't doing things right, the way that waiters were supposed to. As he was leaving the room, the man in the string vest asked him to put a sign on the door so that we wouldn't be disturbed.

When we finished the tea and sandwiches, we settled down to business, with me taking the position of observer again. The other two men also watched and said nothing. All the talking was done by the man in the string vest, and it was on the same lines as the previous meet – about taking over London gaming clubs and arranging for planes to take London gamblers to Las Vegas and bring wealthy Americans to London.

I knew that this was already being done by other syndicates from the West End clubs (groups of businessmen who financed trips to and from New York for gambling purposes) and I didn't think that the firm would want any unnecessary violence through muscling in on other gangs' territories. We had had clashes in the past with others trying to muscle in on ours. The firm had had 'phone calls from clubs and casinos telling them that men had been calling on them for protection money and saying they had been sent by the Krays. When this happened, members of the firm were sent along to sit and wait for these individuals and give them 'a word of warning'. After that we had no more trouble.

Ronnie looked fascinated by the man who was talking, but I don't think he was taking much notice of what he was saying. Reggie, on the other hand, was different. On this meet he sat there smoking and taking every word in, but saying nothing. However, I think that even he was fascinated by the way this man was putting the proposition over.

When he had finished speaking, he looked from one to the other for any comments. Ronnie stood up and lit a cigarette. Then he looked straight at the man who had done all the talking and said: 'It all sounds very nice, but we will have to give it some thought. There is no hurry for this at the moment. We will give you an answer in a few weeks' time.'

The man looked surprised. He must have thought that he was going to get the firm involved straight away. 'That's all right,' he said, 'but I will be going back to the States very soon. Will you get in touch through him?' He indicated one of the other two men with him. 'He will let me know your answer.'

Ronnie and Reggie nodded in agreement.

The meet was now over, and again we relaxed. Drinks were ordered and we all smoked and chatted till they were sent up. When we had finished our drinks we got up and shook hands. Then we left the hotel. The drive back from this meet was again in silence. I had got used to this because it was common knowledge among the members of the firm that the two brothers didn't tell us everything that was happening. There was no sign of a police tail this time but when we got to Vallance Road a red cortina with two men in it was waiting on the corner. Ronnie got out of the car and walked over to them. We could hear him say something about joining us for a cup of tea. When he came back he said to Reggie and me: 'I told them we'd be in Marge's pub tonight.' Then he gave his weird smile. He presumed they were police.

They never let me know whether anything came of these meetings with the Mafia, or whether they made any deals. I did suspect that they made some kind of deal because they had a couple of more meets in the hotel when I wasn't with them and there did seem to be a bit of cash about, though that could have been from any of the pies that the firm had their finger in.

13

The Killing of
Jack the Hat

There was quite a lot of boasting going on in the firm that no matter what they did, nobody could touch them. They wouldn't have felt so secure had they known then that the police were building up quite a case against them!

It was about this time that Jack the Hat's name was brought up again in the pub one night. Somebody told the twins that he was still going around telling everybody who cared to listen that he worked for the firm and that he was with Reggie when he shot Jim in the foot. This didn't go down well with them.

A couple of nights later I popped into a pub on my way home from the club to see some friends of mine and have a couple of drinks with them. Only two people knew that I used this pub, they were Jack and Ian. It was about nine o'clock when Jack walked in and came over to me. He said, 'Can I have a word with you?'

'Sure you can,' I told him.

As usual, he had the glazed look of the pill taker. I took him over to a corner table.

'What's the matter, Jack?' I asked. 'You look worried.'

'No, I'm all right,' he answered, 'but I have just come from the Regency Club and I have heard a whisper that the twins are looking for me. I know I can trust you, have you heard anything?'

This was the first time I had seen Jack scared.

'I know they have the needle with you,' I told him. 'They have been told through the grape-vine that you have been shooting your mouth off.'

He started to get flustered, but I carried on talking.

'You are still going around shouting your mouth off that you know they got rid of Mitchell and you are also telling everybody that you still have the gun that Reggie shot Jimmy with. I know that is bothering them.'

He started to flare up. 'I don't care about those two bastards.' His voice rose, and I had to tell him to keep it down.

'From now on,' he said, 'I am carrying a double-barrelled shotgun with me when I go out at nights. I don't want to use it, but if I have to I will. There are a lot of crooks going around saying that the firm is giving the East End a bad name and taking liberties with people.'

'Yes, I know,' I told him patiently, 'but they are not saying as much as you are. They all know what the twins are capable of doing. Do yourself a favour and keep out of the way.'

He looked resentful for a moment, then he said with his usual bravado: 'I don't care. One day it will be me or them, and as I have told you before, I am tooled-up. If they try to take me I shall most probably take one of them with me.'

As he paused, the waitress came over to clear our glasses and take another order for drinks. She smiled at Jack and said, 'Hello, Jack, I see you're still wearing your hat.'

When she went away to get our drinks, I said to him: 'All I am telling you is to be careful what you are saying. There are a lot of people that will run to the firm with what you are saying to get in their good books. I wouldn't like to hear that you are on the missing list like a few others we know.'

As we finished speaking, Ian walked into the bar and as he approached our table, I called over for another drink to be brought with our order. When the waitress put them on the table, Jack repeated to Ian what he had told me about being tooled-up.

'Don't take any notice of him,' I said to Ian, 'he is talking through drink again.'

After about half an hour, Ian told Jack that we had to go. We had a tough time shaking him off because he wanted to go with us. As usual, we had to give him a few quid, and then we left him in the pub. Ian and I went back to my flat.

I was taken by surprise when he started talking about the last three years with the firm.

'I wish to Christ I had never come down to London,' he said. 'Do you think the police are onto the firm?'

Ian was very quiet and looked a hard man. What with the scar on his face, a lot of people were slightly afraid of him. I often thought that was why Ronnie liked to have him around when he went to strange pubs for meets. He was obviously thick with Ronnie – but not out of choice. I thought he looked worried. I had seen a lot of changes in him since we joined the firm, and I knew that since the Cornell murder he had been drinking more and taking pills. He was obviously under pressure.

'There are a lot of rumours going around,' I said. 'I don't really think that the police are sleeping – too much has happened.' He nodded and I continued. 'Look how many of the firm are still around. If you can remember the first time we ever met them in the pub, they appeared to have an army round them. After the Cornell shooting a lot of the smart ones got out. I know some of them had to leave London, but they still got out. And what about the Mad Axeman? You know what happened to him. I can't understand how I let myself be talked into looking after a complete stranger. You never met him, did you?' I asked.

Ian shook his head, and I said bitterly, 'He was harmless and his life was taken away from him for no reason. Who will be next? It could be one of us. I don't think that the firm have as many friends as they had three years ago.'

We arranged a meet for the next day, and Ian left.

As the weeks passed and we went to our usual local haunts and West End night spots, I noticed that people weren't so eager to drink in our company, although there were a few new faces wanting to get on the firm. These were mostly young up-and-coming villains. I remember thinking back to the time when Ian and I were asked to work for the twins. We were strangers to London and had never heard of the firm and didn't know what they were involved in. We just saw the lure of the night-life.

I could never understand what the fascination of the firm was for men who were small-time crooks and wanting to join it. Perhaps they wanted to get into the big time. However, I was glad to see these new faces because it gave a few of us who wanted it a chance to get out slowly and get on with our lives away from the firm. It was easy to get in, too: all you had to do was be invited for a drink and, if Ronnie liked the look of you, you'd be put on the payroll and then, in exchange, you started collecting money from the card clubs.

Meanwhile, word spread around that the firm had forgiven Jack the Hat, and he started getting round his old haunts again.

One early evening when I was at the club playing cards, one of the firm came in and called me over to one side.

'Ronnie is having a party late tonight at blonde Carol's house,' he told me. 'He wants you to come, but he doesn't want anybody to bring their wives or girl-friends. He said he only wants a few of the firm there. We will all be going to the Regency and then on to the party.'

I knew the house in Evering Road, Stoke Newington,

very well. The party was going to be in the basement flat which Carol lived in. The firm sometimes paid her to let them use it for parties. There were a few houses in the same street where the firm sometimes met for drinks, and I remembered going to Big Pat's house there a few months previously, to deliver the two bren-guns for him to store away.

I thought back to some of the other parties that I had been ordered to attend. They had been more like meetings – it was only different when the women were there. I said I wouldn't be there because I had already made arrangements to meet my girl-friend's family. This was a lie, but I had to think up an excuse fast. I was fed up being at their beck and call.

As he left me to report back to them, I stopped playing cards and walked out of the club just in case there was a 'phone call for me. I never heard from anybody the next day and forgot all about the party that I had missed. Then, a day later, Ian came round to my flat. As I let him in he seemed to be bursting with excitement.

'Have you heard?'

'Heard what?' I asked him, feeling puzzled.

He seemed to take a deep breath. 'Reggie and Hart have murdered Jack the Hat.'

I felt as though time stood still. I just stared at him in disbelief and then sat down to light a cigarette.

'What are you talking about?' I gasped. 'There was nothing in the papers about any murder. Are you sure?'

It took Ian a long time to convince me that Jack was dead. I found it hard to digest. Maybe he had got it wrong.

'Were you there when it happened?' I asked, clutching at straws.

'No, thank Christ,' he replied, 'I didn't go. I didn't want to leave Pat – we haven't been out for a few days.'

'Who told you about it then?' I asked him.

'I had to go to the East End last night and I saw Hart in

the pub on his own,' he replied, 'and when he told me what had happened, I reacted just like you. I just couldn't believe what he was telling me. The way he was talking gave me the impression that he helped Reggie to stab him.'

Ronnie Hart had joined the firm when he came out of the army and was a good-looking guy – dark, tall and strong – who always boasted that he would do anything for Ronnie and Reggie – his cousins, although he used to call them his 'uncles'. He was always good company and lively, with a taste for excitement. Like the rest of us, he had originally been attracted by the glamour of the firm's night-life – not the violence that went with it. I liked him.

Ian still looked a bit shocked by it all even as he told me.

'It looks as though Hart's got himself well involved now,' I told him, 'just like you are with Ronnie.' Then a thought struck me. 'I wonder why there is nothing in the papers about it,' I said.

Ian shook his head and said he didn't know. He started to say that it had happened at a party a few nights ago in Evering Road.

'Christ,' I broke in, 'that's the party they wanted me to go to.'

Ian started filling me in on the sordid details that Hart had told him the night before. It seemed that the party was in full swing when somebody said they were running out of booze. One young man, who was not a member of the firm but who had been invited along, was asked to go round to the Regency Club and get some more drink. He was also told to look around and see if there was anybody there that the firm knew. When he came back he said that Jack the Hat was there shouting his mouth off as usual. Ronnie heard this and told the young man and a new member of the firm to go back to the Regency Club and ask Jack to come for a drink. They were asked not to bring anyone else – only Jack the Hat.

I listened to this without interrupting, then I said: 'Are you sure that it was Reggie that stabbed Jack?'

'Yes,' he answered. 'Hart told me that he started to stab him with a kitchen knife during the party.'

'What happened after that?' I asked.

'They got two of the firm to put the body into a car and take it over to the other side of London,' Ian replied.

'Does Charlie know about it?' I asked.

'Yes,' he answered, 'Hart told me that Charlie was called out to arrange for the body to be taken care of.'

'I wonder what has happened to it,' I said slowly, thinking how my good advice had fallen on deaf ears.

'I don't know,' said Ian, 'but my guess is that it's been cremated.'

'Do you know where Ronnie and Reggie are now?' I asked.

'No, I don't,' he answered.

We both sat thinking for a few minutes, then I turned to him and said: 'So far, none of the firm knows where either of us lives. If they have been looking for us or have tried to get in touch, they wouldn't know where to start. I want to keep it that way. You are the only one who knows my address and I want you to keep it to yourself. After what happened to Jack I don't want any late calls to any parties.'

'Nothing will happen,' he said, 'and they will get out of this – remember that they know a few influential people.'

I looked at him and thought how different he was since Ronnie had taken him on as his right-hand man. He really thought that nothing could touch the twins.

Ian said that Hart had told him we should all stay away from the twins' mother's place for a while. He got up to leave and I offered him a lift. I told him I was going over to the club to try to find out who was at that party. He looked at me but said nothing.

The first person I contacted was a young man called

Tony. I had only met him a few weeks before. He was a likeable man, married with two children, and he enjoyed being in the firm's company. He greeted me with the same story that I had heard from Ian that morning. Jack the Hat was dead.

'How did you know?' I asked.

'I was there,' he told me.

It turned out he was the one who had fetched Jack from the Regency Club.

'What the fuck did you want to get mixed up with the firm for? You're a married man and you go to work,' I said.

He was beginning to look a bit green. 'I didn't know that they wanted him at the party to kill him,' he said. 'I would never have gone and asked him to come there had I known what was going to happen. Poor Jack, he never had a chance. He even tried to jump out of the window on to the path. They tried to shoot him at first but the gun didn't go off.'

He paused for a moment, then I said: 'I liked Jack, I have known him for a long time. If I were you I wouldn't go around telling everyone that you were there. He may have had a big mouth, but he did have a lot of friends. And if they can't get at the twins they might sort out somebody else who was at that flat when it happened.'

He looked as though he was going to be sick. 'I didn't know they were going to kill him,' he repeated miserably.

Another day passed and there had been no word from Reggie or Ronnie. Once again they had decided to go missing for a couple of days till the gossip died down. However, they did send a message for us all to keep away from Carol's house. By now it was all over the clubs that there had been another murder – and this time everyone was saying Reggie and Hart had done it. Some gamblers were even taking bets on whether or not the twins would be arrested before very long. It was a bet that I wouldn't have taken, knowing how powerful they were.

Some of the firm who hadn't gone to the party talked among themselves, saying that if it was true about Jack's murder, then surely this time the police would be asking questions. None of us had any idea then that they were not only asking questions, but also weaving a very deadly web.

It wasn't long before I got to hear the whole gruesome story of what led up to Jack's murder. I was told how the twins involved one of the Barry brothers, who owned the Regency Club. John, the elder brother, was always being called on by the firm for money and was rarely paid for any of the drink consumed in the club. He even had to open up a private bar for the firm to drink in. In this way, he could still keep his other customers coming to the club. Reggie had left a gun at the Regency and he had told John to put it away somewhere safe. On the night of the fateful party, he sent a message saying he wanted the gun brought to the party in Evering Road, which was only a short distance away from the club. Unfortunately for him, the younger brother was in charge that night, and when he received the message he knew he couldn't refuse to take it. Delivering that gun inadvertently got him involved, even though he didn't stay but went straight back to work. Jack was at the party by this time and, apparently, Reggie, spurred on by Ronnie, just opened fire on him. I heard that the trigger jammed on the gun.

When I met Hart, I let him know that Ian had told me what had taken place at the party. Hart said that Carol had worked hard trying to clean the place up, but the firm were arranging for it to be redecorated and carpeted – just to make sure that there was no trace of any blood left there.

It was only a couple of evenings later, while I was sitting talking to a friend in a club, that two men came in. They were strangers to me and I watched them go over to Billy and ask him if he knew where Reggie Kray was. They were big men and didn't look as though they were on a friendly mission. Billy was a little afraid to say too much to them so he came over to me and told me that the two men at the door were asking questions about Reggie, and would I mind asking them what they wanted him for.

I got up and walked over to them and asked if it was important that they see him.

'Yes, it is,' one of them replied, a little grim-faced. 'We want to know if it is true what we have heard, that he butchered Jack the Hat.'

The other man then interrupted and said unsmilingly, 'We did a bit of bird with him, and we don't think he was so bad that he deserved to be murdered.'

I had to be clever here – my answer could well make them decide whether or not to take their revenge on anybody connected with the firm. However, they prevented me from making any answer by repeating that they only wanted to see Reggie. I told them that I couldn't tell them where he was but thought the twins would be about in a few days. I offered to get a message to them and asked if there was any way the twins could get in touch with them.

One of them said: 'We will be around.'

I figured by the time they met up with Reggie they would have cooled off, but I went to see the twins where they were temporarily staying, out of the way, (I think probably I was the only person who knew they were in Walthamstow) and told Ronnie: 'Your uncle is getting worried. I have just come from the club. I just spoke to two geezers that came there looking for Reggie.'

'What do they want him for?' he asked.

'They didn't say, they just told me they were friends of Jack the Hat, and they seem to know that Reggie killed him. I am sure they are tooled-up.'

At these last words, Ronnie's face reddened and he shouted: 'That bastard had no friends. We have done everyone a favour getting rid of him. We were hearing from all sorts of people that he was gunning for us and we were told it was him or us. Those geezers must have been the law.'

He paused for a moment, then he laughed to himself. 'We have heard that they know there's been a murder, but they won't be able to do anyone for it – how can they prove anything without a body? He is well and truly burned up.'

It was kind of frightening, sitting there listening to him speaking so casually about somebody's death. He really thought they would get away with it once again.

Then he changed the subject. 'Where's Ian?' he asked.

'I don't know,' I replied. 'I haven't seen him for a few days. I will be going over to see him later – is there any message for him?'

'Yes,' he said, 'tell him to keep off the booze and be careful. We have a feeling that we are being watched, and tell him not to 'phone us: I think the 'phones are bugged.'

It was getting late, so I left Ronnie and drove over to see if Ian was in. He hadn't been around for a few days and I supposed he had been out drinking in some of his old haunts near to his flat. He was taking advantage of the twins' absence to see his old local pals with his girl-friend. I knocked on his door and waited for a few minutes before he answered. He looked surprised to see me there so late, but I followed him in and said: 'I have just come from Ronnie. He says you're to keep off the booze. He's scared in case you drop him in it over the Cornell shooting. They should be about again in a few days when the heat dies down.'

I reckoned that I had delivered enough messages for one day, so I said so long to Ian and went home, wondering what new events would take place the next day.

14

Old Scores Settled

A few weeks passed, with the usual meetings going on in the pubs and clubs, and the twins came back on the scene again. It seemed as though Jack's murder had been forgotten.

Ronnie received a letter from a prisoner in a top-security prison (he didn't know him personally – Ronnie quite often was asked to help people), who had discovered that, while he was inside, his wife was having an affair with a man who worked in Romford Market, in Essex. He wanted to know if the firm could do something about it because he had still got a few years to serve and the thought of his home being broken up was driving him to depression. Ronnie promised the man that he would do what he could to help.

He called a meeting of a few members and said he would like Connie to go and see this market man. However, Connie wasn't around – he never was when we wanted him. He had been with the firm for quite a few years and lately he seemed to have been clever enough to dodge getting more deeply involved. It looked as if he, too, was trying to pull out before it was too late.

In the end Ronnie decided to get Hart to go over to Romford and tell the man to stay away from the prisoner's wife, or he would find himself in a spot of bother.

'After all,' he said to Reggie, 'he did very well at the party when Jack the Hat got his lot.'

He turned to Hart and said: 'Come into the other room – I want to talk ?"privately".'

They were in there for about ten minutes, and when they emerged Hart didn't look his cheery self. He looked a bit red in the face, but nothing was explained to the rest of us.

All Ronnie said was: 'He is going over to Romford in a couple of days' time.'

Then he looked straight at me and said, 'You will drive him over there.'

As usual, there was no way that I could get out of it, but if anything had been planned, nothing was said to me.

The few remaining members of the firm seemed reluctant to speak their minds to one another. Experience had taught them to keep their thoughts to themselves, but I think we all knew that each day got us more involved and that we would all have to face the day of reckoning sooner or later. It was also getting difficult to keep in contact by 'phones because Ronnie insisted that the 'phones were bugged.

As I left the meeting, Ronnie came out to the door with me and said: 'Make sure that you are about when he has to go to see that geezer in Romford.'

'All right,' I replied, 'I will be at Dodger's club for the next few days. He can get me there.'

Sure enough, two days later, Hart came over to the club to see me. He said that he had just come from Ronnie, who had told him that the market man had his stall out and it would be the best time to see him.

'All right,' I said, 'I will take you over there now.'

We both left the club and, as I watched him get into my car, I noticed how nervous he was.

'What's the matter with you?' I asked. 'You look as if you'd seen a ghost. Are you ill?'

'No,' he said, 'I'm OK, but Ronnie told me to shoot that geezer.'

He stopped speaking and took out a Colt 45 revolver. I

thought I must be seeing things, and my foot hit the brake.

'What the fuck are you doing with that gun?' My voice sounded slightly hysterical, so I tried to calm down. 'Don't you know we might be followed by the police?'

I started the car again and carried on driving towards Romford. Then I took a chance and said: 'Don't get involved by shooting this geezer. You won't get any help from anybody if someone yells for the police – and I don't want to be an accessory. The thing to do is to go back and tell them that this man has gone on holiday for a couple of weeks and has left his stall with someone else till he gets back. I will back you up.'

He was very hesitant about agreeing to this change of plan because he was scared to go against Ronnie's orders, and he didn't know if he could trust me, knowing that I was always with the twins.

'Will you really back me up?' he said, obviously turning things over in his mind. I nodded and he said, 'You had better drive me over there just to get a look at the place in case they have someone following me. At least then nobody can say that I never went there.'

I nodded in agreement, but told him it was only on condition that he either got rid of the gun or unloaded it. I stopped the car again and he tipped the bullets down a drain.

'I can't get rid of the gun,' he told me, 'it has come from Ronnie's arsenal. I will have to give it back.'

'Please yourself,' I said, 'but I shall stop at a café near the market and have a cup of tea while you go and look around. Meet me back there when you are through.'

He wasn't gone long and there was no shooting, but we did stick to our story that the man was on holiday and, luckily, that was the end of it.

Meanwhile, nobody had mentioned the murders for quite some time, and one evening when we were all in the pub Ronnie started talking very seriously about the various people who could go against him. Suddenly he said: 'I hear that Lennie has moved from the flat that we had Mitchell in.'

I was amazed at the way he seemed to get information about everybody connected to the firm. He had an uncanny way of knowing everything that went on.

'It wouldn't be a bad idea if he had an accident,' he continued, 'like falling from his fifth-floor flat.' His face lit up.

'I don't think you need to go that far,' I said. 'He would be too scared to go to the police.'

Ronnie looked at me and unfortunately I didn't see the danger signs, until I said: 'It's a pity you never paid him what you promised him. After all, he did hear the gunshots from outside his flat when Albert took Mitchell out to the van.'

'Don't fucking mention that mad bastard's name again,' he screamed at me. 'It is all forgotten – just like the others. No one will get done for them because no one will dare go to the police and give evidence against me.'

He stared round at all of us, then he simmered down again and decided to change the subject. 'We are going to have someone writing a book about us,' he said, laughing at his words. 'I don't think we can tell him everything when he comes into our company. We will just give him a free hand on all the good things that we do for the old people and for charities.'

Somebody asked: 'Where will he live while he is writing this book?'

'I have been told about a little flat round the corner to Vallance Road. He can stay there for a few weeks to give him the atmosphere of the East End. Tomorrow a few of us will go round and have a look at it and see if it is all right.'

The next day I drove him and a couple of others round to see this flat. As I approached it I remembered that my girl-friend and I had been here with Ian and his girl when they

132

were flat-hunting, but they had not liked it. The flat was dark and dingy-looking and in a decaying block that should have been demolished years before.

As we walked in I said: 'Whoever is going to write this book must be mad to live in a hole like this.'

Ronnie laughed and said: 'He has agreed to stay here for a few weeks.' Then he added: 'We will have to get it cleaned up a bit first. Sammy and Harry Boy will be giving him some stories to write about.'

The following evening, there was a gathering of the firm at the Old Horns pub. We were all asked to be there and bring the women too because we were to be introduced to the man who was planning to write the book about the twins*. He was a quiet-spoken man and very polite. His name was John Pearson. We had been told to give him a free hand and to answer his questions – providing we did not discuss any of the violence that had taken place. The twins had arranged for him to speak to people who knew them in their young days, and I didn't see much of the author because I tended to take my girl to a local pub owned by a friend of mine. The parties with the firm went on and on and everybody seemed to drink too much.

I went round to see Ian one day to try to stop him from being out drinking every night. We inevitably started talking about Jack's murder again, and I said: 'I have heard that some of Jack's friends are out for revenge. If I were you, I would stay away from some of the meeting places.'

'Jack was a pal of mine too,' he said. 'If I had been at that party in Carol's place, I would have tried to stop it happening. Reggie wouldn't have killed him if Ronnie hadn't geed him up, and if he'd kept his mouth shut.'

---

* Although only half-finished when the twins were arrested, the book was published in 1973 under the title of *The Profession of Violence*. I thought it was an interesting book.

'I agree with you,' I replied. 'Whenever there is a party arranged by Ronnie, it usually ends up with somebody getting done up. I bet their own cousin regrets coming out of the army and joining the firm – especially now they have got him involved in Jack's stabbing. Did you know that they even wanted him to shoot some geezer who was carrying on with someone's wife? I managed to talk him out of it.'

We both sat there talking about the past and we both knew that nobody would dare go into a witness stand and give evidence against the twins. But we also knew that unless something drastic happened, things would get a lot worse in the East End.

15

'No One Can Touch Us'

There was an air of discontent among the remaining members of the firm, who seemed to group together, resenting the few new faces that were now a part of our lives.

The protection money still came in, but not much of it seemed to be coming our way. Ronnie kept telling us that he was going to buy a big house in the country and when he spoke this way, I wondered whether he was pulling off deals without the rest of the firm knowing about it. I remembered the factory in Saffron Walden that made purple hearts. He could have made money there with Jeff, the friend who owned the big white Mercedes.

One evening we all decided to go to a basement club in the West End, which was frequented by teams of villains from all over London. It was a club that the firm had an interest in (they put money into it and earned a percentage out of it) and sometimes we used it as a meeting place. When we walked in we noted how crowded it was but, as usual, we stood at the corner of the bar, drinking and smoking. All eyes turned to us and we were very watchful in case there was anybody out for revenge. It was hardly a night for relaxation.

After having a few drinks, Ronnie started egging the firm on to shoot Connie, towards whom he had a grievance; he seemed to suspect he was trying to draw away. Fortunately,

Connie was in the Gents and nobody had any intention of taking up the offer. Ronnie had just started to call his name, when in walked brother Charlie. He listened to what was happening and whispered something to Ronnie, and then all three brothers left the club together. The rest of us stayed, prepared to spend the evening having a quiet drink and a chat.

The new members of the firm had been going round the pubs and clubs boasting to the owners that they were with the twins. At a nearby table, a man who was a stranger to us started shouting that he was now a member of the Kray firm. He had quite a crowd with him who were backing him up. Suddenly, without any warning, one of us drew a gun and shot the man in the leg. All hell let loose. It was like a free-for-all – the whole club got smashed up. When the fight was over everybody left, and what had started out as a nice quiet drink, ended as a fiasco.

The next morning the man who had done the shooting had to report to Ronnie, who liked to have all details of any aggravation that took place. Two weeks later, the club was closed down by the police. Yet each time one of the firm felt a police presence in a club, Ronnie would say: 'Nothing can touch us.'

I was still going to the gaming club where Ian and I had first met the twins' uncle when we had come down from Scotland and Billy also still frequented the club – but only when one of the firm's minders was there. That was the only time he felt safe. My girl-friend was pressurising me to dodge the firm's meetings, though, so I started to make excuses for my absences, mostly blaming my car for breaking down. Somebody warned me that a hand-grenade was going to be thrown in one of our meeting places, but this never happened – although it did create a lot of tension within the firm. There were probably quite a few people in the East End who would have liked to send the firm to Kingdom come, but they just didn't have the nerve. If they failed it would be their turn to face reprisals.

Ian came up to the club to see me one lunch-time with a message from Ronnie.

'He is having a party,' he told me, 'and he wants you there.'

I laughed. 'Who's going to get done tonight?'

It was a standing joke now with the firm whenever parties were mentioned.

'I'll be there,' I said. 'Where is it to be?'

'We will have a drink first in Blondy Bill's pub,' he answered.

I had no intention of going to this party in case it turned out to be another blood-bath. After Ian left the club, I put the party out of my mind and settled down to a game of cards. I didn't go out that evening, but stayed in and watched television with my girl. At about 12.30 a.m. there was a knock on my door. I looked through the curtain and saw it was Hart. I watched for a few minutes before I opened the door, to make sure he was alone.

'What the fuck are you doing here?' I said furiously. 'And who gave you my address? No one but Ian has this address.'

He looked apologetic and replied: 'Ian is at the party, he must have told them where you live. They have the needle with you for not showing up at the party. You and Connie are the only two missing. They sent me over to tell you that they want to see you.'

I shook my head and said: 'I'm not going out at this time of the night. Go back and tell them that you haven't seen me. You owe me a favour for backing you up when Ronnie wanted you to shoot that Romford geezer.' I paused for this to sink in, then I said: 'Look what happened to Jack when he was sent for to go to one of their parties. You know what they are like when they have had a good drink.'

He agreed with me and said: 'I will go back and tell them

137

you are not in. But if I were you, I would move your car just in case they send someone else – now that they have this address. I am going back now – but for Christ's sake don't tell anybody that I saw you tonight.'

He said this last part nervously, so I replied: 'Don't worry, they will not hear it from me.'

After he left I went out and moved my car to a private car park, just in case I got another visitor. Sure enough, at about two o'clock in the morning, there was another knock at the door. This time I was in bed. I got up and checked the window to see who it was. Hart was standing there, so I dressed hurriedly and let him in again.

'They have sent me over again,' he said, looking fed up. 'They are both in the same kind of mood that they were in when Jack the Hat got done. I am marking your card because they are looking for blood and I don't want to get involved. They have even been trying to get somebody to bring Connie to the party.'

'It's not your fault,' I told him, annoyed that they were presumptuous enough to think I would want to get out of bed and go to a party. 'Ian shouldn't have given them my address.'

'I don't think he knew that they were going to send for you,' he said, and looked at his watch nervously.

It seemed to me that he had a lot of regrets about getting mixed up in Jack's stabbing and didn't want to get involved in any more. He had been going out with a nice girl and would have married her, but the twins liked to have her around at special parties to entertain their friends. She was a lively, pretty girl and thought the world of Hart.

When he left, he said that he would tell them I still wasn't home. Meanwhile, I prepared myself in case I got any more visitors during the night. I knew that once morning came and they sobered up, all thoughts of violence would be forgotten. It seemed as if drink brought out the worst in both of them – and unfortunately the worst always occurred in somebody else's house.

The next morning, I decided to go and see them, knowing that they would be in a normal frame of mind away from the booze of the night before. I knocked at their street door and it was Hart who opened it. He was surprised to see me standing there and looked at me in a quizzical way – but I just smiled and walked past him into the living-room. I think he was wondering whether I was going to say something about seeing him the night before. He needn't have worried – I had no intention of dropping him in it.

Ronnie was scowling at me as I entered the room. 'Where were you last night? We wanted you to come to a big party.'

I had remembered that a few days earlier he had asked me to do a bit of nosing around to try to find out who it was that was making enquiries into the killing of Jack the Hat. So I said: 'You told me to go around and try to find out whether it was the law or local villains that were asking about Jack the Hat.'

He seemed to accept that and asked: 'Did you find out anything?'

'Yes,' I replied, 'everyone is saying that it was Reggie and Hart who killed him. There's a bit of talk going round that a little team are out to get them.'

'I have heard all that before,' said Reggie, who had been preparing to go out to see the Yank, who was in hospital. 'I will be back in an hour,' he called out.

Ronnie had now forgotten all about the party I had dodged the night before. We sat drinking and talking until Reggie came back from the hospital. Ronnie told me that the Yank had sent for Reggie to see him. He was in a private room, no nurses were about, and the way he kept on asking questions about the firm made the twins pretty certain that his conversation with Reggie that day was put on tape. When Reggie walked into the room after this visit, he went straight over to the trolley and poured himself a drink, which was unusual for him during the day. He looked a bit puzzled.

'I'm not sure if this is a trap – he didn't seem very ill and he was asking some funny kinds of questions.'

Ronnie sat thinking for a while, then he said: 'We will try to find out who he is working for and we will see to him.'

It wasn't often that he agreed with Reggie about anything, but I could see that this time he was getting concerned.

Meanwhile in a building called Tintagel House, in another part of London, a floor was set aside for the use of a special team of men, headed by Superintendents 'Nipper' Read and Harry Mooney. These were Regional Crime Squad top men, and this team had been working secretly around the clock to clear London of the Kray firm. Those hand-picked men worked efficiently and quietly, ready to pounce when the time was right. They knew that in order to get convictions, they had to get all the firm in custody at the same time. They also knew that if they were successful and were able to crack this most powerful team of villains, then London would be free of large pockets of organized crime and protection – and other people with similar ideas would be deterred.

Unknown to any of the firm, the Yank apparently was helping the team of police from Tintagel House, who knew about his various activities between the States and this country, including the sales of arms.

There was so much speculation among the members of the firm as to whether or not they were being watched and, if they were, by whom. Was it the law? Or people looking for a chance to seek revenge? I myself was only concerned at that time to make sure I wasn't at any parties held in anybody else's house.

Outsiders began to sense our vulnerability. There was some talk about up-and-coming young villains wanting to branch out and extract money from clubs that the firm had interests in. Ronnie reminded us to keep our ears open and to watch and see if any approaches were made to any of the club managers. If we saw anybody trying to muscle in we were to report it to him. However, if any other gangs did have ideas about taking over, they would soon have been put off because the firm were usually ready for any kind of aggro. There were still guns stashed in one of our regular haunts and one club had a gun hidden in the Ladies because the club had been raided by the police in the past and we knew that they wouldn't find it there.

The firm decided to test out whether or not they were being tailed by the police. The twins' mother had a caravan in Suffolk on the coast, and on many occasions she let members of the firm go for the day and use it. Going down to the caravan seemed a good way to find out once and for all. For a few weeks, everyone took it in turns to go and, sure enough, each car was followed. But it still didn't sink in that the firm weren't untouchable. They always thought that no matter what crimes they committed, they would always reign supreme, and although they thought the police were tailing them every so often, they never dreamt that they had a case almost prepared and witnesses ready to talk.

After a few weeks of this cat and mouse game, Ronnie sent for me and said: 'I've been checking up on who has been around lately and I haven't seen Bill. I want you to go round to his house and tell him that I want him to come to the pub tonight. I want to talk to him.'

'OK,' I said, and got into my car.

Bill lived in a small house just off Brick Lane, not far from the pub where we were meeting at that time. He was a man of modest means, with just a couple of suits, and he wasn't one to go round bragging about being with the firm. It was generally thought that the members of the firm all had fine wardrobes and flashy cars, but this wasn't so. We always looked well turned out, but we didn't always have much money in our pockets.

Bill looked very surprised when he answered the door and saw me standing there. I had hardly seen him since the Mitchell affair.

'Hello, Bill,' I greeted him. 'I've just come round to see how you are.'

His face brightened. 'Come in,' he said, 'would you like a cup of tea?'

'Yes, if it's no trouble,' I answered, following him into the kitchen. 'Ronnie wants to see you tonight at the pub. He hasn't seen you around lately.'

As I was speaking I noticed that he didn't look too well. He saw me watching him and said that he had been having a spot of trouble with his heart and couldn't always catch his breath.

'I am finished with them,' he told me suddenly. 'I have had enough. I've been loyal to them for years and now I have been ill and they didn't even send a few quid round for my wife. I don't care what happens, they will never use me again.' His outburst took me by surprise but he hadn't finished. 'I think they are through,' he said seriously. 'All they are getting round them now is a lot of idiots. You should try to get out before it's too late. Do you think they've forgotten about our involvement with Mitchell? Or that bird Lisa or Lennie? We all know too much. Either we will be reading about them in the papers or they will be reading about us.'

He stopped as suddenly as he started and I was amazed at the way he felt. He had never spoken so freely about the firm before and I started to get little warning signals. I thought back to when Reggie visited the Yank in hospital – he, too, had got warning signals. Were we all getting paranoid?

I decided to be on my guard and not talk too much – even

though I had no real reason not to trust Bill. I got up to leave and said: 'Thanks for the tea. I will go back and tell Ronnie that you have been seeing a doctor and you can't go out yet.' I put my hand into my pocket and handed him a ten-pound note. 'Here, take this and have a drink,' I said.

Then I left the house and drove back to Ronnie. I told him that I had seen Bill and he didn't look well. Ronnie looked his usual serious self in the pub that night and although he accepted my story about Bill's illness, I could see he was not too pleased. He mentioned a few more names of people that hadn't been about recently, one of whom was the man called Charlie Clark, who had been given the gun to dispose of on the night Cornell got shot. He said he regretted giving him the gun because he had to take his word for it that the gun had been thrown into the river.

The firm was standing around in the bar just drinking, smoking and listening to Ronnie going through this list of men whom he had once trusted but now doubted. We all did our best to convince both him and ourselves that they wouldn't give evidence against the firm if approached by the police.

Life went on for us and the same routine prevailed, collecting money from the clubs and having meetings to discuss if there were any new deals in the pipeline. If anybody noticed that the big-name celebrities no longer graced our company, they didn't say so. When Harry Boy or Sammy were asked to 'phone up one or two famous names they came back with a message that they were busy 'doing other things'.

Ronnie got bored with the lack of excitement and missed the film stars that we had so lavishly entertained in the past, so he decided that we should all have a night out at the Astor Club. This was a very nice night spot in the West End and we were told to bring our wives or girl-friends along. Arrangements were made for us all to meet first in Blondy

Bill's pub and to then go on to the Astor Club after closing time.

'I think we will show our few new firm members how to enjoy London's night-life,' he said, feeling and looking more like a godfather with every word. I wondered at that moment whether the same words had been said for Ian and me about three years previously when we were the 'few new firm members'.

16

The Dawn Swoop

My girl-friend was excited at the prospect of going to the night club. I had always tried to keep her out of the firm's company when it was 'party time' because I knew it really wasn't her kind of scene. But this was something different and we would just be like any other couple – out to have a good time.

I didn't have to drive Reggie or Ronnie that night – to my relief they had made other arrangements. We all met in the pub, as agreed. I didn't anticipate any trouble, but decided to drink little and keep my wits about me. There was quite a crowd of us and everybody was in a good mood. I looked around to see of any of the local police were about but I couldn't see them. It went through my mind that it was strange that they weren't out drinking. Blondy Bill also noticed that there were none in the pub, and he commented on it to me. I hoped that no one was carrying a gun, especially since we all had women with us.

We left the pub at closing time and drove to the Astor Club in the West End. Everybody seemed to arrive at the same time but I had a habit of never parking my car outside any drinking place, so I stopped outside the club to let my girlfriend out. She went into the Astor with Reggie and his girl. After I had parked the car elsewhere, I walked to the entrance of the club. I had the oddest sensation of being watched, yet I didn't see anybody lurking around or even acting suspiciously. Maybe it was my Marine Commando training making me sensitive, but I had only felt like that once before, when I was in the Malayan jungle. There, too, I had been watched. I shrugged the feeling off and decided to have a good evening.

As I walked down the plush, carpeted staircase that led from the foyer to the main part of the club, where patrons could eat, dance and be entertained by a first-class cabaret, I saw not only the usual scantily dressed hostesses taking photos, but also a few strangers.

I took my seat beside my girl and she whispered to me: 'I think I had my photo taken with Reggie when I came in.'

'There do seem to be a lot of photos being taken,' I replied.

As I said that, Reggie shouted across to one of the girls with a camera: 'Stop taking photos. We don't want any tonight.'

He looked very annoyed. There were no more photos taken after that, but one or two of the firm suspected that some of these photographers were the law. Yet none of us noticed that we weren't offered any photos part-way through the evening. Normally, the practice was to develop the film right away and take them round the tables for the customers to buy photographs as mementoes.

We all ordered something to eat and sat back to enjoy the music and dancing. After the cabaret and a few more drinks, my girlfriend and I decided to leave. Ronnie was in deep conversation with a young man he had brought with him, and the others were all quite happily drinking and enjoying themselves. We called over to Reggie that we were going home – it was about two in the morning.

'Will you be round at the house in the morning?' he asked.

'No,' I said laughing, 'leave it out. I will see you tomorrow night.'

146

My girl and I walked to the car and she commented that the evening had been one of the best nights she had spent in the firm's company. I agreed. It had been a good night. It was very late when we arrived back at our flat and we must have fallen asleep quickly.

It was noon when I woke up and my girl had gone out to do some shopping. There was a sudden banging on the door. I looked out of the window and saw Ian. I let him in – he was in a very excited state and was almost shouting.

'Have you heard what's happened? The twins have been nicked. There were about twenty cops – they broke into their mother's place when they were asleep. Ronnie was with a boy and Reggie was with his girl.'

He paused for his words to sink in. I was stunned. Although we had all felt from time to time that we were being followed, none of us really thought that the axe would fall so quickly. No wonder so many photographs had been taken in the Astor Club the night before – the police must have taken them straight back for developing.

'What will you do?' Ian asked. 'Will you leave London?'

'No, of course not,' I said, trying to look on the bright side. 'Why don't you wait and see what happens – they may not be kept in for very long – it might just be to answer a few questions. How about Charlie? Has he been picked up too?' I asked.

'Yes,' he replied, 'he was in bed, they must have timed it so that they were all in the same place at the same time.'

I thought back to all the little warnings that no one had heeded when we had felt that we were being watched or followed. Ronnie's words kept ringing in my ears. 'No one can touch us' he had said so many times.

'It's a good thing they don't know where we live,' he commented, 'or we would be nicked too.'

I agreed with that, but I knew that it would only be a matter of time before we, too, would be picked up.

'They can only charge me with harbouring Frank Mitchell,' I told him. 'I don't think that is worth hiding for the rest of my life for. I reckon they have already got to Bill. If they have, he will probably help them because he has the needle to the firm at the moment and he has already said that he wouldn't "take the can" for anybody. Not that I blame him – he is a sick man.' I paused for a moment to light a cigarette. 'Have you seen any of the rest of the firm yet?' I asked Ian, going through all the names.

'No,' he answered, 'I came straight round to see you.'

'What will you do if Ronnie gets charged with Cornell's murder?' I asked anxiously.

'I don't think he will be,' Ian replied. 'They may not get enough witnesses to come forward.' He sat thinking and then said: 'He once said that if he got done he would plead guilty and get me out of it.'

I laughed at this. 'No one pleads guilty to murder.'

'What are you going to do?' he asked.

'Nothing,' I replied. 'I am not running away – there is nowhere to go. I will stay here and see what happens. If they haven't been charged after forty-eight hours they will have to let them go. I wish I knew if anybody else has been nicked. If Ronnie does get done for murder, you should give yourself up.'

'What for?' Ian asked. 'They have nothing on me.'

I looked doubtfully at him, then I said: 'I reckon the police have been on our tail for months. I think we had better have a drink, it might be our last for a long time.'

I poured out a couple of scotches and we sat there just thinking our own thoughts and chewing over the events of the past few years since we came to London and joined up with the firm. In a way I was slightly relieved it was coming to an end, because if I did get arrested and had to serve a sentence, at least after that I could settle down and start life afresh.

'I once asked Albert if he shot Mitchell,' I said, 'but he told me he didn't.'

Ian looked up. 'When did you ask him that?'

'Oh, the night you and he had a fight at the Regency Club when you were both drunk. I had to get between you – I bet you didn't even know he had a gun on him that night.'

'No,' he said, 'I didn't.'

As we finished speaking there was a tap on the window and we both jumped. I got up to see who it was, but it was only my girl with Hart's girl, whom she had met while out shopping. They couldn't get in the door quick enough to tell us what we already knew. I asked if Hart had been arrested but she said not as far as she knew. She only stayed a moment, then hurried home.

I went to the 'phone and called the twins' flat – no answer. I dialled the club and asked if any of the firm were there, but got no joy. I decided to leave it for the moment and 'phone the pub later, but as Ian left, I told him to be careful and not go to the pub for a few nights until we were sure of the facts about the twins' arrests.

The next morning I decided to visit the gaming club in Brick Lane where it had all begun for Ian and myself three years previously. I walked up the familiar narrow staircase wondering how long it would be before my visits here would end. I could smell food from the little café next door, and wondered why I had not noticed it before. I suppose I had been too busy thinking about cards and going on meets to give anything else a second thought.

Billy, the twins' uncle, greeted me at the door with a shocked look on his face. 'What are you doing here? Don't you know that the twins have been arrested? The Old Bill have been here – they are looking for you. If I were you, I would stay out of the way till they sort things out. I reckon the twins will be out soon on bail.'

He sounded optimistic, but I wasn't so sure. I had a very

strong feeling that the police had done their homework well and that soon I and the rest of the firm would be standing together in the dock.

I told him that he should stay at home for a while just in case of reprisals by people who could take advantage of the twins' absence by getting their own back on him. He smiled, but I knew I was right.

'Do you need any money?' he asked. 'I can let you have a few quid.'

I shook my head and said, 'Thanks, but I don't need any.'

Dodger, the owner of the club, came over and also offered me some money, but I refused and said, 'What's the good of it? I have a feeling it won't be long before I am picked up.'

As I was leaving, I called out to a few of the men playing cards, 'I'll be seeing you,' but I wasn't very hopeful.

The next few days were spent with my girl, and going to my pal Blondy Bill's pub and chatting to him and his wife. I didn't try to hide. One afternoon, my girl reminded me that we were to go to a family party at her sister's house. I told her that it would be best if she went alone. Her family didn't know about my past and I didn't want them involved in my immediate future. I popped into the pub before dropping her off at her sister's house and I noticed the local cop having his usual quiet pint. Bill asked if many of the firm had been arrested.

'I don't know,' I told him. 'I will be back later – I am just going somewhere.'

When I got back to the flat to pick her up she was looking upset. 'I don't like to leave you,' she said. 'Please stay in while I am gone.'

'I will just have a drink in Bill's pub,' I told her. I didn't mention that I had seen the local cop there in the afternoon.

'The police can't know where I live,' I said, 'or they would have been here by now.'

She brightened up and we got into the car. As she was

getting out of the car at her sister's house, I said: "Phone me when you want to leave.'

But she said: 'Don't worry, I will get a lift back.'

I drove back to Stoke Newington and parked my car round the back of the pub, where I always parked. I looked round and saw two other parked cars; both had men sitting in them. Somehow I knew it was the law, but I felt that if I were going to be picked up, I would rather it was when I was alone and not at home with my girl.

The local cop was still sitting in the same place when I walked in. 'Hello, I see you're still here.'

He looked up and nodded.

I looked around the bar and saw the two strangers at the far end. I called out to Bill: 'I'll have a double scotch.'

He looked nervous, and said: 'Have this on the house.'

The local cop got up and went outside. I suppose he went to tell the others that I was in. As I was having my drink, one of the strangers went to the Gents and as he passed me I could hear his walkie-talkie crackling in his pocket. He was only gone about thirty seconds when the pub doors opened and in burst about ten plain-clothes cops. They took positions around the pub and every one must have been hand-picked – they were all six-footers and looked ready for anything. One man came forward and walked over to where I was having my drink. He was tall, clean cut and very smartly dressed, as were the men with him.

'Hello,' he said, very politely, 'my name is Superintendent Mooney.'

I realized then that this must be the big Irishman that we had heard about months ago, through the grape-vine, making enquiries about the Kray firm. I couldn't believe at first that he was a high-ranking policeman – he looked more like a bank manager and was very quietly spoken.

I put up my hands to indicate that I wasn't carrying a gun and I didn't speak as two of his men searched me. Then he said: 'You will have to come along with me.'

'Of course,' I answered.

He beckoned to a couple of his men to take me outside. I expected them to handcuff me, but they didn't. When we got outside I knew why. There were about twenty police in the street, all quietly waiting. The passers-by must have thought a film was being made, or that a crime had been committed on a large scale. I didn't try to run for it – if I had I would probably have been shot and I presumed they were all armed.

One of them said: 'Where is your car?'

'You must know where it is,' I replied, 'you saw me arrive.'

I pointed to the back of the pub, where my car was parked. When we got round there I saw that the two cars parked there when I arrived were now hemming my car in.

'Where are your keys?' asked Superintendent Mooney. 'We will take care of your car.'

I gave him my keys and told him where I lived. I was told to get in a car, and two of the police sat in the front with one on either side of me in the back. One of them must have wanted to make a name for himself because he told me that if I made a move he would shoot me and then they would say I had been trying to escape. I just looked at him, knowing that he was trying to be big.

'I don't think you will do anything like that – you would have to answer to your chief.'

One of the men in the front turned round and told him to shut up, which he did, but I never saw him again.

I was taken to Stoke Newington police station and put into an office. I was allowed to smoke and after about twenty minutes Superintendent Mooney came in and asked me if I would like some tea, which he must have ordered already because at that moment a policewoman came in with it.

'We have been looking for you for days,' he said.

'I haven't been hiding,' I told him. 'I have been to the club and the pub where you picked me up tonight.'

After a few preliminary questions, I was taken to a police station in the West End, where I was questioned about Frank Mitchell. Everybody was friendly and polite, and having heard so many stories about police brutality, I wondered if perhaps they had orders to be gentle with the firm. I was put in a cell for the night and early in the morning I had my first encounter with Superintendent Mooney's partner, Read. The cell was unlocked and in walked two men. The shorter of the two said to me: 'My name is Superintendent Read, and this is Chief Inspector Cater.'

I looked at him and thought, so this is the famous 'Nipper' Read. I had heard so much about him from Ronnie in the last three years, that I felt I knew him personally. He had been trying to nail the firm for some time – since long before Ian and I came on the scene. Ronnie once had a pet snake and he called it Nipper Read from the Yard. He didn't look like the stereotype policeman. He was short and pleasant-looking. He was also, like Superintendent Mooney, very quiet-spoken and polite.

'You will be going to court this morning, and you will be charged with harbouring Frank Mitchell,' he told me.

I didn't say anything – I didn't have to.

After breakfast they took me to a different cell. Two minutes later the door was opened and in walked the twins and Charlie. They looked as surprised as I felt when they saw me sitting on the bed smoking. I stood up, and was just going to speak, when Ronnie put his finger to his mouth to silence me. The door was closed, leaving the four of us alone. Ronnie then started to check over the cell to see if it was bugged. He looked at the bars on the window, the light bulb and even under the bed. While he was doing this, we stood silently watching. Only when he satisfied himself that it was OK did he relax and start to speak.

'How long have you been here?' he asked. 'What have they got you for?'

At that time none of us had any idea that most of the firm were now in custody.

'I am going to be charged with harbouring Mitchell,' I told them grimly.

Ronnie looked surprised. 'How can you be?' he asked. 'Who has grassed? No one will dare give evidence against us.'

He really seemed to believe his own words. He and Reggie went through the names of the people who could connect them to Frank Mitchell's disappearance. They acted as though he really had gone into hiding and would suddenly reappear. We went over the names, not knowing that the police had already got statements from most of the people connected with the Mitchell episode.

'What about Lennie?' I asked.

The look on Charlie's face told me that Lennie could point the finger at him. He sat on the bed, deep in thought.

None of us spoke for a few minutes, then Ronnie said: 'Do you know if Bill's been pulled in?'

'I don't know,' I replied, 'I went to his house a few days ago but no one was in.'

Ronnie looked more confident and said: 'He is probably keeping out of the way.'

Reggie came over to me and whispered: 'Have they asked you anything about Jack the Hat?'

'Yes,' I replied, 'his name was mentioned by "Nipper" Read just before I was brought down here.'

He looked worried. 'Have they got Hart?' he asked.

'I don't know who they've got,' I answered.

He started to ask something else, but was interrupted by the cell door being unlocked. We were led upstairs and I have never before seen so many policemen in one place as I

154

saw on that short walk. They were all big and in uniform – and they lined the stairway. Then I saw coming out of the other cells various men who had been arrested. Ian was not with them.

We all stood in the dock together at Bow Street, and then the police brought in a witness. It was Bill. There was a shocked gasp from Ronnie and Reggie – they just couldn't believe it. He gave evidence saying he was one of the men who harboured Frank Mitchell for the Kray twins. I thought that he looked ill – he must have had guts to stand there, knowing what power the twins had, he could be dead before he ever went to court again.

As we went down to the cells, Ronnie said: 'That dirty bastard. He won't get away with it.'

We were all remanded for seven days and were separated. After going backward and forward from our various prisons to Bow Street, with full escort and sirens blaring, we were committed to trial at the Old Bailey. Ronnie was charged with the murder of George Cornell; Reggie was charged with the murder of Jack McVitie.

I had plenty of time to think about the predicament that I was in. By now I knew that there was 'no honour among thieves'. It was July 1968 – four years since Ian and I had come to London to start a new life.

Ian had now been arrested and charged with being an accessory to murder. He and his girl had moved to another part of London and didn't get picked up until over a week later, when he went into the East End to drink in one of the places known to the police. We had been kept apart from the twins in the early stages of the trial and one day, while exercising, I managed to talk to him. He said he had heard that the police didn't have enough evidence to convict Ronnie of Cornell's murder and that they would probably both get off.

I looked at him in disbelief and said: 'You are a fool. You

should tell "Nipper" Read the truth – you didn't fire that gun.'

My words fell on deaf ears. He stubbornly insisted that Ronnie would plead guilty which would mean a lesser sentence for Ian, given the fact he did not fire the shot that killed Cornell.

'How did you get picked up, anyway?' I asked. 'I thought you had moved and would stay out of the way until it was all over.'

He looked sheepish. 'I got drunk one night and I saw Charlie Clark. I think he must have told the police what pub I was in because they came for me.'

Ian was eventually sentenced to twenty years, which as far as I know, he spent in Durham Prison. Our paths haven't crossed since.

At about 11 o'clock one evening, I was taken by the warder to an office. When I entered, I saw it was occupied by Superintendent Mooney and a detective. He told me to sit down and I felt quite relaxed. We started talking and he said nothing was going to be written down; it was strictly off the cuff. He told me that Lisa, Lennie and Bill were Crown witnesses.

'Do you really think that you can keep them safe during the trial?' I asked.

He assured me that a lot of money was being spent on protecting the witnesses in case there was anybody around with orders to silence them. It sounded as though they had been protecting some of their witnesses for some time before the firm's arrest. He also told me that Hart and Albert had already given statements. Hart gave a statement about the gruesome murder of Jack the Hat. He saved himself from going to prison by turning Queen's evidence. He really had very little choice. Albert gave evidence about the twins' organizing Frank Mitchell's escape. He was sentenced to three years for his involvement. There was not enough evidence to pin Mitchell's murder on anybody and I was never asked to give evidence on the Mitchell affair. I realized then that the net had closed.

'I shall plead guilty to harbouring Mitchell, but what are my chances for getting bail? After all, I have a girl on the outside and I have to think of her safety.'

Mooney nodded and said: 'We will give her the same protection as the other women'.

I thanked him and went back to my cell. I applied for bail at the next hearing and got it, even though I knew that I would have to serve a short sentence for my part in the Frank Mitchell episode.

The trial that had started at the Old Bailey on 5 March 1969 took place in the Number One Court Room and was presided over by Judge Melford Stevenson. The Court was packed every day – not only downstairs, where the solicitors, barristers and defendants sat, but upstairs in the public gallery, which was lined with the families and many friends of the firm. At the back of the court were the newspaper reporters. The jury sat enthralled.

The trial lasted nine months, and was one of the most expensive and sensational ever. The witnesses and their families and members of the jury were all offered police protection twenty-four hours a day. The police gave them all new addresses (though not new names) and plain-clothes detectives – some male, some female – accompanied the witnesses and their families everywhere they went, right round the clock. All this was paid for by the Regional Crime Squad.

The witnesses never appeared in the stand together. They were brought in one by one by detectives. Out of court too they were kept in separate rooms and away from the photographers and journalists. After they had given their evidence for the prosecution, they were taken away from the Old Bailey. None of them was recalled, but they were protected till the end of the trial.

The witnesses for the Crown, as Superintendent Mooney had told me, included Bill, Lisa and Lennie. They testified that I was in the flat with them when Frank Mitchell was taken out and they heard the shots. I had no option but to plead guilty. None of them received a sentence.

The defendants were quiet during the trial, except once when Ronnie (at least, this is what I've heard) lost his cool and went into the witness box where he called one of the barristers a fat slob. Otherwise he remained impassive as always.

In the end the roll call of sentences for the Krays went like this: Ronnie received a recommended thirty-year sentence which he is serving in Broadmoor; Reggie received a recommended thirty-year sentence which he is currently serving in Parkhurst; Charlie received a ten-year sentence for disposing of Jack's body (he is now out of prison and is a business man). There were no appeals.

By the time I got bail my girl had moved to a different flat, and here I was taken. She had been staying there with a plain-clothes policewoman. I got quite a shock when I got there because it turned out to be in the same block in Finchley as the one Ronnie had stayed in when he planned Mitchell's escape.

After the trial was all over and I had paid my dues to society, I met the club owner who had stood bail for me.

'I am glad that it happened,' he said, referring to the arrests and the trial. 'I am going to make sure that I never pay protection money to anybody again. The police worked hard to make the East End safe for people like me by putting the twins away.'

'Yes,' I replied, 'you are right. If some of the firm hadn't gone down for murder things would have got worse. It's only a pity that Ian went down with Ronnie over Cornell's shooting. He didn't do it.'

'Supposing Reggie had pleaded guilty to Jack's murder?' he said.

'Then Hart would have gone down with him,' I answered. 'He boasted about what happened at that party enough times when he thought they had got away with it. He really wanted to be a big-time gangster like his uncles.'

Rumours continued to circulate in London about the disappearance of the bodies of Mitchell and Jack the Hat. Some said they were taken to a pig farm; others said they had been put in cement and were holding up the Bow flyover in the East End. But my theory was that they were cremated in a proper cemetery. Those questions were never answered.

We started thinking about Albert, and my club-owner friend said: 'Did you know that Albert used to work for me in the club before he joined up with the firm?'

'Yes – I did know,' I replied. 'I think he only came on the firm to wait for revenge after he got shot in the foot by Reggie some time ago.'

I paused, and he broke in with: 'That trial was really sensational. It must have been the most expensive and successful case in history. The protection of witnesses and their families was so well thought out.'

I nodded, but my mind was still on Mitchell's disappearance, and I said: 'I wonder who really shot the Mad Axeman. I know Albert gave a statement to the police, and he didn't do it. No one really knows the truth, except the people in the van at the time. It is a mystery that will probably go down in the files as the murder without conviction.

Index

Other bestselling Warner titles available by mail: